T0413807

Marseille 1940

Marseille 1940

The Flight of Literature

Uwe Wittstock

Translated by Daniel Bowles

polity

Originally published in German as *Marseille 1940. Die große Flucht der Literatur* © Verlag C.H. Beck OHG, Munich, 2024

The translation of this book was supported by a grant from the Goethe-Institut

Polity Press
65 Bridge Street
Cambridge CB2 1UR, UK

Polity Press
111 River Street
Hoboken, NJ 07030, USA

ISBN-13: 978-1-5095-6542-9 – hardback

A catalogue record for this book is available from the British Library.

Library of Congress Control Number: 2024946088

Typeset in 11.5 on 14 Adobe Garamond
by Fakenham Prepress Solutions, Fakenham, Norfolk NR21 8NL
Printed and bound in Great Britain by CPI Group (UK) Ltd, Croydon

For further information on Polity, visit our website: politybooks.com

Contents

Prologue

As a result of the German *Wehrmacht*'s campaign against France in May and June of 1940, eight to ten million people found themselves compelled to flee. It was a mass exodus of scarcely imaginable dimensions and perhaps the most enormous refugee movement Europe has ever witnessed in such a short span of time.

Among those refugees were hundreds of exiles from Germany and Austria who had fled from Hitler after 1933 and taken refuge in France. Now they had no choice but to leave everything behind a second time – their possessions, home, job, friends – and seek safety from the advancing Germans.

Marseille 1940 relates the drama of this second exodus. There is documentation for everything included here; nothing has been fabricated. The evidence stems from the written correspondence and journals, memoirs, autobiographies, and interviews of a number of great authors, theater folk, intellectuals, and artists. These people are the focus of this book. Along with them, countless unknown persons faced the same dangers, but the traces of their lives have been lost in the chaos of war and flight. The fates reported here shall thus stand in for all those we know too little about to be able to tell their stories. I would like to dedicate this book to the unknown refugees who fought for their survival in France in those days – far too many of them in vain.

At the same time, this is the story of a group of astonishing people who attempted, at considerable peril, to rescue as many exiles as possible from the deadly trap France had become for them. The tale of this group, centered around the American Varian Fry, traces back over a significant span of time and to several countries before these helpers ultimately converged on Marseille in 1940. They were to set an example of unflappable humanity in times of the greatest inhumanity imaginable.

Backstories

Two Days in July 1935

Berlin, July 15 and 16, 1935

Hessler, on Kantstrasse, is a somewhat old-fashioned restaurant decorated in dark wallpaper, chandeliers, and ponderous stucco work. The entire rear wall of its dining room is occupied by a massive, dark brown sideboard, the tables before it standing at attention as precisely as if a Prussian sergeant had mustered them for roll call. From Kantstrasse it is only a few steps to the famous Romanisches Café just behind the Kaiser-Wilhelm-Gedächtniskirche. But it is quieter at Hessler and not nearly as packed.

Sitting alone at one of the tables, Varian Fry eats his supper. He is from New York, twenty-seven years old, a journalist. If there is such a thing as the epitome of a classical East Coast intellectual, he comes fairly close to it: slender, of medium height, clean-shaven, with a serious, alert expression and rimless glasses. Fry takes his time with his meal; he has nothing further planned for the day.

The streets are more full of life than they have been in previous weeks. The Berliners are enjoying the pleasant metropolitan evening; up until now, the summer has far too frequently been gray and rainy. Fry came to Germany two months ago aboard the *Bremen*, one of the fastest transatlantic ocean liners. Since then, aside from a few side trips to other German cities, he has been staying at the Hotel-Pension Stern on the Kurfürstendamm, a respectable, bourgeois establishment with rooms at reasonable rates, fifteen marks a day.

Fry is here on a research trip. Some people in New York think very highly of him. He is regarded as one of the promising newcomers among the city's journalists. When he returns to America at the end of the month, he will assume the role of editor-in-chief at *The Living Age*, a

Varian Fry in Berlin, 1935

sophisticated, soon-to-be hundred-year-old monthly devoted primarily to foreign affairs – a tall order for a man as young as him – and he has clear ideas about the issues he wants to highlight for his readers in the future. By his estimation, the greatest threat in international politics is posed by the fascist regimes in Europe, by Italy, Austria, and, above all, Germany. And so he has arranged with the publisher of *The Living Age* to first spend a few weeks in Berlin to form his own opinion of Hitler's new Germany before joining the editorial team.

You need not be a prophet, Fry believes, to realize that Hitler's political strategy will ultimately result in a war. It is sufficient to take his appalling proclamations seriously, verbatim, and not turn a blind eye to what he is doing to the people in his own country. Not many Americans have the courage to do so, however. All the large newspapers between New York and Los Angeles are reporting on the Nazis' martial demonstrations, the military's buildup of arms, the waves of arrests, the concentration camps, but with these stories, they scarcely prompt more than a shrug among their readers. Europe is far away, while the misery of the Great Depression in their own country, by contrast, can be felt acutely. Every attempt to gain control of the tenacious economic crisis occupies the Americans ten times more than news about a far-off despot in a weird brown uniform.

Over previous weeks, Fry has traveled across Germany, conducting dozens of interviews with politicians, economic leaders, and academics, but also with shop owners, with waiters, churchgoers, and taxi-drivers, the so-called simple people off the street. He is also learning German to gain a more direct entrée to the country. His notebooks are full to bursting. Once he is back in New York, he will be able to provide information about Hitler's state not only in abstract numbers and concepts, but also from personal experience, descriptively and concretely, as is proper for a reporter. He has a great deal planned: transforming *The Living Age* into an alarm bell that will ring in the ears of even the deafest and most complacent of Americans.

After eating, Fry settles up and calmly makes his way back to Hotel Stern, just a short evening's stroll away. The boulevards in western Berlin are the city's promenades, flanked by elegant shops, cafés, cinemas, theaters. This is where well-to-do citizens live who do not want to withdraw into the tranquil villa districts, but to know something of the pulse of the metropolis. If, despite the Nazis' narrow-mindedness, Berlin still radiates something akin to international sparkle, then it is here.

Fry enjoys the warm evening, a relaxed summer atmosphere seemingly blanketing everything, until while turning from Kantstrasse toward the Kurfürstendamm he suddenly hears shouting, yelling, splintering glass, screeching brakes. It sounds like an accident.

Fry dashes off – and runs right into a street fight on the Kurfürstendamm. Young men in white shirts and heavy boots are surging into the road from the sidewalks on both sides of the street. They are stopping cars, tearing open doors, yanking the occupants from their vehicles, and pummeling them. A windshield shatters – shouting everywhere, tussling, men lying on the ground being kicked, women collapsing from the blows and crying for help. Fry witnesses uniformed SA men outside a café sweeping the dishes from a patio table with a swipe of the arm, hoisting it up, and throwing it through the shop window into the establishment. One of the double-decker busses is stopped, and several thugs shove their way inside, dragging passengers off and beating them. Again and again the shouts: "Jew! A Jew!" or "Death to Jews!" Intimidated passersby quickly wrest their papers from their wallets to prove they are not Jews. In a panic, a man wearing a dark suit sprints into a cross street as several pursuers chase after him.

Fry stands amid the tumult in disbelief; no one pays him any attention. He sees a white-haired man with a gaping, hemorrhaging wound on the back of his head. Bystanders spit on him. He sees women pushed around by caterwauling attackers until they stumble and fall. He sees trembling, distraught faces streaming with tears. He sees policemen, dozens of policemen, but they do not rush to the aid of those attacked. Men call them "Jew flunkies" or "traitor to the *Volk*." The officers regulate traffic, clearing free passage for busses, but nothing more.

Then Fry becomes aware of the droning chant in the background. A voice grunts a few words, which Fry cannot make out. A second line follows, then a third, then a fourth. Finally, the voice begins from the top, and the hooligans within earshot, in white shirts or SA uniforms, take up the words recited and roar them back rhythmically. It is like the antiphony in a church between cantor and chorus. Fry still cannot understand what is being shouted. Later he will find someone to transcribe it for him: "When the trooper's off to join the fight / oh, he's in a happy mood, / and if Jewish blood sprays from his knife, / then he feels twice as good."

Fry flees into one of the cafés whose windows have not been shattered. From there he observes the street – its entire width now under the control of those bands of thugs, not one pedestrian dares set foot on the sidewalk or the road. Two SA men enter the café and patrol along the tables. A solitary, potentially Jewish diner stiffens, turning his head away in an attempt to avoid being spotted by the uniformed men. The two men bear down on him; one of them reaches for the dagger of honor on his belt and raises his arm, plunging the blade down into the diner's defenseless resting hand, nailing it to the tabletop. The victim screams, shrieks, stares horrified at his hand, while the men laugh, the one ripping the knife back out again. They leave the café smirking. No one stops them.

At this point, the ruffians now gather on the street. A tall young man gives a brief speech, little more than a concatenation of buzzwords and insults, and then a kind of protest procession forms. The men chant

"Jews, out! Jews, out! Jews, out!", raise their arms in the Hitler salute, and march up the Kurfürstendamm.

Fry leaves the café – the situation seems to have settled down – and walks the few paces to Hotel Stern. Back in his room, he tries to think straight. He moves to the window, looking down onto the street. After several minutes, the demonstration procession returns on the opposite side of the street, followed by a single, slowly idling police car. The men still shout slogans. Fry does not understand them.

When the protest march has finally disappeared, Fry takes a seat at the desk in his room, grabs his notebook, compels himself to be calm, and begins writing down what he saw.

At first glance, Varian Mackey Fry comes across as a young man spoiled by good fortune: the son of a stockbroker, talented, exquisitely educated, successful, worldly. But this first glance deceives. A crack runs across his seemingly so very affable existence. Since his birth in 1907, his mother has suffered from severe depression; she has spent a great deal of time in clinics and was, perforce, unable to care for her son as she would have wanted. Her illness has left its mark on Fry. In spite of his outstanding abilities, he leads a precarious life. The feeling of having been cheated out of something to which he was entitled has made him irritable.

Those who get to know him more intimately occasionally experience that dealing with him can be difficult. He has an unpredictable, rebellious side. Sometimes he behaves like a bulldog that latches on and cannot let go. In moments such as those, he shows no timidity about becoming unpleasant, polemical, or hurtful, although doing so does his intentions more harm than good.

Such outbursts have been part of him from an early age. Three times he was expelled from expensive boarding schools to which his father sent him. He numbered among the good students, in some subjects even among the superb ones. He loved the classical languages, Latin and Greek, most of all. Yet with some regularity he was overcome by the urge to rebel against the venerable, frequently somewhat ridiculous traditions of those fancy academies. And irrespective of which school he attended, he was always quickly viewed as a loner who set no store by endearing himself to others. On the contrary, he was often haughty and made others feel what little regard he had for people who swim with the tide.

With one exception: at Harvard University, he met Lincoln Kirstein, the son of wealthy Jewish parents from Boston. Like Fry, Kirstein was an enthusiastic proponent of avant-garde art, of new literature, music, and painting. While still in high school, Fry, upon learning that James Joyce's novel *Ulysses* was on the index of banned books in the United States for pornography, had ordered a copy directly from the publisher in Paris. When he received it, his pride knew no bounds. He felt it was a badge of honor to possess it: a rebellious book for a rebellious young man. He could scarcely bring himself to put it down, reading from it to his fellow schoolboys, which swiftly prompted the next scandal, because the teachers did not think much of one of their pupils disseminating pornography in their boarding school.

Even then, Fry adored the provocative element of the avant-garde, its uncompromising nature, its willingness to break radically with conventions. When he found in Kirstein a like-minded soul, the pair founded a magazine, *Hound & Horn*, largely paid for with money from Kirstein's father. They wanted to make their heroes of modernism popular at Harvard; they printed Joyce, T. S. Eliot, Ezra Pound, Gertrude Stein, or pictures by Picasso. Kirstein traveled to England with his parents, visited T. S. Eliot, and after his return attempted to persuade the university president to invite Eliot as a visiting professor. From its first issue, *Hound & Horn* made a tremendous impression – among the professors, too. In the blink of an eye, Fry and Kirstein were regarded as budding intellectuals, were praised, promoted, and passed around from party to party.

Much of the recognition Fry enjoys as a journalist still stems from this time. That magazine lent him the aura of a young man with a mind of his own and a keen eye for the issues of the future. He is considered a pugnacious man, but a certain intellectual rebelliousness is virtually to be expected of someone like him. Colleagues have dubbed him "Varian the Contrarian."

Naturally, Fry at some point also clashed with Kirstein. Their magazine had an elitist reputation, and in order to appeal to a broader readership, Kirstein wanted to place more popular articles in the publication. Fry thought that lowbrow and staunchly defended its ambitions. In the end, an argument erupted, and Fry left the editorial team. He is not one for compromise.

In spite of his successes, he is eventually also in danger of being expelled from Harvard. He had stolen a "for sale" sign and erected it in front of the university president's office because he considered him corrupt. This had been the last in a whole series of provocations with which he tried everyone's patience. If the university nevertheless gave him one final chance, he owed it to the petition from an especially benevolent professor, and from an editor at *Atlantic Monthly*, Eileen Hughes. The letter from Hughes in particular made an impression; she mentioned his mother's illness and insinuated that a bit more guidance from an "older and more sensible person" – she was six years Fry's senior – could quickly set him back on a prudent path. What she left unmentioned was that the two were lovers, which had to remain secret until Fry sat for his exams. The week after, they got married.

That very night Fry sent his account of the street battle on Kurfürstendamm by cable to the *New York Times*. The editorial team is grateful to have found in him an independent witness to this largest antisemitic eruption of violence in years. To be sure, abuses against Jews have been taking place in Germany continually, but nothing of this magnitude. The newspaper prints the story about the bloody riot right on the front page; Fry's description continues on page four.

The next morning, Fry telephones the Nazi Party's informational Foreign Press Bureau to learn more about what prompted the disturbances. He harbors no great hope, expecting instead to be put off, but to his surprise, he receives an appointment for a conversation – he is to come right away. When he leaves the hotel and steps out onto the street, he sees that the building façades along Kurfürstendamm are practically plastered with anti-Jewish posters. He scrutinizes them: the distorted faces with their hook noses, wanton mouths, and bug eyes. When he tears down two posters, policemen walk up to him with the intent of arresting him. They shove him into the foyer of a cinema and ask for his identification papers. He has no time to lose – he has an appointment at the Nazi party office – so he pretends to be the clueless tourist claiming he took the drawings for newspaper advertisements. Could he keep the posters? He would like to take them back with him to America as souvenirs. As soon as the officers hear his accent, they become more agreeable and issue only a warning; it was party propaganda that must not be removed. To his question about whether the commotion from yesterday was also party propaganda, he receives only a vague nod.

The office of the Foreign Press Bureau is located just behind the Brandenburg Gate on Wilhelmstrasse. There, a different mood prevails than in the German administrative offices Fry has so far visited. No one barks "Heil Hitler" or thrusts out their right arm; the atmosphere is more civilian. The press chief himself, Ernst Hanfstaengl, approaches Fry. He is a hulking man nearly two meters tall, his hair slicked back and parted severely down the middle. He comes across as a circus director about to brandish his top hat to announce the big animal act.

Hanfstaengl speaks English beautifully, so well that Fry can make out the cadence of the typical Harvard graduate. He comes from a rich Munich publishing family and worked for a while as an art dealer in New York after his university studies, before becoming Hitler's henchman back in Germany. But he does not fit in with the other party vassals. He has nothing of their brutality and their consciousness of power. His office, half scholar's cloister, half chaotic editorial parlor, is stuffed full of file folders, books, and stacks of old newspapers, and has a piano in the corner.

The conversation takes a different course than Fry expected. Hanfstaengl is no diplomat, no man of subtle undertones. Apparently, he wants to impress his guest – who comes from the same university as he – with the autonomy with which he brushes aside all conventions of political speech. The claim on the part of German newspapers that the riots were a spontaneous outburst of popular anger he dismisses out of hand. Everything, he says, has of course been organized by the folks in the party. The Gloria-Palast on Kurfürstendamm is currently screening a Swedish film, *Pettersson & Bendel*, a cheap whodunnit, in which a smarmy Jewish baddie tries to get the better of a radiantly blond Aryan businessman – and fails, naturally. On the previous Friday, three days before the riot, there were attendees in the theater who pretended to be scandalized by the film's antisemitic bias and disrupted the show with heckling and loud hissing.

The hecklers were of course not Jews, but provocateurs, Hanfstaengl says, SA men in civilian clothes under orders to act like Jewish trouble-makers to provide a paltry pretense for the long-planned pogrom. *Der Angriff*, far and away the favorite paper of Joseph Goebbels, then went to print on Monday afternoon with a fiery lead article warning the Germans about the allegedly brazen behavior of Jews and calling on them, finally, to fight back. After that, Goebbels only had to send his people outside the Gloria-Palast and let them start swinging fists as the whim took them. Most had worn white shirts, likely as a disguise, and not their SA uniforms.

Fry listens to Hanfstaengl, amazed. It is not the SA's duplicity that surprises him – on the contrary, there were many indications that the riot was staged – but the fact that a press officer would so unguardedly spread his party's secrets, and in front of a foreign journalist, to boot, who might easily escape censorship? Fry did not expect that. Naturally, Hanfstaengl every so often drops hints that some of his comments are confidential and may not be quoted by Fry publicly. But he clearly has no desire to phrase the key points with circumspection. He lunches regularly with Hitler! They have been friends since the early years of the movement! He was even there for the march on the Feldherrnhalle in 1923, Hitler's attempted putsch. Why shouldn't he say bluntly what he thinks?

Hitler, Hanfstaengl is convinced, puts up with the wrong men in his ambit. Göring and Goebbels? Both fanatics pushing him in a sinister direction. It hardly goes unnoticed that Hanfstaengl considers only one man capable of advising Hitler competently: namely, Hanfstaengl himself. And it is of the very greatest importance, he insinuates, that he in fact get through to the Führer. There are, he explains to Fry, two contentious camps among Hitler's paladins. A moderate group would like to house the Jews in specially designated reservations in order to segregate them systematically from the Aryan population. The radical group, on the other hand, wants to solve the Jewish question with a bloodbath. Fry hears Hanfstaengl's words echo in his mind as the two men shake hands goodbye. He said *bloodbath*.

On the way back to Hotel Stern, Fry realizes that he has heard something seldom uttered so explicitly and of which almost no one in America is aware. If Hanfstaengl speaks of a bloodbath, then what is meant is murder – mass murder of the Jews. How many hundreds of thousands of Jews are there in Germany? Does the radical faction of the Nazis actually want to kill them? Can a bloodbath of such magnitude even technically be carried out? Hard to imagine. Hanfstaengl, however, moves within Hitler's innermost circle. What a man like that says, Fry cannot discount as nonsense.

He does not know what he is to make of this conversation, but two things are clear. First, it would be better for his health were he not to speak of Hanfstaengl's remark while still on German soil. And second, he must not withhold it from American newspaper readers. In his next article for the *New York Times*, he has to mention what Hanfstaengl divulged. Perhaps that will finally open Americans' eyes to the sort of people currently holding power in the middle of Europe.

Briançon, July 16, 1935

Heinrich Mann no longer sports a goatee. He shaved the narrow band of hair between lower lip and the tip of his chin that gave him a mildly rakish aspect; his mustache, which has since gone gray, was all he kept. This makes him appear more courtly, perhaps even younger, but also a bit prudish.

On the same day Varian Fry learns of unfathomable plans in Berlin, Heinrich Mann takes the time in the French Alpine town Briançon to draft a long letter to his brother Thomas in Switzerland. Heinrich is staying in the venerable Hôtel du Courts with his companion Nelly. They are here for a respite; in midsummer, Briançon is refreshingly cool, the mountains offer wonderful vistas, and in the Old Town the little houses huddle against the mighty collegiate church like chicks beneath the wings of their mother hen. Nelly, nearly thirty years younger than he, is not especially bothered by the summer heat of Nice, where they have been living since their escape from Germany, but he, now sixty-four, needs a break. The past two years in exile were trying for him.

He has long put off writing this letter to Thomas. There are all sorts of things worth relating, but Heinrich wants to dress up the news with a diplomatic tone so as not to imperil in any way the reconciliation between them – a reconciliation that too often seems as though it were nothing but a non-aggression pact.

During the First World War, they had burned all the bridges between one another. At the time, Thomas was trumpeting his enthusiasm for war throughout the country, indulging in ethnic-psychological clichés about the soulfulness of the Germans, the mercantilism of the English, and the merely expedient, pseudo-civilized nature of the French. A pacifist and admirer of French literature, Heinrich could not stomach that much nationalistic bigotry. In public, both exercised restraint; for the uninitiated, the few printed allusions to their rift were nearly impossible to decipher. In private, however, they exchanged contemptuous letters that left deep wounds. Not until four years after the war, in 1922, did the pair call a party truce within the family – which proved sustainable also because Thomas had done a radical about-face in matters of politics, having finally committed himself to the republic and democracy. But very warm their relationship is not. Their dealings with one another are cautious, almost a bit ceremonial, and they endeavor not to provoke their old divisions.

After more than two years of hard and concentrated labor, Heinrich has just finished *Young Henry of Navarre*, the first of two novels about the man who rose to become king of France in the sixteenth century. It is his most important and best book in years, confirmed for him by everyone permitted to read the manuscript in advance: a diligently researched, grand historical apologue, dedicated to a ruler who not only led his country to newfound strength, but who also cultivated within it unprecedented tolerance and liberality in matters of religion. At first it sounds as if Mann had dreamed his way back from the politically dark present into an inviolate, humane past, but in the novel, he lends the antagonists of his wise King Henri IV some easily identifiable features of Hitler and Goebbels, making the book a reckoning with the Nazis as well.

In his letter to Thomas, though, he makes no mention of any of this. It would not interest his brother or, worse, might reinflame the literary rivalry between them. He would much rather give an account – in the most innocuous way possible – of the spectacular Writers Congress that he, but not Thomas, attended three weeks earlier. More than two hundred fifty authors from all over the world had traveled to Paris, among them such illustrious colleagues as Bertolt Brecht, André Gide, Lion Feuchtwanger, Anna Seghers, Aldous Huxley, André Breton, and Boris Pasternak. Despite the scorching heat blanketing the city, more than three thousand auditors packed into the large hall of the Maison de la Mutualité. The goal was to establish a united front of protest against the Nazis within the cultural milieu. The many quarreling mini-factions of communist, socialist, Social Democrat, emphatically Christian, or bourgeois-liberal authors were finally to be committed to a strong alliance of resistance against Hitler and Mussolini.

The congress had been the idea of communist authors, or more specifically: those loyal to Moscow. Suspicion quickly spread that it was secretly tasked with securing a better reputation and more influence among intellectuals for Stalin's regime; the Soviet Union wanted to be regarded as the only morally acceptable alternative to the fascists' terror and the capitalists' exploitation. Heinrich Mann was aware of the organizers' poorly concealed intentions, but he put up with such propagandistic ulterior motives. In his eyes, without the backing of the emergent Soviet Union, bourgeois Europe is a lost cause as it is.

Of course, not every one of the two hundred fifty authors attending was able to say his piece at the congress. But the organizational committee had expressly requested that he, Heinrich Mann, speak. When he approached the podium, the entire hall rose to its feet, among them Europe's most important writers, honoring him with sustained applause. In the galleries, where the communists had placed their rank and file, some began singing the "Internationale" but were silenced immediately by the shouts of others. The swelling song would otherwise have made all too clear the extent to which the convention was dominated by Stalin's people. Even so, the imperative tone that stifled that spontaneous gesture like a shot was essentially just as telling.

After Heinrich's appearance, he was joined on stage by Thea Sternheim, the ex-wife of Carl Sternheim, whose satiric dramas had impressed him again and again. They knew each other well but had lost contact with one another for several years. Thea Sternheim had possessed sufficient foresight to leave Germany months before Hitler's assumption of power; now she was living in Paris. In contrast, Heinrich Mann had realized only at the last minute that his renown was unable to protect him from the Nazis. From Berlin he had traveled as inconspicuously as possible by train to the Rhine, disembarked in the tiny border hamlet of Kehl, and walked across a bridge to France, a valise in one hand, an umbrella in the other – he could not manage to salvage more for his exile. It had almost been too late. One day after his escape, SA men stormed his Berlin apartment to take him into custody.

Thea Sternheim and he soon found their way into familiar conversation, exchanging recollections of their Berlin years. Then, however,

André Gide approached them, and thus began a peculiar game. Gide had also known Thea Sternheim and Heinrich Mann for quite a number of years, and he requested they leave the overheated auditorium for a quick half hour at the café Les Deux Magots on the Boulevard Saint-Germain. They went with him, but Gide was continually distracted, compelled to greet acquaintances here and there and yonder while exiting the building, and he kept the two waiting. Even when they arrived at the café, he invited a married couple with whom he was on friendly terms to join them at their table, conversed only with them, and spared hardly a word for Heinrich Mann. Heinrich quickly realized what he was to make of this. Gide was regarded as France's most important writer and thus also viewed himself as the star of the congress. As a result, the audience's salutes to Mann had offended him in his sense of rank, and now he intended to make him feel who in fact was the most celebrated author here in Paris.

There is no way Heinrich can write his brother about all of this. Needless to say, Thomas Mann considers himself the literary sovereign among German expatriates – even if he has been keeping a low political profile and still has not yet publicly broken with the Nazis. If Heinrich were to mention in his letter the enormous show of respect bestowed upon him at the congress, Thomas might react as jealously as André Gide.

The newspapers, however, have reported on Heinrich's triumph, so he cannot completely hide this fact from Thomas, just try to mitigate it. And so he mentions how spectacularly the congress went. The uniting of all non-fascists, by no means only the communists in thrall to Stalin, proved a success. "Whenever a German appeared on stage," he continues, "the whole house rose to its feet, and from above they began singing the Internationale. But the singers were met with shouts of *Discipline, camarades!* – and then they stopped." It is admittedly a rather unlikely scene for every German speaker to have been given an ovation, for the "Internationale" to have been struck up each time, and each time for it to be cut short. All the same, however, it disguises Heinrich's success without completely concealing it.

At the conclusion of his letter, Heinrich offers one last admission to his brother. In May, Thomas and his wife Katia, a couple as urbane as they are implacable, visited him and Nelly in Nice. At the time, Heinrich was writing the final pages of *Young Henry of Navarre* but dropped everything to fetch the two from the train station and drop them at their hotel. It was simply impossible, however, to hide that Nelly came from a very different social stratum than their guests.

Heinrich had met Nelly six years earlier in Berlin, at the Bajadere, a nightclub near the Kurfürstendamm where she worked as a bar girl. Her real name is Emmy Westphal, but she goes by Nelly Kröger. She is a strawberry-blond, voluptuous beauty, fun-loving, often quite loud, and a touch forthright. She knows nothing of literature or art, she is the daughter of a maidservant, she was born out of wedlock, and her stepfather is a simple fisherman. Never did she have opportunities for a solid school education. In other words, the conventions of intellectual conversation are alien to her. On top of this, she drinks more than is good for her.

This does not bother Heinrich. He has never cared a whit about the rules of bourgeois respectability. He loves Nelly for her youth, for her candor, and not least for her courage in sharing his emigration with him. She only landed on the Nazis' radar because she had been living with him in Berlin and had helped him escape. That would probably not have been an insoluble problem; one of her stepbrothers is a squad leader with the SS. With his connections, she would surely have been able to find a way, in spite of it all, to remain in Germany. Instead, however, she opted for Heinrich, for life at the side of a much older writer whose future prospects in exile are now very uncertain.

Thomas and Katia brought a bouquet of roses to Nelly for their first meeting with her in Nice. They were intent on establishing friendly relations with her, but once the four of them were sitting at dinner at Régence, one of the city's finest restaurants, and Nelly drank uninhibitedly and prattled on, she got on Thomas's nerves. In his eyes, she is nothing but a silly, terribly vulgar person.

The following evening did go better. Heinrich had invited his brother and sister-in-law to the new flat on the Rue du Congrès. Nelly prepared a first-rate dinner, they conversed with one another in the drawing room late into the night over red wine and coffee, and the mood was fantastic. Nelly, however, spent the majority of the evening in the kitchen tending to the pots such that she was hardly able to participate in the conversations, which was a huge relief to Thomas.

Heinrich noticed that. These days he is especially gentle, almost humble when engaging with his brother. He does not want any tensions at all to arise, and so he ends the letter he is now writing him in Briançon with an emphatically formal final line: "Frau Kröger sends thanks for your greeting and reciprocates it." This sounds as if Nelly were his housekeeper, not his companion. But Heinrich is aware that his class-conscious brother, the Nobel Prize winner, would rather abstain from informal familiarities with Nelly.

Sanary-sur-Mer, July 16, 1935

Marta is merciless when it comes to his work. She would never tell him what he wants to hear. For Feuchtwanger, that is important; he knows he can rely on her judgment. For much too long now, he has been torturing himself with the final chapter of his new novel, *The Sons*. A week earlier, on his fifty-first birthday, Marta was especially lovely and loving throughout the day, but when he read to her from his manuscript that evening, she rejected it stridently. Not even a birthday can put her in an indulgent mood, not in matters of literature. Afterward, he slept poorly and spent the next few days making endless changes and emendations.

Today the newspapers contain awful reports out of Germany. Evidently, the SA in Berlin organized a veritable witch hunt for Jews, not secretly in some remote district, but right in the middle of the Kurfürstendamm, in front of the world. Here at their home in radiant Sanary-sur-Mer, beneath the skies of southern France, such accounts take on an unreal aspect. It is difficult to believe them possible. All day long, Feuchtwanger has continued working on the manuscript with Lola, persistently and plagued by doubts, until finally everything seemed to cohere. Then, in the evening, he reads the new ending aloud to Marta, but this one, too, she dislikes. She is still not satisfied.

Lion Feuchtwanger long ago stopped drafting his novels himself; he dictates them, which goes faster. Together with Lola Sernau – she will soon have been his secretary for ten years – he has developed a method of advancing the manuscripts in several steps and readying them for print. This is the easiest way for him to proceed with work. So as not to mix up the various versions, they use colored paper. He dictates the first version to her on blue paper, then the second on red, the third on orange, the fourth on yellow, and then finally the fair copy on the usual white. In this manner he can expeditiously expand, rework, and tweak his text, from one step to the next, until it is right.

Fortunately, the relationship between Lola and Marta has recently improved somewhat. Marta is usually pleasant to the women with whom Feuchtwanger sleeps, but as soon as they attempt to contest her, his wife's, place in his life, she mans the barricades. Then she strindbergles, as Feuchtwanger calls it (thus likely comparing her to Swedish playwright August Strindberg's volatile character Miss Julie). It sounds ironic, but when Marta's wrath is unleashed, it gets uncomfortable for him, too.

For around two years now, Lola has been one of the women on the side with whom Marta has to come to terms. Once she caught Lion and Lola in the act, which was awkward for everyone, but for Marta was not actually a surprise. There was never any talk of sexual fidelity between herself and Feuchtwanger, and he makes no secret of his incessant erotic appetite. The usual secrecy and uptightness associated with screwing around are not to his taste. She, too, occasionally has affairs, yet is much more discreet than he and not as indiscriminate.

When Feuchtwanger was still slogging along as a critic toward the beginning of his career, he limited himself to brief flings or prostitutes. Then came his first successes as a writer with his theatrical works, and he met Eva Boy, an expressionist dancer, very boyish, very athletic, and only just turned nineteen, not even half as old as he. Eva was a complicated woman who skidded from one crisis to the next. Once she attempted to kill herself with sleeping pills, but Marta noticed in time and was able to save her.

When Marta and Lion moved to Berlin from Munich, Eva went along; her relationship with Feuchtwanger went on for years. In Berlin, he rose to the rank of a bestselling author, and while his novels made him not only world-famous but also filthy rich, he became almost sexually insatiable. Sometimes he had five or more paramours at the same time, without forgoing prostitutes. He is a short, wiry man and certainly not handsome. But his intelligence and his uninhibitedness in getting right to the point when flirting have an animating effect on many women. For the villa he and Marta had built for themselves back then in Grunewald, they planned separate bedrooms, which accommodated Lion's escapades.

Fleeing from Germany has changed their lives astonishingly little. Of course it was a tough loss when the Nazis confiscated their home in Grunewald, but the Villa Valmer, which they rented here in Sanary, is ultimately even more beautiful. Brilliant white, it is situated on a hill in the town amid a large, lavishly burgeoning garden with a clear view of the sea. The curving coastline, with several ornamental islets as well as Sanary's tiny fishing harbor, comes across as the setting in a dream. Rambling up the slope to the right and left of the house are olive trees, fig trees, and stone pines. The house has generous high-ceilinged rooms, a wonderful terrace, a bright, airy office for Lion – you cannot live much better than this. While moving in, Feuchtwanger was initially skeptical, but now he has practically fallen in love with the house.

Naturally, there are other women besides Marta and Lola here, too. Since Hitler's assumption of power, Sanary has transformed into a refuge for many German emigrants, men and women alike. In addition, the town has for decades been the chosen home of a considerable gaggle of artists and bon vivants such as the gorgeous American illustrator Eva Herrmann or the opera singer Annemarie Schön, who sleeps with Feuchtwanger now and again, but expects a monetary gift in exchange each time.

The Côte d'Azur has a further allure, moreover, that he finds hard to resist. There are a number of casinos here. Feuchtwanger loves to gamble, which has been his second vice since his youth. Most of the time he loses. In the past, his gambling debts occasionally reached worrisome levels, and Marta had to learn to shepherd him through nasty financial straits. The days are over, however, when publishing houses throughout the world would wire him truly princely fees for his books.

Like Heinrich Mann, Feuchtwanger also visited the Writers Congress in Paris. For weeks beforehand, author friends of his had importuned him to attend – most of all authors who maintain stellar connections with the Soviet Union. At first he hesitated, because a sordid incident that grew into a real tragedy had taken place during the preparations for the meeting.

The quarreling all began with one of the slanders common to the literature business. Ilya Ehrenburg, a Russian writer who lives primarily in Paris and who was among the organizers of the congress, badmouthed the French surrealists in a newspaper article using the typical tone of

Stalinist functionaries. He labeled them mentally ill and indolent, called them "young lads who make a business out of insanity," waste their time with "pederasty and dreams," and shamelessly fritter away their parents' or wives' money.

A cheap, parochial polemic, but within the Parisian literary world, it caused a considerable scandal and provided plenty of fodder for conversation. It was mostly André Breton, who sees himself as the inventor and pioneer of surrealism, who felt defamed by the attack. He is a proud, power-conscious man who unfortunately lacks any sense of humor and – perhaps also for this reason – reacts with particular irascibility to criticism.

Although Breton, like Ehrenburg, lives in Paris, the two have never met. Yet they happen to cross paths on the Boulevard du Montparnasse just a few days before the congress is set to begin. Both of them are pugnacious men with sweeping black manes they comb back severely. Ehrenburg had just left a café and was about to cross the street when Breton walked up to him and addressed him:

"I have come to settle an affair with you, monsieur."

"And who are you, monsieur?" Ehrenburg asked.

"I am André Breton."

"Who?"

At which point Breton repeated his name several times in a row, always together with a slap in the face and one of the insulting appellations Ehrenburg had given to the surrealists. He was the mentally ill Breton. *Slap*. The indolent Breton. *Slap*. The insane Breton. *Slap*. The pederast Breton …

Ehrenburg mounted no defense against the blows, only protecting his face with his hands and threatening: "You're going to be sorry for this."

Indeed, Ehrenburg subsequently managed to force through the organizational committee of the Writers Congress that neither Breton nor any other surrealist would be permitted to give a speech or even set foot on stage during the meeting. He wanted to banish Breton's people from public life, literally to revoke surrealism's literary right to existence. Vehement disputes broke out on the committee over this. The young poet René Crevel in particular, who, like Ehrenburg, was a member of the Communist Party but at the same who worshipped André Breton as his literary "god," attempted to prevent Breton's exclusion by all available means. When Crevel was forced to realize after hours of exhausting debates that he could not reverse the decision, a tragedy occurred. He left the committee's office, went to his apartment, wrote on a slip of paper "burn me," opened the gas valve, and killed himself.

It quickly became apparent that Crevel had probably not been driven to suicide by the conflict between Breton and Ehrenburg. Rather, he had been suffering from tuberculosis for years and had learned from a doctor shortly before the deed that the disease was now destroying his kidneys and he did not have much time left. Nevertheless, wild rumors about Ehrenburg's campaign of retaliation against Breton circulated immediately. To take the wind out of their sails, the organizational committee had no other choice but to find a compromise. In Paul Éluard, they put on the speakers list a well-known lyric poet and close friend of Breton's who was now officially permitted to speak on behalf of the surrealists.

Feuchtwanger does not care for such quixotic feuds. He is not as involved in political matters as Heinrich Mann; in the end, he did not find the congress very enticing. But when word got out that Lilo Dammert would be there, he decided to travel to Paris for a week after all. Lilo is a scriptwriter; he has known and admired her since they met in Berlin. Nevertheless, he has still not yet been able to get her to sleep with him.

The weather is radiantly beautiful when he arrives in Paris. The city presents itself in its full glamour. He has hardly arrived at the hotel when calls from the organizational committee reach him. A few days earlier he was told he could of course give his speech in German. Now, suddenly, it turns out that he is to speak French. Right away he hires a secretary and a translator and begins to rework his text in a frantic hurry; his appearance is scheduled for the very next day. Even so, he keeps the evening free for Lilo Dammert. They go out, and of course he flirts with her. She has a grand time but resists his attempts at seduction.

Back at the hotel, Feuchtwanger cannot sleep. The translation of his speech preys on his mind. In the morning, Bertolt Brecht stops by briefly. They have known one another from their years in Munich and Berlin, and he, too, will speak at the congress. Then Feuchtwanger continues working on his text. That afternoon he brings in a second translator. By evening, the speech is finally ready. He has stage fright, walks into the boiling hot convention hall, but is made to wait. When he finally gets to speak at around midnight, his talk falls flat. No one takes up his ideas. No standing cheers like for Heinrich Mann, just minor obligatory applause.

Perhaps that is because of the commotion French writer Henry Poulaille caused beforehand. Surrounded by kindred spirits, he tried to interrupt the speaking order to tell of the fate of dissident Victor Serge, who was being held in a Siberian labor camp on Stalin's orders. Only after some tussling with the security personnel could Poulaille be silenced and escorted out of the hall. The organizers reacted as if spooked; they want to paint an ideal image of a harmonious Soviet society at the congress. News about Stalin's opponents disappearing in camps are unhelpful to them.

To salvage what could still be salvaged, Anna Seghers rose to speak. She is not just a fantastic storyteller, but also a loyal Stalinist, and she planned the congress with Ehrenburg and others. "The Serge case has no place here," she announced, pitting the perils of fascism for the entire continent against fate of an allegedly wayward individual. "In a building that is on fire, you can't help a person who has sliced his finger" – as if incarceration in Siberia were nothing more than a minor laceration. But the debate can no longer be suppressed. Victor Serge is too well known for that and the distrust of Stalin among many writers too great.

Feuchtwanger, of course, had higher hopes for his lecture. Yet, as a sort of consolation, the authors from the Soviet Union are now especially friendly to him. Maxim Gorky, they say, praised his novel *Success* to the heavens, and for them Gorky is a literary demigod. The Soviet embassy in Paris invites Feuchtwanger to a reception, and he even receives an invitation for an official visit to Moscow. All of his novels, so they lead him to expect, are to be published in Russian and sold in large numbers.

It is a charm offensive the likes of which Feuchtwanger has never experienced. The trip to Moscow does not entice him, though the offer to translate his books into Russian does, all the more. He is not a communist and does not intend to become one, but with such prospects, Stalin's regime cannot help but rise in his esteem.

On the following days, Feuchtwanger meets with many other German authors in Paris. Like him, they have all fled from Hitler: Alfred Döblin, Anna Seghers, Alfred Kantorowicz, and last but not least, Ernst Toller with his wife Christiane, a very young, ravishing actor. The couple married in London five weeks earlier, right after Christiane turned eighteen. His two final evenings in Paris, however, Feuchtwanger has set aside for Lilo Dammert. On the first of these, he invites her into his bed again after dinner, again she turns him down, and so he goes looking for a prostitute that night in Montmartre. But on the last day, his luck is finally better. With satisfaction, he notes in his diary: "This evening Lilo. Finally fucked her."

Vienna, July 16, 1935

Flanked by wreaths and tall candlesticks, the coffin lies on a massive catafalque in the dim light of Hietzing's parish church. Officers of the Ostmärkische Sturmscharen [Stormtroopers of the Eastern Mark] form an honor guard on both sides. As bells peal, the cardinal-archbishop of Vienna steps before the casket and utters the benediction. The church is overcrowded; thousands were unable to find a seat among the rows of pews and are standing in the forecourt and along Maxingstrasse to pay their respects to the deceased on her way to Hietzing Cemetery.

Three days earlier, Herma Schuschnigg, wife of the Austrian federal chancellor, died in an automobile accident on her way to a family vacation. Outside of Linz, the state coach, a limousine of make Gräf & Stift weighing two metric tons, went off the road, lost control, and crashed into a tree. Like her husband and her nine-year-old son, Herma Schuschnigg was thrown from the vehicle. While the other two escaped with minor injuries, she broke her neck upon impact.

Chancellor Kurt Schuschnigg reigns with dictatorial powers. Both parliament and the constitutional court have been sidelined since 1933. Partially to secure his own rule, he attempts to defend Austria against Hitler's greediness and prevent a looming annexation by Germany with all available means. He has had his wife's funeral staged as an act of state. Hietzing parish church directly abuts the park at Schönbrunn Palace, the summer residence of the Austrian imperial family. Banners of mourning hang from the buildings along Maxingstrasse. A mounted police division leads the funeral procession to the cemetery, followed by several flower carts overloaded with wreaths, then the hearse, drawn by six black horses, with the cardinal-archbishop processing in front and Schuschnigg walking behind it by himself. A lonesome ruler. Only then, at some distance, come relatives, members of government, diplomats, and officers from various armed services.

While Alma Mahler-Werfel and Franz Werfel are good friends with Schuschnigg, they do not participate in the burial service. Alma never goes to funerals. Ten weeks earlier, her favorite daughter, Manon, died of polio at just eighteen years of age. Alma did not appear at the cemetery for her burial either.

Yesterday, however, on July 15, Franz Werfel published an obituary for Herma Schuschnigg. In it, he writes surprisingly little about the deceased and primarily congratulates Austria on its chancellor's survival of the accident. He calls Schuschnigg a "pure, extraordinary man" who embodies "Austrian humanity" and who undertakes his office not "for his own power, his own fame, his own fanatical ends, but out of selfless love

Alma Mahler-Werfel and Franz Werfel, 1935

for the fatherland" – not a word about the cold calculation with which Schuschnigg brought about the destruction of democracy, reintroduced the death penalty, and had insurrectionary leftist workers court-martialed and shot dead.

During the First World War, Werfel still wrote for leftist newspapers, but toward the end of the war, he met Alma, eleven years his senior, fell in love, and rejiggered his life to accord with her ideas. The two make a striking couple, shaped by seemingly irreconcilable differences. He is a frequently somewhat strident entertainer driven by a love of storytelling, short, corpulent, perpetually sweaty, and always a bit shabbily dressed. He comes from a Jewish family and cannot imagine life without religious underpinnings. To be sure, he seldom if ever visits a synagogue, but instead flirts with Christianity and Catholicism. In his books he raves about high ideals and grand gestures, albeit without being a champion for his own convictions. Outside of literature, he tends toward a willingness to assimilate and compliance. Ultimately, Werfel has truly fuzzy notions of what is happening in Europe politically. He speaks of humanity, peace, and justice, but when the Prussian Academy of the Arts demanded a written affirmation of Hitler's politics from its members in 1933, Werfel could not move fast enough. He sent a cable to Berlin requesting the appropriate form, returned it posthaste with his approval – and barely two months later was expelled from the Academy as a Jew.

In her mid-fifties, by contrast, Alma now numbers among the dominant personalities in Viennese cultural life. She is tall, very present, and always draped in flowing, ankle-length gowns with which she conceals how much her pleasure in food and alcohol have bloated her. In no way, however, does this lessen her vitality or her power to assert herself; she possesses astonishing abilities to steer people according to her will. Although she never cut a graceful figure, she has long managed to inspire in men the notion that she is the most beautiful woman in Vienna. The list of her famous lovers and husbands is long. In her youth, she seduced Alexander von Zemlinsky, who gave her composition lessons, while also mocking him for his ugliness. Then she married the much-celebrated, nearly two-decades-older Gustav Mahler, who forbade her to compose, cheated on him with the young, highly talented architect Walter Gropius, plunged into an affair after Mahler's death with painter

Oskar Kokoschka who was feared for his fits of temper, before ultimately marrying Gropius after all, whom she again double-crossed with Werfel.

When Gropius had himself transferred from the front-line battle to a safe military school during the First World War, Alma was horrified at his unheroic conduct, admonishing him in a letter: "My husband must be first-rate." She seems always to have chosen her favorites according to this motto. While she enjoys working herself up over the idea that she subordinates herself to her famous husbands to serve their successes, her instinct for power remains on high alert at all times. Total submission on the one hand and complete contempt on the other blend seamlessly into one another in her romantic relationships. She therefore makes no secret of her antisemitism and regards her marriages with the Jews Gustav Mahler and Franz Werfel as self-abasement – from which she derives the right to humiliate and insult her husbands in return.

When she met Werfel for the first time, he did not outwardly accord in any way with what she had imagined. He was, she thought, a fat, bowlegged Jew with fleshy lips and watery slit-eyes. But, she added, he grows better the more he reveals of himself. She recognized his enormous literary potential and, with her idiosyncratic powers of suggestion, coaxed him to unimagined discipline in work. Before, he had spent a considerable portion of his time on extended benders with friends and almost exclusively wrote poems or seldom performed plays. Under Alma's influence, he then switched to prose, with phenomenal success; his novellas and novels reach high print runs and earn him fabulous fees.

Money that the both of them desperately need for their extravagant lifestyle. They own a country home in Semmering, a small mansion in Venice, and a palace-like villa in Vienna. The latter is where Alma celebrates the high art of maintaining social contacts. Her home is one of the city's prime addresses, with an elegant hall for receptions, a representative dining room, a study for the men in dark green, as well as a marble-paneled salon for the ladies with an oval floor plan. Her soirees are legendary. She invites those of distinction in economics, culture, and politics, and everyone – *everyone* – comes. Alma brings together people who never would have met without her assistance; she is a matchmaker for marriages and other erotic connections, spreads rumors that facilitate or ruin careers, and in spite of all of this never loses sight of her own interests and those of Werfel.

It was on one of these occasions that she established a connection with Schuschnigg, when he was not yet chancellor. His overtly autocratic ambitions did not bother her. On the contrary, she admires men who ruthlessly make use of their power. Werfel also turns a blind eye to Schuschnigg's political crimes, preferring to see in him a sort of kind and strict national father figure. In his most recent novel, *The Forty Days of Musa Dagh*, he tells of the fanatical nationalism of the Turks during the First World War, which erupts into the genocide of the country's Armenian minority. The book is a tour de force of historical storytelling: tremendously vivid, thrilling, precisely researched in every detail. Published in 1933, it quickly became a global bestseller. Critics and readers alike viewed it as a visionary warning against the violence of fascist rulers like Hitler, Mussolini – and Schuschnigg, too. Yet Werfel cannot find the energy to distance himself from Schuschnigg.

To Alma's delight, the connection to Schuschnigg rapidly grew closer. The chancellor was crazy about Anna Mahler, Alma's eldest daughter, and relatively soon a romance developed between the two. When Anna traveled to Italy with her mother and Werfel, the lovestruck Schuschnigg followed them and met up with them in Viareggio. An incumbent head of government, however, he could not keep his private sojourn in Italy a complete secret, but rather had to declare himself to the government in Rome through diplomatic channels. As a gesture of friendship between dictators, Benito Mussolini made his own state limousine available to him for his vacation. And so Werfel, the antifascist author of *Musa Dagh* celebrated the world over, took excursions to Tuscany on subsequent days, accompanied by the fascist ruler of Austria and in a vehicle belonging to the fascist ruler of Italy.

Le Désastre

May 1940

Northern Eifel, May 10, 1940

At first light, German troops decamp for the battlefields in France they left twenty-two years earlier. So as not to get bogged down in a paralyzing trench war as they had been then, Hitler and his generals look to deploy fast tank units. For two days, these now barrel through the forests of the Ardennes like an avalanche of steel. The French defenders are completely surprised by the vehemence of the attack. By May 13, the Germans have broken through the defensive lines at Sedan and are crossing the Meuse. From there, the tanks advance farther westward, on the move day and night, fighting their way through the weak defenses of northern France toward the English Channel coast.

Sanary-sur-Mer, May 14, 1940

In his villa by the sea, far removed from the realities of war, Lion Feuchtwanger is lying on an ottoman, following the evening news over the wireless. In the gathering twilight, a glorious early summer day comes to an end. But what Feuchtwanger hears does not gibe with the tranquil evening mood. The German troops are charging forward; the French and their British allies have been forced to concede bitter defeats. Hitler, from whom he fled to France, is about to conquer the country of his exile.

While Feuchtwanger is still pondering the horrifying state of military affairs, an official statement is read by the radio announcer. All Germans and Austrians between the ages of seventeen and fifty-five living in Paris and its environs, as well as all stateless persons of this age range born in Germany or Austria, must report to certain rendezvous points in order to be transported to internment camps. The French government sees in them potential Nazi sympathizers and wants to avoid the risk of possible acts of sabotage behind the battlefront.

Feuchtwanger is all too familiar with this precautionary measure. He was detained once already, when France and Great Britain declared war on Germany for invading Poland eight months earlier. What grotesque harassment. As most others in exile, he is an avowed opponent of the Nazis. To suspect him of sabotaging France is absurd. But the French authorities proceeded in accordance with strict bureaucracy and permitted no exceptions. Only when it became clear that no *acts* of war followed the declarations of war did they let everyone go again.

This peculiar state of abeyance has held for more than eight months. The enemy armies had taken up position along the German–French border and tracked one another closely, but had not fired a shot. An eerie quiet lay over everything. German grunts referred to this as *Sitzkrieg*, a sitting war, and in France the newspaper wrote of *la drôle de guerre*, the comic war. Yet the war is not comic anymore, but rather brutally serious, and the French government swiftly calls to mind its internment order, which it had never rescinded.

For a few minutes, Feuchtwanger continues to lie on his ottoman without moving. It is quite tempting, of course, to persuade oneself that the order might remain limited to Paris and its environs and that he might be spared, here, in the fortunate south. Feuchtwanger is too intelligent, however, to delude himself. If eight months ago the measure pertained to the entire country, now, after the enemy has overrun the borders, it will not turn out to be any more moderate.

He gets up, realizing to his surprise that it is now already dark. Clearly he has been occupied with thoughts of the military situation longer than he imagined. He steps out onto the terrace, strolls through the garden, but is capable of seeing the blossoming glory of the flower beds only as something of the past. The instinctive process of saying his goodbyes has already begun. Then he returns to the house, looks for Marta, who is in the kitchen making up the food for the cats, and shares the bad news with her. The order to report for internment also applies to women from Germany and Austria. At the northern edge of the Pyrenees, near a village called Gurs, there is an enormous camp for women. It is very damp there, quite filthy, and cold – that much Marta and Lion know. A dreaded place.

Marta immediately begins planning which of his influential friends Lion should write the very next day, or better yet: wire, so that they can intervene on their behalf at the highest levels. It has got to be possible to obtain an exception, at least for Lion. After all, the edict is valid only for men up to age fifty-five, and in just a few weeks he will turn fifty-six.

Suddenly, there is a knock at the front door, then at the kitchen door. Lion and Marta give a start. A visitor this late is unusual, and yet still they answer the door. Anton Räderscheidt, a painter from Cologne, and his wife have been driven here by their concern: "Have you heard?" Both of them are also refugees from Germany and live just next door. Räderscheidt is a difficult man, a loner who even in placid conversations can all of a sudden turn irascible and acrimonious. Feuchtwanger mostly avoids him, and Räderscheidt in turn does likewise. This night, however, is different. Today it seems obvious to them to seek each other's company and deliberate together about what to do.

It would have been more prudent, of course, to have left France a year or two earlier and sought safety somewhere in America. After the annexation of Austria by Germany and after the destruction of Czechoslovakia by Hitler, the imminent threat of war in Europe was palpable. Thomas Mann did not delay when he was offered a professorship at Princeton.

But Feuchtwanger was afraid of the endless bureaucratic impediments. Getting a residence permit for the United States is not easy for anyone – and in his case, there is an additional obstacle. After the big Writers Congress in Paris in 1935, he did in fact garner an invitation to the Soviet Union, and in his book about the trip, he described how reasonably, peacefully, and justly everything worked in Stalin's empire. Now he is regarded as a fellow traveler of the communists, which has not increased his popularity with American immigration authorities.

What's more, two years earlier, he was still deeply immersed in work on his most recent novel *Paris Gazette*, a sort of political thriller about a cleverly devised Nazi covert operation against emigrants in Paris. While working on it, he did not want to be interrupted for any reason. And then another sentimental obstacle arose. Feuchtwanger fell madly in love with southern France. He enjoyed the magic of the landscape to the fullest, the climate, the light, and, not least, life in their villa above the sea. It would never have occurred to him to leave this place voluntarily. Sanary was his paradise.

Only war and internment managed to change that. No one expected it, but all of a sudden, all the borders were closed. Expatriates were no longer permitted to leave the country. From one day to the next, they were stuck in a trap. Feuchtwanger tried to obtain exit visas, but he was denied them for no valid reason. All at once, the government of the country that had so kindly taken them in after their escape from Hitler showed an entirely different side of itself.

The camp outside Aix-en-Provence where Feuchtwanger had been incarcerated eight months earlier, Les Milles, is no concentration camp. No one is beaten, tormented, or tortured there. There is no forced labor, there are no prison cells, there are no death threats – just tolerable food and businesslike, unagitated guards. The filth and the hygienic conditions, however, are dire. Les Milles is an old, defunct brickyard, fenced in by an entanglement of barbed wire. In the factory buildings, a layer of red brick dust covers literally everything, finding its way into the seams of clothing, the folds of skin, the hair, the ears, the eyes. And yet for the two thousand men in the camps, there are only twenty faucets and seven primitive latrines on wooden planks. Long queues form at each of these at every hour of the day; internees often have to wait in line for hours to satisfy their most basic needs.

This is more than an unpleasant nuisance. It is barbarity, a violation of human rights. The overfull latrines, the filth, the scarcity of water are concrete health hazards for these penned-up men. There is no malicious calculation behind this, just the indifference and overextension of the authorities. No one was prepared to incarcerate so many people in such a short time. And now, after the battles with the Germans have begun, there is little inclination to improve the conditions of German prisoners in the camps – especially since there are neither the resources nor the personnel to do so.

What is in store for them will not be an easy time – Räderscheidt and Feuchtwanger should be under no illusions. At Les Milles, the former storage areas in the two upper levels of the factory building serve as dormitories, grim halls with loose straw on the ground for the prisoners to drape their blankets over. The windows are boarded and nailed shut so that no light penetrates to the outside that might provide orientation to German bomber pilots at night. There are no bedsteads, no pieces of furniture, no nooks for privacy; whatever Räderscheidt and

Feuchtwanger take with them to this camp they must store there in their suitcases.

The situation is ludicrous – surrounded by the bounty of the Feuchtwangers' villa, the two men and their wives must plan for an almost destitute period of time in mass accommodations that the summer heat will soon transform into furnaces. And there is nothing they can do about it.

London, May 15, 1940

At seven thirty in the morning, the French prime minister Paul Reynaud telephones his British ally Winston Churchill in London, beginning the conversation with the line: "We've been beaten."

Because Churchill, who has only just woken up, must first collect himself and does not reply immediately, Reynaud repeats: "We're conquered. We've lost the battle."

Churchill attempts to calm his French counterpart: "All experience shows that an offensive will come to a standstill after a while." The constant advance will push the men in the tanks to the brink of collapse and force them to rest. They must halt, Churchill says, "and then the possibility of a counter-offensive will present itself."

But the German tanks do not halt. They continue thundering forward, seemingly unstoppable.

Paris, May 15, 1940

Hannah Arendt takes the Metro – it is easiest that way. For four months now, she has been married to Heinrich Blücher, whom she accompanied yesterday to the Stade Buffalo on the outskirts of Paris, where the men are to gather for evacuation to the internment camps. Next up today: childless German and Austrian women. An exemption clause is in effect for mothers, who may remain with their children. Everyone else, however, must report to the Vélodrome d'Hiver, a cycling arena near the Eiffel Tower.

The decrees are pedantic in their precision; every internee is to bring food rations for two days, her own mess kit, and a blanket. Luggage may not weigh more than thirty kilos total. It is not actually very far to the

Vélodrome from the Rue de la Convention, where Arendt and Blücher live, just a short stretch along the Seine, but because of her suitcase, Arendt prefers taking the Metro.

She has been living in Paris for almost seven years now. At first glance, she still comes across as girlish and fragile, despite being in her early thirties, but one should not be fooled: those who get to know her better quickly experience her determination, for which she is held in high esteem by many women, and also by some men. In Germany, she worked for a long time on a postdoctoral project, but when, as a Jew, she was forced to flee in 1933, she purposely set the manuscript aside. Today she still mentally grapples with her experiences at universities in the weeks following Hitler's seizure of power. Even some of her closest friends suddenly pledged themselves to the new rulers and their hatred of the Jews. They dissociated themselves from her as if she were a leper; it was as if a void had formed around her. It had little to do with antisemitic beliefs; the people concerned merely did not want to endanger their careers. She did not experience anything similar with other, less educated friends.

Thereafter, at first, she found the academic sphere abhorrent; she initially wanted nothing more to do with the university. In Paris, Arendt sought out a job as a social worker and organized transports of children to Palestine for the Zionist Youth Aliyah, a meaningful, practical occupation in which she could have become engrossed. Ultimately, however, her theoretical interests could not be forsaken. While she did not register as a student at the Sorbonne, she did attend political discussion groups there, gave lectures, and met with other German exiles. In one of these roundtable discussions, she also met Heinrich Blücher, a former supporter of the German communist party who now preferred to devote himself more to Kant than to Marx. And she met another man there, who became a good friend: literary critic and philosopher Walter Benjamin. With touching awkwardness, he slogs his way through life, but writes incomparably sophisticated, poetic essays.

The Vélodrome d'Hiver is a gigantic sports arena capped by a glass cupola. When Hannah Arendt arrives there, lines have already begun to form at the entrances; the women must stand and wait for police officers to lock them inside. Each of them receives a sack of straw for their overnight stays on the bare concrete floor of the stands. The hall is hot

Hannah Arendt, around 1930

and dirty, the air stale, the toilets and washing facilities few. On top of that – and this irks Hannah Arendt – smoking is strictly forbidden. But because there is dry, loose straw everywhere, in every alcove, hallway, and stairwell, she can accept the prohibition.

At night, the women hear the drone of German airplanes first, then the explosions of the bombs and the muffled booming of the antiaircraft guns. Every now and again, there is a sharp bang whenever splinters of the flak shells fall onto the glass cupola from high altitude. The Vélodrome has no air-raid shelter; the internees are at the mercy of the bombs. Only a few spectator boxes have half-height walls and seem halfway safe. Arendt speaks with the women sleeping there and asks whether she might climb behind the partitions with them if a bomb hits. "But of course," they reply.

After about a week, dozens of buses stop at the arena entrances. Word gets round fast among the women that they are to be transported to Gurs, the dreaded internment camp in the Pyrenees. The buses drive them along the Seine to the Gare de Lyon. It is a perfect spring day; the sun is shining, the sky is blue, and the trees are blooming. The city in which many of these exiled women have lived for years presents itself to them in all its beauty. A number of them burst into tears. None can be sure she will ever see Paris again. Hannah Arendt also assumes it is a farewell forever. She loves this city, but the final accounting is bitter. The protection she found here was withdrawn again all too capriciously.

New York, May 16, 1940

Late in the morning, Varian Mackey Fry receives an alarming telephone call in his office not far from Times Square. He has since left the magazine *The Living Age* and has become chief editor for the Foreign Policy Association, a wealthy foundation that publishes a book series on matters of foreign policy with Headline Books. It is a dream job; the foundation manages a considerable fortune, is headquartered in the middle of Manhattan, and is interested not in profit, but above all in persuasive essays on the current state of the world. Without having to pay overly much attention to sales, Fry can publish books on all matters of politics – and has written several of them himself.

On the telephone is Paul Hagen, a psychoanalyst and journalist with a checkered political past. Like many leftist intellectuals in Austria and Germany after the First World War, he traveled the long path from communism in the Soviet model via moderate socialism to membership in the SPD [Social Democratic Party of Germany]. Immediately after Hitler's ascension to power, he was forced to leave Germany and since then has been trying to make life difficult for the Nazis while in exile.

Hagen's real name is Karl Frank – that Fry knows. Out of consideration for family members who still live in Germany, however, he has adopted a code name. He is an energetic, brawny man who led a clandestine resistance group in Europe called Neu Beginnen [Beginning Anew]. He is well acquainted with the plight of exiles in Europe. For his underground work, he was forced to change cities and countries continually, from Vienna to Prague, from Paris to London. He even returned to Germany with forged identity papers for a few missions and, fortunately, got out again. He has now been living in New York since the winter and has founded an organization with other activists that calls itself American Friends of German Freedom.

Right after arriving, Hagen began establishing contact with politicians and pundits with whom he could continue his fight against Hitler, including with Varian Fry, who has been issuing warnings about the Nazis for so long now that his journalist colleagues deride him as a Cassandra. The Americans are still not interested in the tattered state of political affairs in Europe and want to avoid being drawn into the war carnage there at all costs.

Over the phone, Hagen sounds even more passionate and more worried than usual. Since the German tanks broke through near Sedan three days earlier, news has reached him from France that preys on his mind. He asks Fry to meet him at Childs', a diner on 42nd Street where they have had lunch together a few times before, to discuss the state of the war.

When Fry arrives at Childs', Hagen gives him an account from his own negative experience of what the Nazis do when they overrun one of their neighboring countries. In the wake of the advancing military, Gestapo search parties systematically comb through the country. Furnished with prepared lists, they track down Hitler's adversaries, arrest them, deport them to concentration camps, or murder them right then and there. In Poland, which Germany invaded the previous year, they have now proceeded to kill off not just the resistance fighters, but also the country's entire elite: physicians, teachers, merchants, politicians, engineers. Only a nation of worker-slaves is meant to survive.

Because Hagen has also lived in France for a time, he knows the situation there. Thousands of exiles, almost all of them avowed foes of the Nazis, live primarily in Paris and in the country's south. If German tanks continue driving off the French and the Brits as they have, the manhunters moving in from the rear will very soon fan out throughout the country and reap a rich, bloody harvest.

Hagen does not need to talk for long to persuade Fry. Among the artists and intellectuals Hagen names who have fled to France are many whose work Fry has known and admired since *Hound & Horn*: celebrated painters like Marc Chagall or Max Ernst, world-famous writers like Heinrich Mann, Franz Werfel, and Lion Feuchtwanger, or Anna Seghers, Alfred Döblin, and Walter Mehring. Some of the most significant proponents of modernism are included; a whole generation of important European cultural figures is in danger of being exterminated over the next few weeks. Fry gets whey Hagen is so agitated. If they want to help those in danger, they have to act very quickly, faster than the Gestapo.

They begin drafting the outline of a rescue plan. Fry has experience working with political aid organizations – just not good experience. In recent years, he was a member of the Spanish Aid Committee, which tried to support Spain's Republican government in the civil war against the troops of the fascist General Francisco Franco. But the organization failed on two counts. Franco triumphed in Spain, and the committee was infiltrated by a small group of Stalinist adherents who, in Fry's eyes, were no less dangerous than the fascists. And so he ultimately left the committee.

For a rapid rescue initiative in France, they need three things, on this Fry and Hagen agree: prominent allies who will draw public attention to their cause, along with a small, hard-hitting organization, and, not least, money. A lot of money. On this last, most difficult point, Fry might have a solution.

He gets up, goes to a telephone booth in Childs', and calls up Harold Oram, whom he met while working for the Spanish Republicans. Oram is a man with a pronounced sense of social commitment, though no metaphysical dreamer. Half a year ago, he founded a company that does professional fundraising. With the help of well-trained people, he mounts effective donation campaigns, but only for causes he finds convincing and morally justified. As payment, he lays claims to a percentage share of the donation pot for himself and his team.

After only a few sentences, Oram understands the gravity of Fry's and Hagen's undertaking and that they have no time to lose. He sets off and is soon sitting at the table with the pair in Childs'. Together, they compile a list of potential advocates, only well-known people, including writers, clergy, presidents of various universities, important news anchors, journalists. Over the next few days, they aim to speak to these people and win them over to their cause. Then, in the name of these supporters, they will send out invitations to a fundraising gala at one of Manhattan's grand hotels to found a committee to rescue persecuted artists and intellectuals in Europe. They even decide on a date for their event: June 25. Five weeks remain until then. That is short notice for the tremendous amount of work before them, but it is a miserably long time for everyone in France waiting to be rescued.

Abbéville, May 20, 1940

The first German tank units arrive at the English Channel coast near Abbéville by evening. Hundreds of thousands of French, British, and Belgian soldiers are thereby trapped in a gigantic corral around the harbor town of Dunkirk. They are in danger of total annihilation.

In the end, there is a pharmaceutical reason for the speed and endurance of the German tank forces. Since 1938, the chemical plant Temmler in Berlin has been producing a high-potency stimulant: Pervitin. A form of methamphetamine, it eliminates any need for sleep, curbs fear, and enhances both concentration and self-confidence – the perfect drug for wartime deployment. The *Wehrmacht* carefully oversaw its development, tested its efficacy, and had the medicine produced by the millions and distributed to soldiers. Pervitin makes possible a multi-day advance without breaks for sleep. It provides the Germans with enormous strategic advantages and earns them the reputation of superhuman performance ability. Just ten days after hostilities began, France finds itself at the brink of defeat. The country seems to be completely at the mercy of its attackers. Panic begins to spread among the populace.

Les Milles, May 21, 1940

To save his energy, Feuchtwanger takes a taxi a hundred kilometers from Sanary to the camp at Les Milles. Ever since he heard the internment order for all Germans and Austrians on the radio, he tried to obtain an exception from the decree for himself and Marta. But all letters, telephone calls, and telegrams were in vain. In light of the daily horror of war and the growing chaos in the country, no one has time anymore to deal with his case. And so Marta and he must submit to the inevitable. He is not alone in the taxi, though; he has given a lift to a writer friend, the Spanish Civil War combatant Alfred Kantorowicz, as well as his neighbor, the painter Räderscheidt, and Räderscheidt's seventeen-year-old son.

When they arrive outside the camp, the trio watch him pay the taxi driver. Then they drag their luggage through the barbed-wire gate. Feuchtwanger, with his slight build, struggles in a clumsy manner. He is carrying far too much: two suitcases, a folding chair, and a large blanket for the straw bed. It is impossible for him to carry everything at once, and he keeps dropping something. The sentries at the gate become impatient. But then a couple of young Austrians who have known him since his first stay in Les Milles several months earlier catch sight of him. They walk right through the open gate toward him, paying no attention to the "halt, get back!" commands of the soldiers, welcome him, and carry his luggage to the camp's orderly room, where he is to report.

The spontaneous help delights Feuchtwanger, and since he has brought enough money not to have to scrimp, he promises the boys payment if they assist him in the future as well. One of them is an especially strong man, a former boxer. Apparently he suffered brain damage from his bouts and has slowed down a bit since then, but he is very devoted. Happy to have something to do finally after months of boredom in the camp, he declares himself Feuchtwanger's personal manservant and hauls his luggage up the narrow, filthy wooden staircase to the gigantic dormitory on the second floor.

Feuchtwanger has no luck here. He is allocated an especially dark, cramped place to sleep, far from the windows. As he soon realizes, however, he will not be able to complain about the lack of conversational partners in this camp. Two writer friends from Sanary have already settled in: Wilhelm Herzog, a close friend of Heinrich Mann, and Franz Hessel, whom Feuchtwanger knows from his time in Berlin. Hessel was an editor at Ernst Rowohlt's publishing house, a short, gentle man who writes wonderfully elegant stories and who, together with Walter Benjamin, translated the first two volumes of Marcel Proust's novel of the century, *In Search of Lost Time*.

With great diffidence, the painter Max Ernst turns up, almost incognito; he had been living in remote Saint-Martin-d'Ardèche with the young English painter Leonora Carrington, heard nothing there about the internment order, and was brought to the camp by gendarmes. Franz Schoenberner is here, too, the former editor-in-chief of the famous Munich satirical magazine *Simplicissimus*. And just a few meters from Feuchtwanger's straw bed is that of Walter Hasenclever, one of the most important writers and dramatists of Expressionism.

Kantorowicz had more luck with his berth. It is located in a window alcove that is brighter and airier than all the others. Kantorowicz has an alcohol stove as well. When he makes coffee at midday, many of the authors and painters assemble around him. Their gatherings then seem like bitter parodies of the gatherings of artists that once took place in the Parisian Café du Dôme or in the Romanisches Café in Berlin.

Gurs, late May 1940

From the first, Hannah Arendt is dumbfounded at what an enormous role cosmetics play in this camp, which has little else to offer but squalor and heat. Many of the women spend hours each day on their morning toilette, applying makeup, combing their hair endlessly, and putting it up in complicated hairdos. Then they parade around between the barracks in short pants or beach suits, spruced up as if for a summer festival.

Arendt quickly realizes that this all has nothing to do with vanity, but with self-therapy. Gurs is not a labor camp; there is nothing to do here. It is a place of vacuous time. Whoever lets herself go will soon sink into depression. The cosmetic efforts serve to improve not appearance, but psychological health.

The Gurs internment camp in the Pyrenees, 1939

The French constructed Gurs a year earlier after the Republicans had lost the Spanish Civil War and their combatants fled from Franco's troops across the border to France by the thousands. It is a huge compound, three kilometers long and almost as wide, enclosed by a tall barbed-wire fence. There are more than four hundred wooden cabins, arranged in strict rectilinear order like on a chess board. Every thirty to forty of those are combined into blocks and again fenced in with barbed wire. In each cabin there are sixty berths with straw sacks; the women are so cramped together that at night they bump up against their neighbor with every movement. Otherwise, there is literally nothing in these sheds: no cabinets or chairs, no shelf to put anything on, no nail to hang anything. They do not even have windows, just narrow portholes with closeable wooden shutters.

Nowhere in the camps is there a tree or a bush. Almost everywhere it reeks of urine. The worst is the loamy soil. After each rain shower – and it rains often in the foothills of the Pyrenees – the ground transforms into a squelching quagmire. Those who do not want to get their shoes stuck have to walk barefoot, then let the mud dry, and rub it off their skin. There is scarcely any water; at best, a trickle comes from the taps. None of the washing facilities has a privacy screen, so every morning several guards will assemble at the barbed wire to watch the women attend to their hygiene. The latrines are ghastly: tall wooden pedestals with circular holes – also without privacy screens – with open metal barrels underneath to collect the feces. Dysentery and other diarrheic diseases are going around; one needs a robust constitution to survive here.

As in the camps for men, there are also prominent prisoners in Gurs. Thea Sternheim arrived on the transport from Paris. In spite of her fifty-six years and her excellent connections to André Gide, she was not spared from internment. Marta Feuchtwanger and Annemarie Herzog, Wilhelm Herzog's wife, have been brought here from Sanary-sur-Mer. Hannah Arendt also runs into Dora Benjamin here, Walter Benjamin's sister, who is gravely ill; she suffers from ankylosing spondylitis, an especially painful condition that deforms the spine.

Likely the strangest fate is that of the women married to former combatants in the Spanish Civil War. Many of them know Gurs from the tales of their husbands who were incarcerated here until a few months ago. Shortly after their release, the men were re-arrested and interned in other camps, their wives, however, in Gurs – married life to the beat of internments. One of the prisoners finds a slip of paper with a few hastily written lines in her straw sack: "Sweet girl, I don't know you, but I stuffed this straw sack for you. Sleep well on it. Heinz, a Spanish fighter."

Ljubljana – Paris, late May 1940

A few weeks ago, Miriam Davenport traveled to Ljubljana to join her fiancé, a Yugoslavian university friend, and prepare for her final exam there in peace. She is an American, a young woman in love, twenty-four years old, studying art history in Paris. She likes braiding her hair into pigtails and pinning these up in coils on both sides. She then looks a little like a dark-blond Mickey Mouse with a pert nose and cheerful eyes. But now she must make an important decision.

Her examination date is approaching, and she has landed in a sticky situation on account of her trip to Yugoslavia. On the one hand, it is pure lunacy to return to Paris now, while the battle around the corralled troops at Dunkirk is raging, to sit for her exam. On the other hand, she is under tremendous pressure. Her parents died three years ago, and they left her and her ten-year-old brother penniless. With the scholarship for her studies, she can only just keep herself and her brother, living with relatives in America, afloat, but now both her scholarship and her visa for France are expiring, and both will not be extended in the middle of the war. In other words, the impending exams are her only chance at a decent degree, and without a degree she will never get a job with which she can support herself and her brother.

And so, feeling queasy, she boards a train in Ljubljana that takes her straight across Italy back to France. In Paris, she rents a room in cheap lodgings with a pompous name: the Hôtel de l'Univers. It is close to the Sorbonne and right next door to a bordello with a jauntily blinking red light. The following day, she is about to add her name to the list of examinees at the university, but she does not encounter another soul there. To escape to safety, the professors have long since left Paris. The exams have been moved to Toulouse, in the southwest of France.

Miriam has no choice but to follow them there. She wants to pack her suitcase right away and head to the train station, though now – it is made clear to her – strict regulations are in effect in France. Foreigners may not travel outside their place of residence without a *sauf-conduit*, a kind of official permit. To obtain this travel permit, she must visit various government offices. That, she is warned, may take several days.

While gathering together all the necessary forms and stamps, she spends dreary nights in the hotel and gets to know four exiles, three men and one woman. Once, they tell her, a fifth exile had lived in Miriam's room, a great dramatist and novelist, Ödön von Horváth, who was struck dead by a falling tree branch on the Champs-Élysées during a thunderstorm two years earlier. They are amiable but anxious people. Among themselves they only speak French, despite hailing from Germany and Austria. They do not want to be recognized as foreigners. If the French catch them, they will end up in an internment camp; if the Germans get their hands on them, they will all be killed.

All four of them are writers. One of them, Hans Natonek, a journalist and novelist, is a huge charmer and probably did not flee Germany solely from Hitler, but also from the wrath of his wife, on whom he cheated countless times. The second one always has a bottle of wine with him in some pocket or bag whenever Miriam runs into him. Walter Mehring is a short, slender man with a large head, as fidgety as a child. A few couplets he wrote for the cabaret have become genuine popular hits. His volumes of poetry have prompted the likes of powerful critics like Kurt Tucholsky to sing hymns of praise. Ever since his escape from Berlin, however, his once so radiant, quick wit has grown increasingly bitter. He writes less and less, and what he writes gets darker and darker. The woman in the group, Hertha Pauli, has long been friends with Walter Mehring, but they are no longer a couple. She comes from Vienna and was formerly an actor. Now, as a literary agent, she tries to find new publishers for her own books and those of other authors who have been forced to flee abroad from the Nazis – an almost futile business.

Ernst Weiss, the oldest of the four, could really use Hertha Pauli's help. He studied medicine, worked for a few years as a surgeon, but then chose literature. Writer colleagues like Thomas Mann and Joseph Roth hold his books in esteem, but none of them has ever had success with readers. His most recent manuscript, *The Eyewitness*, lies in a drawer, unpublished; no publisher wants it.

The novel tells the ingeniously fictionalized life story of a doctor. During the First World War, he has to treat people with hideous injuries in field hospitals behind the front. When Germany's defeat looms large, a fanatic suffering from hysterical blindness is brought in. The man, a simple private, is so distraught at the outcome of the war that his eyes would rather see nothing at all than witness Germany's collapse. The doctor heals him by appealing to his fanaticism. He convinces him that he must overcome his psychological blindness so that he, Private A. H., can save Germany and restore it to its former greatness. Years later, A. H., in whom readers of course recognize Adolf Hitler, has risen to become the country's dictator. So that no one learns that he was once seen as a hysteric, he intends to make his medical record vanish at any cost – and preferably the doctor who cured him along with it.

Weiss has never numbered among the optimists, but ever since being unable to find a publisher for his *Eyewitness*, he has descended into black despair. Natonek and he do not live in the Hôtel de l'Univers, but they come and go daily to see Mehring and Hertha Pauli. The horrifying successes of the German troops have virtually pulled the rug out from under their feet; they seek each other's company as though they could protect one another. Miriam senses their fear and realizes what a stroke of luck it is for her to have an American passport.

Dunkirk, May 26 to June 4, 1940

The last chance of the Allied troops surrounded at Dunkirk is a hastily improvised rescue mission. As many British, French, and Belgian troops as possible are to be evacuated to England across the Channel with an armada of large, small, and tiny vessels. All their military equipment, however – weapons, ammunition, vehicles, artillery, tanks – will remain behind on the beach. On May 27, during the final, fierce battles with the British rearguard, SS troops murder ninety-nine injured prisoners of war with machine guns in a village named Lestrem. In the Belgian town of Vinkt, west of Ghent, German soldiers execute eighty-six civilians on the same day. On the day after, in the northern French town of Oignies, eighty civilians are shot dead by the Germans. Panic grows among the population. Hundreds of thousands abandon their homes and flee southward.

Paris – Sanary-sur-Mer, late May 1940

Alma Mahler-Werfel and Franz Werfel have only one goal in mind: get out of France. They have spent the past few weeks in Paris, though not in such modest accommodations as the Hôtel de l'Univers, but in a suite at the Royal Madeleine, one of the city's finest addresses, situated between the Tuileries and the monumental Opéra Garnier.

In truth, they have been residing in an old windmill in Sanary-sur-Mer for two years. The locals call it Moulin Gris. Decades earlier, the windwheel was dismantled and the former mill tower, together with the outbuildings, was remodeled into a kind of country house. Alma is ill at ease there. In the summertime, the mosquitos and the heat plague her. The aged structure is perched on cliffs directly above the coast, however, and the room at the top of the tower has twelve wraparound glass windows. This is where Werfel works, as Feuchtwanger does in his villa, with an unobstructed view of the Mediterranean Sea. The vista is spectacular.

Alma cannot forgive her husband for making her leave her beloved Vienna. The thought of being banned from Germany because of her marriage to a Jew is hard for her to bear. In her diary, she notes, "Now I will have to wander to the ends of the earth with a people alien to me." For her, this is especially nonsensical because, in her heart of hearts, she reveres Hitler and considers him "a genius at the pinnacle of a great people." With "the greatest admiration," she writes, she observes "this heroic man … striding victoriously over humanity." Secretly, she toys with the idea of divorcing Werfel.

After the beginning of the war, the mood in Sanary foundered. In prior years, the locals treated the exiles with a kind of business-minded hospitality. Now, though, many see in those who speak German a potential enemy to the nation or, worse, an agent of Hitler. One day, Werfel was stopped by a gendarme on the market square right in front of Sanary's town hall and searched like a criminal in broad daylight.

"Are you a communist?" the officer barked at him.

"No!" replied Werfel, who had long since put the leftist ideals of his youth behind him.

"You do write for the poor, though?" the mistrustful man insisted, which he obviously viewed as clear proof of Werfel's communist convictions.

"I write," Werfel gave as his Solomonic retort, "for everyone, poor and rich."

Naturally, nothing impermissible was found during this body search, and the gendarme had to let Werfel go. But after this violation, the Werfels did not feel safe in Sanary and relocated to the Royal Madeleine in Paris. Here, however, airstrikes by German bombers forced them to leave their beds every other night and descend into the – in Alma's opinion – stinking cellar of the hotel. There they would sit for hours among half-asleep people in rumpled nightshirts.

This is no life for Alma, and so they are now heading back to Sanary. There they intend to liquidate their household at the mill and travel onward to Marseille. In that city, there are good hotels, an acceptable opera, and, most importantly, an American consulate where they can apply for visas for the United States. They have heard this will not be easy. But Werfel's novels achieve huge print runs in America as well. The consul, they believe, will surely issue at the drop of a hat a prominent writer such as himself all the papers necessary to leave this now inhospitable country.

Loriol, late May 1940

Having to wait, pointlessly letting time tick away, is the worst thing for Golo Mann. Never would he have expected to end up in an internment camp. The French government's decrees are exasperatingly mindless: war in its stupidest form.

When the pocket closed around the Allied troops at Dunkirk, Golo Mann could no longer take it in Switzerland. He had worked in Zurich for almost a year as the editor of *Mass und Wert* magazine, which his father publishes from Princeton. Within this one year, Switzerland has transformed itself before his very eyes into a fortress. Men between the ages of twenty and fifty were called up to military service, thoroughly trained, and stationed at the borders. New weapons were acquired, all public buildings barricaded, bridges set with blasting charges, and antitank barriers set up at strategically important locations. Golo Mann is now thirty-one years old. He cannot idly watch such preparations for war; he wants to fight against Hitler. The Swiss army, however, refuses to accept him – it has no place for foreigners.

For he is, officially, Czech. In 1936, the Nazis collectively expatriated Thomas Mann's family and revoked their German passports. Through diplomatic channels, the Czech president Edvard Beneš subsequently offered to make them citizens of his country, an offer they gratefully accepted – with the exception of Erika, the oldest daughter, who married the English poet W. H. Auden and thereby became British.

In Zurich, Golo Mann was so very ashamed of his country of birth that he hardly ever ventured out and would feign a Czech accent in conversations so as to go unrecognized as German. Once he learned there was a Czech Legion in the French army, he wanted to join it at any cost. He obtained a travel permit from the French consul general and even received from him – since the consul was an admirer of Thomas Mann – a personal letter of recommendation to boot.

But none of that interested the French border officials. They took him into custody just past the boom gate and transferred him, like all the other German and Austrian exiles, to an internment camp. Golo Mann could not even muster any resistance, because the officials initially led him to believe he was being transported to his future brigade for training.

The Loriol camp where they have taken him is located somewhere in Provence and does not differ appreciably from camps like Les Milles or Gurs: barbed-wire fences, filthy latrines, vermin, straw mattresses, water scarcity. Golo has of course written letters of protest to the military authorities. But will they now take the time, during war, to resolve the case of a native German with a Czech passport who has entered the country via Switzerland and wants to fight with the Czech Legion?

A young Czech in the camp with whom Golo Mann gets to talking offers him little hope. He is a resolute, brave man. Months earlier, he left his family in Prague to join the Czech Legion, but he, too, was arrested at the border, taken to the camp, and wastes his time here while the news from the front gets worse and worse. "My nerves," he shouts, smacking himself on the forehead in a barely controlled outburst of rage. "My nerves. It's unbearable."

June 1940

Paris – Toulouse, June 1, 1940

When Miriam Davenport has finally collected all of the documents she needs to follow her examination committee to Toulouse, she packs in

Miriam Davenport

a mad dash at the Hôtel de l'Univers. Not for a second does she think of saying goodbye to Hertha Pauli or Walter Mehring in the adjacent rooms.

She hurries to the train station. Outside the entrance and on the platforms, dense clusters of people are jostling around. Apparently, the desire to leave Paris is now widespread. But that is not Miriam's concern; she is happy to catch the night train to Toulouse. It, too, is overfull, but in one of the compartments, she discovers a narrow spot on a bench seat, just big enough for a small woman like her. Dog-tired, she falls asleep and awakes the next morning in the arms of the man whose shoulder she apparently used overnight as a pillow. She apologizes; the man waves dismissively – it was a pleasure for him.

Toulouse is flooded with refugees. Every bed, every sofa, every cubbyhole is taken. People sleep overnight in the chairs of hotel lobbies, in the alcoves beneath the stairs, outdoors in the parks. The city's only movie theater, the Cinéma Pax, serves as a reception camp and a dormitory. When Miriam reports to the university for her exams, she is told the tests were moved up by two weeks; she is to sit for her finals the very next day. She is at once happy and stunned – happy to have arrived at the right place just in time, stunned because she now lacks any time to prepare. For days now, she has been fighting against bureaucratic or other travel-related obstacles and has spent not one second thinking about her testing material. How odd to immerse oneself in art history while the country is being torn apart by war.

Paris, June 4, 1940

In the morning, clouds of smoke drift over the city. German bombers have attacked the Air Ministry, the Citroën plant, and the Seine bridges. The streets are filled with hectic bustle. Waves of refugees are pouring through the city.

Walter Mehring is sitting at the Hôtel de l'Univers with his friends, weighing their remaining options. The antiaircraft battery in the neighboring Jardin du Luxembourg fired throughout the night, shaking their hotel and rattling the windows with every round. The war has now moved closer to them than ever, and their prospects do not look good. Where could they escape to if they are no longer safe in France? Italy and Spain are ruled by the fascists, and Austria, half of Poland, and Czechoslovakia are occupied by the Nazis. The Netherlands, Belgium, and Denmark have already surrendered to the Germans, and Norway is about to. And since Mehring and three others are not communists, the Soviet Union is out of the question as a new place of exile. America, however, could be a refuge.

Ernst Weiss shakes his head. "No one will take us across."

Hans Natonek is more optimistic. He has an idea. "Thomas Mann – he's over there. Let's write him to send someone for us."

Thomas Mann as the all-powerful savior in times of need. For Mehring that sounds too easy, too fantastic. "Natonek," he laughs, "you are the true poet among us."

But Natonek remains obstinate and will not let the idea go so easily. He thinks they must finally make clear to German authors in America what a terrible situation they are in here in France. "A telegram," he says, "a telegram to Thomas Mann – we have to get out, we need a visa ..."

"Of all people, the four of us," Mehring mocks. But then he hesitates and turns to his friend Hertha Pauli. "Perhaps I could – I know Thomas well ..."

For a moment, they all sit in silence. Then Ernst Weiss says, "Yeah, leave me out of it. There's no point."

"No," Pauli protests. "All or none ..."

For a while they consider the plan from all sides. In the end, they land on the idea of sending a cable not just in their own names, which would come off as selfish, but in the names of all writers stuck in France. There is a tremendous number of them.

Ernst Weiss remains despondent. He has no faith in the idea. Such a telegram, he says, would reach no one and achieve nothing. But he adds his signature anyway.

Dunkirk, June 5, 1940

Some 340,000 soldiers, the bulk of the Allied troops surrounded at Dunkirk, have escaped across the Channel to England. Over 80,000 remained behind on dry land; they are taken prisoner by the Germans. All of them, those who escaped as well as the prisoners, are now absent from France's defense.

From June 5, the *Wehrmacht* turns southward from Dunkirk to continue its conquest of the country. Again, the tank units tear ahead, again intoxicated by Pervitin. To the east, they circumvent the so-called Maginot Line, the French bunker fortifications along the Rhine, and push forward to the Swiss border. Once more, they thereby corral half a million French soldiers. To the west, they also overwhelm the weakened defenders within a few days and advance toward Paris.

The attacking troops continue driving fresh waves of refugees before them: Belgian, Dutch, and French civilians who attempt to reach safety from the combat zones – but also British and Belgian soldiers trying to escape to the south to avoid capture by the Germans. At this point, eight to ten million people in overladen cars, on horse carts, on bicycles, or on foot are traveling on the congested roads. To fuel the panic more, German bombers and hedgehopping aircraft attack the convoys of refugees, killing thousands. In the traffic chaos, French troops lose all freedom of movement and are barely still capable of carrying out military operations.

Les Milles, early June 1940

Feuchtwanger has been in the camp for two weeks now. Without much resistance, he has submitted to the daily routine: being awoken at five thirty by reveille, early lunch at eleven, then the miserably hot, empty hours of the afternoon, and finally dinner at five when the courtyards have gotten cooler again. In between: queueing up forever at the few washing facilities and latrines and the half ridiculous, half admirable attempts of many inmates to preserve their dignity by addressing each other with their titles: "How do you feel today, Herr Professor?" – "How did you sleep last night, Herr Direktor?" A few of the scholars marooned here even offer brief lectures in their fields of expertise to fill the dull afternoons.

The dust and the heat beset Feuchtwanger. His servants, the former boxer and another young man, lighten his load in many respects, however, tending to the straw for his berth or washing his laundry. In the evenings, when Feuchtwanger changes clothes for the night, they provide a little privacy and hand him his pajamas – a somewhat pretentious ritual that his fellow captives make fun of.

Relations with the guards are almost always good. They wear a fez despite not coming from the French colonies in North Africa. Whenever they patrol outside the barbed-wire fence with their red covers and the glittering bayonets on their rifles, they cut a painterly picture against the verdant hills in the background. They do not take their task particularly seriously. Where are the prisoners to flee? There are roadblocks throughout the country, passports and *sauf-conduits* are checked everywhere, and, what's more, the borders are closed; no one can leave France.

A kind of friendly coexistence has developed between the guards and those under guard. Whenever the prisoners play soccer during the cooler hours, the soldiers enjoy watching. Once, when the ball flies out over the barbed wire, the players ask their chaperone whether they can go get it. That, he replies, was strictly forbidden. But then his sympathy for the men prevails, he thrusts his rifle into one of the prisoner's hands, runs out, fetches the ball, retrieves his rifle, and the game can continue.

It is the bad news about the war that bothers the internees most. With each French defeat, Feuchtwanger grows more nervous. The speed with which the Germans keep pushing the front farther south is incredible. Feuchtwanger is one of the most prominent anti-Hitler writers; he is close to the top of all the Nazis' wanted lists. He cannot wait here in the camp until he falls into the hands of the advancing troops. That would be a feast for the Gestapo; either he would be shot dead on the spot or taken to a concentration camp from which he would not come out again alive.

Erquinvillers, June 9, 1940

In the village of Erquinvillers, a hundred kilometers outside Paris, *Wehrmacht* soldiers shoot dead a hundred fifty primarily Black French prisoners of war. In total over the course of the Western campaign, about three thousand Black soldiers, so-called *tirailleurs sénégalais*, are segregated from their French comrades in war captivity and murdered by the Germans.

Rome, June 10, 1940

In the afternoon, Benito Mussolini declares war on France and Great Britain in a theatrical speech from the balcony of his seat of government. Italian troops attack France near Menton and in the Maritime Alps. Because German troops are now only a hundred kilometers outside Paris, the French government abandons the capital and retreats to Tours on the Loire.

Paris, June 11, 1940

Walter Mehring learns from an employee at the Ministry of Foreign Affairs in the morning that the government has fled. He goes weak in the knees. Idling along the Boulevard Saint-Michel are transport trucks meant to follow the ministers with the Republic's files aboard. The Germans are perhaps only eighty or ninety kilometers from Paris, which is to be declared an open city – open for the Germans. The French want to avoid destruction from street battles and further bombings. Then, the rumor suddenly circulates that the first German tanks have been sighted in Montmartre already. Presumably a false report, but no one knows anything for sure.

Hertha Pauli gets ahold of a French friend by telephone who is loading up his car, about to head to Orléans. On the far side of the Loire, he says, the French army will establish a new defensive line. She must come immediately; he still has one free seat. Hertha Pauli stuffs a few things into a rucksack. Mehring brings only his manuscripts. They have to run through the Jardin du Luxembourg. The park lies deserted. Even the streets in the city center are dead. Whoever has not yet fled is in hiding.

Hertha Pauli's friend is still waiting on others, a married couple from Romania who also want a ride. "Oh," he says upon seeing Mehring. "I hope we still have room …" He secures his suitcases on the car's roof. When the pair finally arrive, Mehring squeezes himself between the others in the back seat, the valise with the manuscripts on his lap. They are winding through the desolate Boulevard Montparnasse when Hertha Pauli realizes: "We didn't say anything to Weiss and Natonek …"

"Why should we have?" her friend asks. "We can't help them anyway."

Already at the Porte d'Orléans, the municipal border, they end up in a traffic jam. Like a gigantic caterpillar, the convoy of those fleeing inches forward, creeping along a few meters, followed once more by gridlock. Their progress is terribly slow. They would move faster on foot. In the skies above them, they spot German planes, but since, as an open city, Paris may not be defended, they are also no longer attacked by the bombers.

Farther afield, the fighter planes buzz so low over the southbound N20 that the swastikas on their airfoils can be made out. All of a sudden, the pounding begins. The pilots unleash their first volleys, sending everything and everyone diving for cover off the road. The hands of the driver operating the vehicle in which Pauli and Mehring are riding tremble so much that Pauli takes the wheel. She may not have a driver's license, but who cares? "You mustn't look up," she says, driving stubbornly onward to the next snarl of traffic, until they are stopped on the road again like a target and the next strafer starts firing.

Their fuel runs low. None can be found anywhere as all the gas stations have been pumped dry. In the end, they are forced to push the car. In a village, Hertha's French friend purchases a bicycle for a great deal of money and desperate pleading with which he intends to procure gasoline in the next town over. They are all to wait at the car.

Stuck bumper to bumper between the other cars, they do not move a single meter overnight. In the skies ahead of them, they see a faint glow in the dark. Their friend with the bike does not return. Instead: the news, sometime next morning, that the Germans have marched into Paris – not forty kilometers behind them!

Mehring can stand it no longer. He means to continue on foot. The other couple protests: "We have to wait. We mustn't abandon the car."

"You are Romanians," Mehring says, "they'll do nothing to you." He, however, is a Jew, and if they get their hands on him, he is a goner. "Walter can't stay here," Hertha explains to the other two. She grabs her rucksack, he his valise, and at first light, they hit the road.

When the sun rises, they reach Etampes, the place their friend with the bicycle wanted to get gas. The town was bombed, hence the glow they saw in the night. Outside one of the ravaged houses, a gruesome encounter: a woman, scared stiff, appears to be standing in the door, but as they approach, they see the woman is dead, jammed between the doorframe, her eyes wide open. Gendarmes move from house to house, banging on the doors with the butts of their rifles, shouting, "Get up, pack, take only the bare necessities with you!" The entire town is to be evacuated, for the Germans are coming; the tanks are not stopping in Paris. They are rolling onward.

The gendarmes' commands increase the mass migration southward. Farmers yoke their horses or oxen, load up their carts with household items, strap infants to their backs, and walk beside their wagons with their older children.

Pauli and Mehring plod along for hours in the convoy. Toward evening, Hertha is at her limit. She cannot go on any longer. Her feet are bleeding. She remains sprawled out by the roadside. "I've had enough. You go on," she says to Mehring, "Just let me lie here ..." He tries to lift her up and encourage her. "There'll be coffee in Orléans." But that is unable to entice her. "I just need a bed."

And so Mehring knocks at a house with smoke rising from its chimney. A woman answers the door; he prevails upon her, pointing at Hertha. Then he comes to get her. The woman lost her husband, killed in the battle against the Germans. Hertha may sleep in the dead man's bed. The next morning, the woman makes the two breakfast – coffee and bread – after which they rejoin the bleak column of people fleeing.

Mehring summons all his rhetorical skills to cheer up Hertha and paint her a picture of the peace awaiting them beyond Orléans. Suddenly, they hear a German reconnaissance plane tracing a circle in the sky above them with black coaldust – a marking for higher-flying aircraft to drop their payload here.

In frenzied horror, everyone dives off the road, runs into the fields, drops to the ground, just seconds before the hail of bombs comes raining down. Craters open up all around them, blasting fountains of dirt into the air. Then the machine guns begin rattling away. Strafing planes sweep past them overhead. When it is quiet again some eternal seconds later, they raise their heads. They are lying in a scene of devastation: tattered corpses, tattered animal carcasses strewn about them, burning cars on the road, upturned wagons, scattered household goods.

Paris, June 11, 1940

On the morning Hertha Pauli and Walter Mehring clear out for Orléans, Hans Natonek and Ernst Weiss meet in a café for a late breakfast. They sit on one of the large boulevards in the June sunshine, watching the cars depart. Weiss drinks his tea leisurely, almost lost in reverie. He watches the things happening around him as if from a great distance. Natonek, by contrast, is quite agitated. He senses that their time is up. "You can't stay," he urges Weiss. "Hitler could be here tomorrow."

But Weiss shakes his head. As a Jew, he knows what awaits him if the Nazis occupy the country. In 1933, he fled Berlin for Prague and then continued onward to Paris. This time, though, he lacks the strength. He does not want to set off for a foreign country yet again.

No longer able to stomach sitting still, Natonek leaps up, pays for his breakfast, and dashes off. In his apartment, he packs two suitcases despite not even knowing how he is to get out of the city. As he checks one final time what he must leave behind, two winter coats catch his eye, two furs. It is a real shame about those. He grabs them and hurries to a furrier nearby to pawn them. While he is haggling with the fur dealer about the price, a car stops outside the store. The driver is a Polish officer in civilian clothes who wants to say goodbye to his sister, the furrier's wife, and then slog his way through to the Loire or, better yet, to the Spanish border. There is still room in his car. Natonek seizes his opportunity and exchanges the two coats for a place in the backseat of the car. Moments later, he is at the Porte d'Orléans, in the same convoy in which the car containing Pauli and Mehring has been inching along since morning.

New York, mid-June 1940

The news from France is devastating. Varian Fry and Paul Hagen have since been meeting regularly at Childs', feeling at once vindicated and depressed. The series of German victories leaves no doubt about the justness of their rescue mission for Hitler's foes in France. From week to week, even from day to day, it becomes easier for the two to garner supporters for their idea. Before America's eyes, a nation regarded as the epitome of civilization, enlightenment, elegance, and *joie de vivre* is imploding. That leaves no one indifferent. The willingness to help and donate money is enormous.

But Fry and Hagen also realize that time is not on their side. The speed with which reports of the successes of the German offensive come flowing in leaves them aghast. The French government on the run. German tanks only a hundred, eighty, fifty kilometers from Paris. Millions of people on the roads. Is their attempt to render aid not coming much too late? Why establish a rescue committee if the people who are to be rescued have long since been caught, arrested, perhaps even murdered by their enemies?

The pair try to comfort one another at Childs' in spite of everything. By no means do they intend to be dissuaded from their course of action, but neither must they delude themselves. Even under the best of circumstances, they will still need five or six weeks until their organization is operational. They cannot make their way to France before then, and it is possible that at that point they will arrive at a cemetery.

Toulouse, mid-June 1940

Miriam Davenport dutifully reported to her examination – and failed. She still cannot believe it. It was all for naught: her journey from peaceful Yugoslavia to a Paris at war, the battle for the *sauf-conduit*, the ride to Toulouse, all of it pointless. Her visa will expire, and she will have to return to America. Without a diploma, she will not find a job. How is she supposed to explain that to her little brother?

But that is only the first part of her misfortune. When she goes to buy a ticket to Ljubljana, where her fiancé is waiting, it is pointed out to her that all borders to Italy are closed on account of Mussolini's declaration of war. There is no longer any way for her back to Yugoslavia. She petitions for an exception – it is an emergency, her marriage date in Ljubljana has already been set – but nobody knows whether it will work out for her. Miriam is stranded in Toulouse.

It is a boy who cheers her up somewhat, a nineteen-year-old Jew from Danzig [Gdansk] named Justus Rosenberg. He looks young for his age and reminds her of her brother. She met him at the Cinéma Pax, the city's emergency dormitory, where he entertains the other refugees with clownish pranks and little tricks for a few sous. Three years earlier, when he was sixteen, his parents sent him to a boarding school in Paris to get him to safety from the Nazis. When the Germans were just now marching into Paris, he was fleeing to Toulouse by bike. He found barely anything to eat, had only the clothes he was wearing to his name, and during his getaway slept on the bare ground beside roadside ditches. Miriam admires his optimism and his obviously irrepressible good mood. If his situation were not so hopeless, people would call him a rascal. Yet his name irritates Miriam. To her ears, Justus Rosenberg sounds much too staid, almost like "Judge" Rosenberg. She prefers to shorten his first name to "Gussie," which she says suits him better.

Tours, June 13, 1940

Churchill is flown to Tours with an escort of twelve fighter planes for a final meeting with the French government. He urges Prime Minister Reynaud to continue the resistance against the aggressors. But Reynaud's deputy, Marshal Philippe Pétain, views the war as lost and makes the case for offering the Germans an armistice. On the sidelines of the conference, Churchill notices a relatively young general called de Gaulle, who has just been named Under-Secretary of State in the Ministry for National Defense. Then he flies back to London.

Paris, June 14, 1940

Ernst Weiss is alone in Paris. Pauli, Mehring, and Natonek have fled Paris, and all other friends have long since been in internment camps. The hotel room in which Weiss has been living for years has ugly, garishly colorful wallpaper, its only window looking out not onto the street, but into a dim inner courtyard, a sort of light shaft. Hardly a sound issues from the city; the streets are dead, the buildings locked, the stores barricaded. Not a thing moves. Almost half of its residents have left Paris. Ernst Weiss can see nothing from his room; he gazes into the light shaft and listens to the silence.

The Germans are coming today. Since early this morning, they have been moving down the large boulevards into the center in endless convoys. There are no shootouts, no skirmishes – everything remains calm. The troops swiftly occupy some of the large hotels, which are to serve as future command centers; they declare the Hôtel de Crillon, right on the Place de la Concorde, their command headquarters. Paris, the open city, belongs to them. They may take what they want. With the military band leading it, an infantry division marches down the Champs-Élysées. Beneath the Arc de Triomphe, two German generals pay homage to the Unknown Soldier entombed there, after which they review their troops. A swastika flag is hoisted atop the Eiffel Tower.

Ernst Weiss does not care about this. He is not only a writer, but also a physician, and knows what to do. He has pills that work unfailingly. In his hotel room, he draws himself a bath, swallows the pills, lies back in the tub, and slits his arteries.

A woman friend, an employee at the Théâtre Pigalle, finds him a short while later and alerts the emergency services. But it is too late. Ernst Weiss dies in a nearby hospital. He is buried in a mass grave.

Meudon – Pithiviers-le-Vieil, mid-June 1940

When they reach the village Longpont-sur-Orge, they spot the tank. It sits motionless at an intersection. It is a French one, thank God. Anna Seghers and her two children already saw it from a distance, a hulking monster made of steel right in the middle of a deserted little village, not forty kilometers south of Paris. Not a sound is to be heard; the small houses, the gardens, the street – everything seems as if it has been emptied out. A ghost town. Apparently, all of the residents have fled.

Seghers carefully steps toward the tank with her children. They have to walk past it – there is no other way. As it is, they are making much too little forward progress. They have to get faster or else the German troops will catch up with them.

Three days earlier, when news came that the government had absconded for Tours, Anna Seghers was no longer able to endure the passivity. For seven years, she had been living in Meudon, a quiet suburb of Paris. Her husband, László Radványi, whom she calls Rodi, had been arrested by the French back in April and taken to the internment camp Le Vernet. Now she had to decide what to do without him. She packed one rucksack and a small suitcase for each of them, for Ruth, too, even though she is only twelve. Just as they were about to set off, they heard over the radio that train services had been suspended. That made Seghers' trepidation even worse; at that point it seemed impossible to her to remain in Meudon for even one more day.

They thus struck out on foot. Peter, her fourteen-year-old, loves maps; she gave him the only map she owns, along with the task of finding the shortest path to the N20, the large highway southward. Perhaps they would be able to wave down a car there that would give them a ride.

They have been on the road for three days now, slept in haystacks or barns, but had to stop for breaks much too often because of their exhaustion. In Longpont-sur-Orge, the ghost town, Peter pauses once more just outside the intersection to check the map for which of the roads they must take. Suddenly, they hear a hollow sound from inside the tank. There is a jolt, the roof hatch swings open, and a French soldier wearing a leather uniform climbs down to them from the turret. He walks up to Peter and asks to look at the map – he has taken a wrong turn and must get his bearings. Finally, he returns the map to Peter, offers his polite thanks, and scrambles back into the tank. The motor roars to life, and the colossus rumbles away.

Anna Seghers is a prudent woman. She is not prone to impulsive decisions. Her precipitous flight from Meudon on foot was a mistake, she now understands. But what was she supposed to have done? They are Jews, and she has been a member of the Communist Party for years. She knows that the Gestapo will search for her. If she is caught, that will also be a death sentence for the children.

The prospect of initially slipping through the Nazis' net without being recognized is not something she believes possible. She is too famous for that. Her very first short story, written when she was twenty-four, was printed in the venerable *Frankfurter Zeitung*, and for her very first novel, *Revolt of the Fishermen of Santa Barbara*, she

Anna Seghers with her husband László Radványi and their children Peter and Ruth in Meudon

received the Kleist Prize, one of the country's most important awards. At the time, she was twenty-eight and regarded as a new master storyteller. Ultimately, her books are almost always about the defeats suffered by crusading workers, about failed strikes, abortive revolts, unsuccessful revolutions. But she has a fabulous talent for allowing a glimmer of hope for a better future, in spite of everything, to shine forth in her stories.

Now she wants to make it to Orléans with her children and, from there, to cross the Loire, as the others do, too. The extent of the horrible situation they have landed in becomes clear to Seghers when they finally reach the N20. The sight of the endless stream of refugees dully inching forward is a shock. All the cars and horse carts are overladen; no one will be able to give them a ride. After only a few kilometers in this chaos, Peter guides them with his map onto smaller side roads where they will make better forward progress.

In Brétigny, a village somewhat east of their route, they see a freight train waiting for permission to proceed. Together with other refugees, they climb into the open boxcars, but just as soon as the train has begun rolling, it stops again. The railroad lines are overburdened. If they move, then it will be at a walking pace at best. Hitler's tanks are faster, Seghers knows, but the children are so tired they have to rest.

When German airplanes soon appear above them, everyone panics. An older man, a reservist, explains that in case of an attack, they must jump from the cars without hesitation and lie flat on their belly along the railway embankment. But then the planes veer away, and moments later, Seghers and her children see the bombs hitting along the convoy of refugees on the N20. The fields here are completely flat; the road lies before them as if on a giant stage. The explosions send fountains of mud, smoke, and wreckage into the air.

On the sixth night of their getaway, when the train comes to a stop once more, nervous voices can suddenly be heard in the dark. All refugees must disembark immediately and continue on foot, they shout; the Germans might be here any moment. Seghers shakes her children awake. They are to leave everything behind, get down from the train, and start walking with her. The only thing that counts now is getting away as fast as possible. When day breaks, they have managed over twenty-five kilometers.

So as not to give hedgehoppers a target, they avoid the roads and walk on farm lanes. In the afternoon, it begins to rain. By then, they are completely drained. Trucks packed with French soldiers race past toward the south. Seghers waves, but no one stops. In the tiny village of Pithiviers-le-Vieil, finally, they see a house with its doors open. It is empty. Only the beds are still there. As if numb, they collapse onto the bare mattresses. Moments later, they have fallen fast asleep.

The next morning, they are awoken by the engine sounds of a military convoy. *Wehrmacht* trucks pull up. Soldiers jump out and begin ransacking the houses. In mortal fear, Seghers burns her identification papers and decides to act as if she does not understand a word of German. She also impresses upon Peter and Ruth to speak only French. By that point, the soldiers are already rattling at her door. They shout their commands, but Seghers does not react and shrugs at all of their questions.

Since many other refugees, French and Belgian, are also stranded in the village, Seghers and her children do not attract unwanted attention. The soldiers hardly notice them; they have their hands full with scraping together food and shelter for themselves. Seghers discovers a farming family that has not left the village, buys milk, a few eggs, and a chicken. Odd – the worst has come to pass, what she feared most: the front has overrun them, and she and her children are at the mercy of the Germans, but the soldiers do not have time to worry about them. Life goes on as before.

They remain in the empty house. No property owner comes to drive them off. After a few days, placards from the new French government appear, directing refugees to return to their hometowns. With the children, Seghers packs up the few items they still have and finds a truck, the driver of which is willing to give them a lift.

The return is comfortable, but also sobering. In the seven terrible days of their flight, days on which they exerted themselves to the brink of collapse, they covered only around ninety kilometers. It takes two hours for their driver to bring them back to Paris.

Bordeaux, June 16, 1940

Since there is considerable doubt whether the new defensive line on the Loire can be held, the French government has fled from Tours to Bordeaux. There, Prime Minister Reynaud resigns, and the eighty-four-year-old Marshal Pétain takes over from him. As his first act in office, he inquires with the German High Command around midnight regarding the conditions for an armistice.

Les Milles, June 16, 1940

Golo Mann is in a perfectly bad mood. A week ago – while then still in Loriol camp – one of the officers approached him, shook his hand, and said that a small miracle had occurred. In spite of the miserable military situation, the review committee had met and accorded him the right to join the French army. Finally. Golo Mann was happy for a moment. He had the end of his inaction and internment within sight.

Two days later, he was locked in a closed cattle car with thirty others. Their train was bound for Marseille. Sweltering heat plagued the railcar.

Filth was everywhere, and thirst plagued the men to the point that they were always getting into fights. Rumor had it they were being taken to Africa, to one of the colonies, to Algeria perhaps. But in Marseille, their boxcar sat idle, exposed for hours to the summer's blaze. Because of Italy's declaration of war, all crossings to Africa had been canceled. An encounter with Italian warships would have been too dangerous. In the end, the train rolled back out of the city into the hinterlands – and took them to the camp at Les Milles. They remained internees.

The camp is now irredeemably overfilled; more than three thousand men throng into the much-too-small dormitories. Lately, Italian exiles are taken here, too. There is only one cup of water per day for washing. No one has thought to build additional latrines.

By and by, Golo Mann runs into acquaintances from Berlin and Munich. With a bitter laugh, he greets Feuchtwanger. "Do we meet again in hell?" Franz Hessel, Alfred Kantorowicz, and Walter Hasenclever are also here. But these encounters cannot dispel Mann's bad mood.

The circumstances become ever more grotesque. German troops are getting closer and closer, and the day the first tanks pull up to the camp's gate is imminent. At this point, some of the staunch Nazis interned at Les Milles already feel like victors. They speak unabashedly of capturing the "politically compromised" on their own and detaining them until the Gestapo arrives. Some openly raise their right arms in the Hitler salute, and this in a French camp! No one prevents them from doing so. The guards apparently do not wish to get on their bad side. In short, the exiles cannot count on French protection once the Germans have arrived.

Orléans, June 16, 1940

When Hertha Pauli and Walter Mehring reach Orléans, the German air raids have cut swathes of ruin through the city. Torrents of refugees tumble past ravaged buildings toward the two bridges leading over the Loire. Rescue parties search the ruins for buried survivors and the dead.

Suddenly, sirens blare. Wedged among the mass of people, Pauli and Mehring are pushed into a cellar. They stumble into the dark, their eyes still blinded by the daylight. From a corner, the muttering of bearded men. "Kaddish," Mehring whispers. The men are saying the Jewish prayer for the dead.

Outside, the bombs hit. A young mother next to Pauli leans over her baby at each impact to protect it with her body. The child screams. Mehring screams, too. "Don't frighten the kid," Pauli snaps at him. The mother looks at her: "This evening, both Loire bridges will be demolished." Another explosion, and she leans over her baby once more.

Once the bridges have been demolished, the refugees will be stuck in a trap. The French want to curb the German advance at any cost, so they are destroying the bridges to gain time. If Mehring and Pauli have not crossed the Loire by evening, they are lost.

As soon as the sirens give the all-clear, everyone bolts out of the cellar. It is already evening. Time is running short. Wreckage must be shoved aside; shards cover the ground, slicing up shoe soles. Everyone is pushing their way toward the bridges. At a gas station, Pauli and Mehring see a truck loading up with fuel, not just filling its tank, but huge gas cans as well. Three refugees huddle onto the loading bed between the cans. Without asking, Pauli and Mehring climb into the cab and squeeze into the passenger seat. The man at the wheel hardly bothers with them. He drives toward the teeming street, attempting to shoehorn his way between the other vehicles, but is only able to bring up the rear.

As they inch toward the bridge, Pauli spots airplanes in the sky, flying in long, sweeping loops. The motorcade crawls forward at an excruciatingly slow pace, then halts. Everything is stopped. Pauli sees the airplanes banking, returning to the city, coming ever closer. Their truck has just reached the midpoint of the bridge, its loading bed full of gas cans, the tank freshly filled. One direct hit will transform the vehicle into a fireball. A fighter bomber plunges toward them from the sky. Mehring screams, leaps out of the cab, and runs in between the wedged-in vehicles across the bridge, toward the far side of the river. The driver also loses his nerves, steps on the gas, and rams into the car in front of him. Metal crunches.

Suddenly, the plane veers off withing firing. The convoy moves forward a few meters, stops again, moves ahead a bit more, stops. The plane banks, returns, hurtles toward the bridge, but does not fire this time either. Apparently, the Germans do not want to damage the bridge, nor do they want to block it with wrecked cars. The pilots are just playing with the panic of those fleeing.

On the opposite bank of the river, the driver stops and pushes Pauli out of the vehicle. No sooner is she out than he steps on the gas. It has now gotten dusky. Pauli gets her bearings, then follows along the road, and walks up a gentle incline to a wooded area. All of a sudden, a flash of light, followed by thunder: the ground shudders. She whips around and in the half dark sees a dust cloud rising into the sky and, beneath it, the bridge collapsing into the river. Pauli's eyes catch sight of a lanky man lying on the ground beside the road, exhausted. It is Mehring.

Nice, mid-June 1940

Heinrich and Nelly Mann live in seclusion on the Rue Alphons Karr. They had to give up their imposing flat on the Rue du Congrès, where Katia and Thomas Mann visited them in 1935. Heinrich Mann has since published the second volume of his novel about King Henri IV of France, perhaps the most important book of his life. In Nazi Germany, however, it is allowed neither to be printed nor sold and consequently reaches very few readers. Since then, he has mostly written political essays and articles for French newspapers to supplement his scant earnings.

Heinrich and Nelly married nine months ago. They are an exceptionally dissimilar couple, he the son of a Grand Burgher, she the daughter of a maidservant. He increasingly comes across as a man of the nineteenth century: dignified, but also a bit lost. She is overwhelmed by life in exile, almost always drunk and, of late, addicted to sleeping pills.

Since the beginning of the war, their situation has quickly gotten uncomfortable. At sixty-nine years of age, Mann may not need to fear being locked away in a camp, but the French press stirs up hatred against all Germans – not only against Hitler's soldiers, but also against the exiles. They are suddenly regarded as Nazi supporters in disguise, as a fifth column that prepared the way for the advance of the troops.

The claims are far-fetched, but not without consequences. The newspapers for which Heinrich Mann wrote no longer want to publish a single line of his anymore. His financial circumstances are thus becoming increasingly more precarious. On top of that, their landlord has sent them a notice to quit; he wants to lease his "apartment only to Frenchmen and allies." Heinrich is furious, replying that he accepts the termination of their lease, but not the stated rationale. Both he and Nelly have Czech passports and, he writes to the lessor, "as Czech citizens, we are allies."

Ever since Italy's declaration of war, the thunder of artillery from the front lines can be heard in Nice, depending on the direction of the wind. The fear of bombing raids is likewise growing. At night, curfews and strict blackout regulations are in effect. Police officers patrol the empty streets, and as soon as they spot even a glimmer of light in a window, they blow their whistles until no ray of light can be seen.

At this point, Heinrich Mann places his last hopes in Great Britain. As long as Churchill continues the fight against Hitler, everything is not yet lost. By night he sits in the dark apartment, listening to the news on Radio London.

Nelly and he cannot remain in Nice for much longer, that much is clear. They must relocate to Marseille and join the queues outside the consulates to get their hands on a visa for a halfway safe country. For Heinrich, though, the thought of leaving Europe, the continent of culture, reason, and enlightenment, is horrible. Although he has written his brother in Princeton requesting Thomas obtain American visas for him and Nelly, he wants to go to the United States only in case of emergency. For him, that country is the realm of stark, uninhibited materialism. He would rather go to Morocco, which is a protectorate of France after all. There, in close proximity to Europe, one might be able to lead a suitable life until Hitler is defeated.

Bordeaux, June 17, 1940

In a radio address around midday, Marshal Pétain announces that he has entered into negotiations with the Germans on an armistice. Large portions of the French army subsequently believe all battles are over. Entire regiments lay down their weapons and disband. The soldiers mix with those fleeing or are taken captive.

Washington, D.C., June 17, 1940

President Roosevelt is stuck in a political double bind. Since at least the German troops' invasion of Paris, the American press has been following the fate of the anti-Hitler exiles in France with horror.

Pressure from humanitarian organizations that would enable their escape to the United States has increased massively. On the other hand, the vast majority of Americans want nothing to do with the war. Even the State Department under Secretary Cordell Hull resists admitting refugees, for reasons of national security. It would be, Hull says, completely irresponsible to bring these politically active European intellectuals into the country; many of them belong to socialist or communist parties.

Roosevelt is almost on the campaign trail. In November he hopes to be the first president of the United States to vie for a third term in office. It is thus important to him not to put himself at odds with either refugee-welcoming or refugee-wary voters. To politically defuse the topic as quickly as possible, he has convened representatives of the State Department and the Department of Justice today. He charges them with finding ways to rescue the exiles under threat, while also factoring in the security interests of the United States. Within the next month, he expects actionable results from them.

Marseille – Narbonne, June 18, 1940

Alma Mahler-Werfel and Franz Werfel are now lodging at the Hôtel Louvre et Paix, one of Marseille's finest houses. As a precaution, they have registered there under the name Mahler so as to be harder to find.

One morning, they were awakened by the radio from one of the adjacent rooms announcing in stentorian tones that Hitler's troops moved into Paris without a fight. Werfel regarded this as a propagandistic lie from the Germans and their next-door neighbors as Nazis spreading false reports. But when he discovered pictures in the newspapers of *Wehrmacht* columns marching down the Champs-Élysées, he went into a state of shock and could hardly contain his agitation.

Alma loses her patience with him. She says she had predicted all of this and had wanted to move to America years earlier. But he was firmly convinced of the invincibility of the French army and deep down thought the United States was an uncivilized country. "I won't lose my grip," he had said, "on the last corner of Europe," with the result, Alma says, that like mice in a trap, they now have to look for any sort of way out, though none is open to them any longer.

By now, it is clear that the new defensive line at the Loire will not hold either. The French army is clearly in the middle of disbanding. German troops are already bearing down on Lyon. Once again, Alma and Franz have had to spend half the night in the hotel cellar because of a bombing alert. Exhausted, they struggle to maintain their composure. The most recent rumors speak of ships carrying refugees, bound for England or America, and departing from Bordeaux, the new seat of the French government.

Suddenly, Bordeaux seems to them their last resort, Marseille a death trap. Hotel staff track down for them a driver with a car and large gasoline reserves willing to take them to Bordeaux for eight thousand francs. They set off by late morning, though it takes considerable effort to be able to stow their luggage – twelve suitcases and various bags – in the car. It is simply too small. A large standing trunk has to be stowed on the back seat where Alma also sits. With each curve, it is in danger of toppling onto her. She is afraid of being crushed to death by it. Franz occupies the front passenger seat.

The journey quickly becomes torture. At midday in Avignon, there is so little time that they must eat lunch in extreme haste. Their driver is an obstinate, intolerable fellow who cannot find the right directions. For inexplicable reasons, he takes a route via Narbonne and from there hopes to go west, toward Bordeaux. But on the far side of Narbonne, he takes a wrong turn and meanders around tiny roads until they arrive once more in Narbonne again at eleven o'clock at night. They have driven in circles.

By this point, Alma and Franz feel half dead and decide to suspend their escape. All hotels are booked up, however. Only a hostel for refugees can accommodate them. Alma is appalled. There is no dinner, just garlic sausage and stale bread, and the rooms are musty and ratty. Franz has to spend the night in a dormitory for men, she herself in a room with several women and children. They ask her not to turn on any lights. The cots they are assigned have neither blankets nor cushions; they are likely dirty. In brief, it is a nightmare.

Chasselay, June 20, 1940

After fierce battles about twenty kilometers outside Lyon, French troops surrender to the *Wehrmacht*. After capturing them, the Germans segregate about a hundred *tirailleurs sénégalais* from their white comrades. They force them to line up in an open field with their arms in the air. Two tanks aim machine-gun fire at them and then roll over the injured and dead.

Les Milles, June 21 and 22, 1940

By now the fear is palpable. News that Marshal Pétain has opened armistice talks with the Germans has shaken the camp like an earthquake. For many of the exiles, it sounds like a death sentence. In their despair, they begin estimating their rapidly waning chances of survival in percentages. Is it still twenty percent, or only ten now? They feel like a herd of sheep waiting for their butchers.

In the halls and courtyards, fierce debates flare up, along with a lot of screaming and jostling, long speeches, angry outbursts. A few bricks and wooden slats are quickly assembled into improvised writing desks and, depending on the writer's mood, pleading petitions or blazing letters of protest drafted. Soon the agitation is so great that the guards position machine guns on some of the buildings' roofs. One of the prisoners yells up at them that they should go ahead and shoot; he would rather die by French bullets than from the Gestapo's torture.

Feuchtwanger is elected by his fellow prisoners to a committee whose aim is to make the camp commander see their dramatic position. At first, the officer listens calmly, then with increasing annoyance. For days now, he assures them, he has been fighting by telephone for a train that would take these threatened men to a safe part of the country, in spite of the overburdened transport routes. The committee is merely robbing him of the time he needs to persuade the military authorities of his plan. He is a captain in the reserves; before the war, he was director of a soap factory in Lyon. He expects people to trust him, he says. After all, as a businessman he is well versed in organizational matters.

Most prisoners remain skeptical, though. Only a few dare to believe in the train coming to rescue them. And even if it were to come, there are still nothing but questions. Where can the train take them? Will the armistice make Hitler the ruler of France? Where else could they hide then? Is their fate sealed as soon as the French army lays down its arms?

Feuchtwanger mentally settles his affairs. Soberly, he takes stock of things. He is now fifty-five years old and will turn fifty-six next month, if he lives to see his birthday. In retrospect, he acknowledges a number of mistakes and wrong turns in his biography, and, if he adds it all up, he still has fourteen concrete ideas for novels in his head that he will likely be unable to realize. To his credit, on the other hand, are nine books with which he is satisfied and which he regards as literarily viable. Is that an acceptable lifetime achievement?

Feeling dead tired, he looks for a place in this overcrowded camp where he can be alone for a few minutes. He is headed for a remote, musty supply building when Walter Hasenclever addresses him, that writer colleague whose fortune resembles his in so many respects. They are both Jews and avowed enemies of Hitler; both enjoyed huge successes before the Nazis expatriated them and burned their books.

How did he size up the situation, Hasenclever asks him, after negotiating with the camp commander? "My dear Feuchtwanger, we need courage today. What percent chance do you give us?"

The two men are standing in the sun. A gentle wind is blowing, and the hills around them are a vibrant green – it is a glorious summer day. But the threat of being murdered looms larger with each passing hour. Feuchtwanger is in a despondent state of mind. "How much hope?" he asks back. "Five percent."

"Really only five percent?" Hasenclever exclaims. He then accepts Feuchtwanger's words as a verdict. "I fear you are right."

Is it better, they wonder, to kill themselves once the Nazis take over the camp? Hasenclever ponders this frequently, and he has thought up a new method for suicide. He suggests they could speak to one of the German soldiers, give him whatever money they still had on them, and say, "Listen, comrade, I'm going to try to escape now. Aim true." – A macabre, self-torturing notion, but they both know they are not the only ones in the camp thinking dismal thoughts.

Then, that afternoon, the sensation. The commander announces by a posted notice that the promised train from Les Milles will depart the following day at eleven in the morning. All endangered prisoners are to pack only the barest of necessities. More than one bag is not permitted. They will be awakened bright and early and must then be ready to decamp.

Again, the agitation is great. In one stroke, many of the exiles are no longer certain whether their prospects would be better by escaping with the train to an unknown destination or perhaps, after all, by waiting in the camp for the German troops and disguising themselves as supporters of Hitler. While Feuchtwanger packs his things to flee, those seeking advice besiege him with questions; he is regarded as a man of foresight and good intel. His straw pallet turns into a kind of information clearinghouse for all matters of survival. Hasenclever visits him again, too, but because he is caught up in conversation, Feuchtwanger can only ask him to be patient, and Hasenclever waves him off: "Don't let me disturb you. It isn't important. Good night then."

Later, Hasenclever speaks with Franz Schoenberner, the former head of *Simplicissimus*, and with peculiar solemnity shakes his hand before the lights in the dormitory are turned out. It is a restive night. Many of the men toss and turn for a long while on their sacks of straw. It rustles as in a stable.

Quite early the next morning, a young Austrian doctor visits Feuchtwanger, worried because no one has been able to rouse Hasenclever. "Come, come quickly. I fear something's happened." Schoenberner also hears that something has taken place with Hasenclever. Several doctors are gathered around the unconscious man. Hasenclever is pale, his breathing shallow and wheezy. Apparently, he has taken so many sleeping pills that his stomach has to be pumped. A small empty bottle of Veronal is found in the straw beside him. If he took all the pills right after lights-out, then the poison has already been in his body too long; then there is no hope for him, the physicians all agree.

Two soldiers arrive with a stretcher. Through the narrow wooden stairs, they hoist Hasenclever down to the ground floor and take him to the sick barrack where the French camp doctor is to attend to him. Feuchtwanger, Schoenberner, and the others have no choice but to assemble in the courtyard for departure and wait.

At around seven o'clock in the morning, a very, very long train pulls up. Among the cars hitched together are a smattering of old passenger coaches and, apart from them, transport cars bearing the label "eight horses or forty men."

Before the march to the train begins, Feuchtwanger pays one more visit to the sick bay and asks whether Hasenclever is fit for transport.

The doctor is skeptical; Hasenclever is in a coma. His head is bright red, and his tongue is hanging out of his mouth, blue and swollen; his condition is ultimately hopeless. Feuchtwanger returns to the men waiting in the yard, looks for the camp commander, and confronts him about Hasenclever: "What's going to happen?" he asks. "We can't leave him behind like that."

The commandant reacts gruffly. To lose such a famous detainee to suicide does not leave him cold either. He is a soldier in a defeated army, but he defends his pride. "What do you take us for?" he replies, snapping his riding crop against his pantleg. "I give you my word of honor as a French officer: the man shall not fall into the Nazis' hands. If there is no other way, then we'll stuff the papers of a fallen French soldier in his pocket."

A short time later, the roughly two thousand men are led to the train and jammed into the railcars assigned them. Golo Mann and Franz Schoenberner find their place in one of the passenger coaches; Feuchtwanger has to go to a transport trailer. The car is so overcrowded that no one can sit down. Everyone has to stand, body squeezed against body like in a streetcar at rush hour. It immediately begins to reek. Grime and brick dust are everywhere. Suitcases are tossed out of the car to make more room. Many have nothing left but the clothes they are wearing. At around eleven o'clock, the train departs – exactly where to, no one knows.

Walter Hasenclever, forty-nine years old, remains behind. His dramas dominated German stages after the First World War, and his comedies were performed in the best theaters in Europe. He dies that same day and is laid to rest in a mass grave in Aix-en-Provence. "Catastrophe is closing in," he wrote two days earlier in a letter to his wife Edith, "today or tomorrow the end may be here … I want to take the final step of my own free will. And in the final moment, *this I swear to you*, I will think of you."

Bordeaux, June 22, 1940

Marshal Pétain accepts the conditions dictated by Germany for the armistice. The agreement seals France's defeat, which shall go down in French military history as *Le Désastre*. The Germans occupy the northern part of France and a strip along the Atlantic coast in the west: sixty percent of the country in total. The south thus becomes the last refuge for exiles and those opposed to Hitler. Pétain, the head of state, rules the unoccupied zone from Vichy, a small spa town in Auvergne. He is no liberal, not even a democrat. Instead, he establishes an authoritarian rule that flirts with fascist ideas.

New York, June 22, 1940

It is a bright early summer's day in Manhattan. Varian and Eileen Fry live on Irving Place, not far from Greenwich Village, the artist and nightlife district. It would be a nice morning for a relaxed brunch for two in one of the many cafés, but as soon as Varian Fry picks up the *New York Times*, he loses his taste for the genial aspects of the day. He does not even need to open the paper: the worst news imaginable is staring him in the face right on the front page: "Hitler Demands Full French Surrender" – a fear-inducing headline. Hitler does not do things by halves; he demands France's unconditional surrender. The agreement is to be signed this very Saturday; the French have no leeway to speak of. It is a total defeat.

In three days' time, on Tuesday, Varian Fry and Paul Hagen intend to present their rescue plan to their supporters in the banquet hall of the Commodore Hotel, found the Emergency Rescue Committee, and ask for donations. What are they supposed to tell people? That they want to rescue persecuted people from a country that has fallen into the hands of the Germans? From a country where the Gestapo rules? That sounds like the operational plan for a guerrilla army, not like one for an aid organization.

Princeton, June 22, 1940

Thomas Mann reads different newspapers, the *Herald Tribune* and *New Leader* magazine, but his horror is no less than Fry's. For him, it is perhaps the war's darkest hour. He cannot complain about his own circumstances. As a visiting professor at the university, he has moved into a brick villa in Princeton with his family, just about an hour's drive southwest of Manhattan. They have ten rooms at their disposal, a generous reception hall, as well as a comfortable studio in which he can work undisturbed. Here he is regarded as one of the greatest writers of the age. Those in charge at the university and his filthy-rich benefactor, Agnes E. Meyer, take pains to make his life as pleasant as possible.

Yet after France's collapse, Mann now thinks anything possible, not just a swift defeat for Great Britain, but also a fascist revolution in America. He no longer feels safe in the United States. But where else could he flee now? To Japan? Heinrich and Golo have been missing for weeks. No more letters have arrived from Nice, where he suspects his brother to be, and ever since his son left Zurich, there has been no news from him either. Rumors are circulating, which contradict one another. In one, Golo is stuck in a French internment camp, and in another, both succeeded in escaping to Spain or Lisbon. But nothing reliable can be ascertained. The Germans are said to have already given lists to the French authorities with names of exiles they demand be handed over. In that case, Thomas Mann's last and most terrible hope is that they both will simply be shot dead by the military straightaway and will not also be tortured by the Gestapo.

His two oldest children, Erika and Klaus, are relentlessly active, working like mad. They have written a book, *Escape to Life*, about the misery of German artists in exile. They give lectures, write open letters, travel to conventions. He, too, writes quite a bit about the political situation himself, but in reality he harbors little hope. The European continent is probably lost. Recently, when he was listening to the Prelude to Wagner's *Lohengrin* on the gramophone one evening, he could not help but weep. He was overwhelmed by the feeling of listening once more, now, amid the downfall, to what he loved most fiercely in his youth.

Yesterday, he took stock a bit in his diary. He sees no future for France anymore. After the Nazis occupied it, it was definitively over for that country: "It will no longer be permitted to think, speak, write. Its eyes put out and its tongue cut off – this is how it will live."

Bordeaux – Bayonne, late June 1940

Hertha Pauli and Walter Mehring stand on a small bridge that leads directly to an intersection. From here, the signpost says, there are only fifteen kilometers left to Bordeaux. Mehring hopes to get on a ship to

England or North Africa there. Pauli is convinced that their only chance to obtain passage out of France is in Bayonne, much farther south. Since they cannot agree, they toss a coin: heads means Bordeaux, tails Bayonne. The coin spins through the air, rolls on the ground, and lands on – tails.

A few minutes later, a vehicle speeds toward them on the road to Bayonne. Pauli succeeds in stopping it. She implores the two French officers to give them a lift south. The pair do not hesitate, point to the empty backseat, and a few hours later, Mehring and Pauli arrive at the harbor in Bayonne. From an inky sky, a cloudburst rains down over the city.

An English ship is in fact anchored off the coast. In spite of the rainstorm, shuttle boats struggle back and forth through the choppy seas to get passengers aboard it. The harbor is cordoned off by English soldiers. Pauli nevertheless manages to elbow her way through to the

Walter Mehring, 1929

British captain standing on the pier in his gold-braided uniform. He seems not to notice her, declining even to turn his head when she implores him for spots for herself and Mehring.

"Are you an Englishwoman?" he asks. And when she shakes her head, he answers simply, "Sorry."

A few women fling themselves into the water from the pier, intending to swim to the ship, but they are pushed back by boats and forced to return to shore.

At dawn, the storm lets up, and Mehring and Pauli watch as the ship hoists anchor and vanishes in the haze between water and sky. They find seats in a harbor bar to warm themselves with a few glasses of wine and to let their clothes dry. At this point, they wonder whether they can get poison from an apothecary without a prescription. Then, suddenly, sailors rush into the bar, saying the British ship hit a mine out at sea and sank like a rock. There are, the men say, apparently no survivors.

Hertha Pauli

Gurs, late June 1940

The camp commandant is a pudgy, somewhat vain man, crude and conscious of his power. Usually, he is quite mindful of his uniform and his militarily rigid bearing. Since the defeat of the French army has become apparent, however, his discipline and that of his crews of guards have declined rapidly. No one feels responsible anymore for order in the camp. One morning, the commandant is seen stumbling drunk down the central camp road with a young prisoner on his arm, with whom he clearly spent the night.

This is the sort of opportunity Lisa Fittko has been waiting for. She is thirty, a Jew with a narrow face and black curly hair, raised in Berlin-Neukölln. Already as a schoolgirl, she joined the Young Communist League, managed to escape from the Nazis to Prague, and for years has smuggled propaganda material into Germany and persecuted people out of the country, together with her husband. The couple only survived this because they strictly abide by the rules of an inconspicuous underground existence, leaving almost no trace.

In the camp, too, Fittko immediately began establishing a communist resistance group. One of her friends works as a message runner in the camp commandant's office, where she was able to steal over a hundred official discharge forms and travel permits. Together with a third friend, a talented forger, they furnished the documents with the commandant's signature and then distributed them to all those intent on fleeing.

One of those is Hannah Arendt. A number of prisoners have qualms about leaving the camp; they do not know what awaits them on the outside, where they are supposed to hide, and what they are to subsist on in their illegality. Arendt is in particular luck, however, because two of her friends live with their children in a small house in Montauban, just about two hundred kilometers from Gurs. She thinks she can manage to get there on foot. Outside the camp, she absolutely wants to remain solo. As just one person, she hopes to be able to slip through the many roadside checkpoints better.

The escape succeeds in a quite unspectacular way. In the morning, around sixty prisoners set out in small groups, in twos, threes, or alone, and report to the camp gate. The mayhem in the camp is so great by now that the guards do not even hit on the idea of checking with the commandant. They examine the papers of only the first couple of women more closely, then wave all the rest of them through.

As promised, Hannah Arendt immediately peels off from the others and takes the road to Lourdes. The city is only two days' trek distant, halfway to Montauban. On the other hand, Lisa Fittko, who has also fled, searches for a hiding spot for the coming days along with Paulette, a friend from Paris. On a country road, they wave down a vehicle, and the officer at the wheel gives them a ride. Overcome with exhaustion, Fittko falls asleep in the backseat and does not wake up again until the man abruptly halts outside the constabulary of a village called Pontacq and gets out. Then they hear the man addressing the police officers in a commanding tone. "I turn over to you two women," he says. "I am making the constabulary of Pontacq liable for the safety of these women. They are Belgian refugees being pursued by the Nazis. You are responsible for ensuring they do not fall into the hands of the Germans."

New York, June 24, 1940

With Monday's edition of the *New York Times*, a glimmer of hope returns. The weekend was awful for Fry. Whenever he feels helpless in the face of glaring injustice, his predisposition for depression makes itself known; he was almost catatonic. In moments like these, the role of the caring wife who tries to cheer him up again falls to Eileen, and she has done her utmost.

The *New York Times* was able to learn the conditions of the armistice for its Monday edition, even before they were published in France. On the front page, the newspaper prints a map, three columns wide, showing France divided in two; the graphic artist shaded the north and a thin region along the Atlantic coast with dark vertical lines that read like the bars on a prison window. He has left the rest of the country white. The border between the two parts is serpentine in its curves, but at the moment Fry is little bothered by it. What interests him is the southern, unshaded part, because it, the newspaper reports, does not fall into German hands according to the agreement, but will continue to be administered by the French, by the government of Marshal Pétain.

At lunch in Childs', Fry pores over the map with Paul Hagen. If the people they want to rescue from France have fled to the unoccupied

South, he says, the case is not hopeless. There is still a chance, then, of finding them and getting them out. Hagen agrees with Fry; he also does not want to give up hope. Nevertheless, he warns, they must not pretend the situation is more favorable than it is.

The price the French must pay to keep the South unoccupied is high – the Germans have imposed strict requirements on them. The *New York Times* has printed the first portion of this armistice agreement right at the bottom of the first page. But those who turn the page will find the second part on the newspaper's third page – and it packs a punch. Article XIX, for instance, targets Nazi detractors among the exiles: "The French Government is to hand over all German subjects indicated by the German Government who are in France [...]." If this section is carried out systematically, Hagen says, then the Gestapo will not even need to send out their search detachments; they will only have to present the French with lists containing the names of their favorite adversaries and let them do the dirty work.

New York, June 25, 1940

The Commodore is no run-of-the-mill hotel. Many New Yorkers see in it something akin to Manhattan's calling card. It is located directly adjacent to Grand Central Station and boasts twenty-two floors, two thousand rooms, and perhaps the grandest hotel lobby in the world. The foyer is three stories tall and festooned with flags from all over the world. In the middle, it also provides enough space for a small palm garden along with a waterfall and a café. To the sides of the lobby, there are entryways to the hotel's various banquet halls.

Fry, Hagen, and Oram have consciously selected a somewhat pompous locale to establish their Emergency Rescue Committee. The banquet at which they want to collect their seed capital ought to be clearly recognizable at first glance as a fundraising gala. By no means should the gathering seem like the meeting of an activist group secretly pursuing political aims as, for example, the Spanish Aid Committee. The three of them want to rescue internationally recognized artists and intellectuals from persecution, not peddle an ideology.

Over two hundred guests come. At each of the tables' formal place settings is a check form, specially printed for the occasion, waiting to be filled out by generous donors. At the start of the event, the famous advocates whom Fry and Hagen were able to attract to the committee give brief but riveting speeches. On behalf of her father, Erika Mann tells of calls for help, in letters and telegrams, that have reached him from France. Frank Kingdon, a well-known newspaper commentator and president of the University of Newark, declares himself willing to assume the chairmanship of the new organization, while Varian Fry offers his office at the Foreign Policy Association as temporary headquarters. A hopeful mood of swinging into action spreads around the ballroom – especially when the announcement is made that over $3,400 in donations have come in, the equivalent of four or five well-equipped mid-range sedans.

Then, however, Erika Mann speaks up again with a very simple, immediately evident thought: "We mustn't forget that money alone cannot rescue any of these people. Most of them are trapped. They have neither visas nor passports they can show to get to safety. They can't simply board a ship and leave. We need someone to get them out of there."

Now that money is available and the committee is taking shape, problems come into view which Fry and Hagen have not yet had to consider. Most of the imperiled artists they want to help are in internment camps or in hiding. Who can procure the required exit documents for them? How can the committee aid people whose addresses it does not have? People who are currently doing everything possible not to be found?

Paul Hagen has a reassuring answer at least to the last question. From his underground work in Europe, he knows how attentively those persecuted keep watch for routes of escape. As soon as word gets around that there is an aid organization willing to assist them, the helpers just need to wait. It is not they who must find the persecuted. Rather, the persecuted will report to them. Indeed, they will break down their doors.

Bayonne – Nîmes, June 25 and 26, 1940

For three days and two nights, the train from Les Milles has been trundling through southern France. It travels so slowly that men leap from the open sliding door of their railcar to relieve themselves next to the tracks, then run after the train, and are able to jump back inside. For hours upon hours, they stand in the boxcars, squeezed tightly together. It is so cramped that they are only able to huddle up on the floor to sleep in shifts. All the while, an indescribable stink hangs in the air. And ever since they reached the Pyrenees, a torrential downpour has been pounding on the railcars' metal roofs. The noise grates on the nerves.

When they arrive in Bayonne, the train remains stopped at the train station for hours, yet the men may not disembark. Fellow prisoners try to persuade Feuchtwanger to walk up to the locomotive and ask the train commandant when they will finally depart so they can board a ship at the harbor. Feuchtwanger's legs are swollen from the incessant standing. Every movement hurts. Awkwardly, he climbs onto the platform from the sliding door and hobbles the length of the train. The commandant, a captain, is standing on the footboard of the locomotive, speaking with other prisoners. They are staring at him in horror. "Tell your comrades we have to turn back. In two hours, the Germans will be in Bayonne. Avoid causing panic."

Shouting erupts right away, loud wailing, accusations – their train was traveling much too slowly, no wonder the Germans are faster. The horrible news spreads rapidly through the cars, and two thousand men are seized by a feverish flurry of activity. So that they cannot be identified, they search their luggage for identification papers, documents, and letters, tear them to shreds, and toss the scraps onto the tracks – better to have no passport than one by which you would be recognized as a Jew or an enemy of Hitler.

Not until the train begins moving again, back into the country's interior, does the tumult subside. Along the route, not a trace of the *Wehrmacht* is to be seen. Forward progress is again only halting; the train is stopped more than it is moving. Through the railcar's open sliding door, Feuchtwanger catches sight of the endless stream of people fleeing, listlessly dragging themselves forward in the rain. They all hoped for a ship to England, America, or North Africa. Now the Germans occupy the Atlantic ports without a fight, and so the caravans have made an about-face and press onward, full of trepidation, away from the places they had only just recently wanted to reach.

The rain grows more intense and seems to wash away every sense of order. The younger, sturdier prisoners in particular want to take charge of their own fate. The border with Spain may be high up in the mountains, but it is not very far away. And so with every stop of the train, men slip away on foot to try their luck. The guards do not stop them. On the contrary: now, after their country has capitulated, some of them follow the fleeing men to make their way home to their families.

Feuchtwanger's two Austrian helpers, too – his attendants who have supported him as well as they could during the journey – no longer wish to remain on the train. They have scared up a map and are trying to persuade him to flee. But Feuchtwanger knows that he has no chance at his age and with the condition of his legs. He has to stay.

The train travels back on almost the same route it had come. The railcars have emptied a little, making the trip for the remaining men more bearable. They can sit on their suitcases now and then at night sleep half outstretched on the floor.

The next morning in Toulouse, Golo Mann succeeds in leaving the train and scrounging up a newspaper in a dank street behind the train station. The scene is ghostly. Hundreds of ragged, bearded soldiers stand in the rain, waiting for orders. Many *tirailleurs sénégalais* are among them. Evidently, there is no one left in the country that plucked them from the colonies to fight the Germans who feels responsible for their destiny.

Now, finally, with more than four days' delay, the newspaper may report on the armistice agreement and the division of the country into an occupied and an unoccupied zone. On the front page, a map is printed that roughly sketches the course of the border. Back on the train, Mann realizes with the others that Toulouse is located in the unoccupied portion of the country, that they are no longer within reach of the *Wehrmacht*. At one stroke, the dismal mood lifts like a fog. The men joke and laugh. Again, some leave the train. Golo Mann, too, plans to head for Marseille on his own, hoping from there to escape by ship to northern Africa. The rest of them look forward to the dumbfounded looks of the guards at Les Milles when the same prisoners who departed five days earlier step off the train once more outside the camp.

As soon as the train approaches Provence, the incessant rain lets up. It is like the final scene in a cheap film; dangers have been overcome, clouds part, and the sun emerges, radiant. Around evening, the train deviates from the route of the outward journey, trundling slowly around the city of Nîmes and finally coming to a stop in a secluded meadow idyllically nestled between hills. All the men are allowed to leave the train. Feuchtwanger alights, knowing that nights in southern France can still be cold, even in June, but he would rather freeze in the open air than spend one more night on the filthy wooden planks of their railcar. He takes a few steps back and forth. In the dusk, the meadow has a fairytale-like beauty about it: a magical meadow. He lies down, stretches out, extending his body, and wraps himself tightly in his blanket, gazing at the stars and relishing the good fortune of having survived.

Narbonne – Bordeaux – Biarritz – Bayonne – Hendaye, late June 1940

Their panicked attempt to flee France becomes an odyssey for Franz Werfel and Alma Mahler-Werfel, costing them a fortune. It is like a curse. Everything they endeavor to do fails. On the morning after their night in Narbonne's refugee hostel, their chauffeur picks them up and begins a second attempt at finding the route to Bordeaux. But after only a few kilometers, the street is blocked off, and the driver claims there are no other ways to the Atlantic coast. Happy to be rid of them, he unloads them and their twelve suitcases outside a miserable little train station, collects six thousand francs, and vanishes back to Marseille.

The Werfels spend the night on the train platform, for the last train bound for Bordeaux is announced again and again but does not depart until dawn. When, another twelve hours later, they arrive in Bordeaux, the city has just been bombed. The streets are full of wreckage. All the ships have long since sailed. And their suitcases have gone missing on the journey, a terrible loss because contained in one of the bags were precious original scores by Gustav Mahler and Anton Bruckner. They were going to sell them in America to have seed capital for their new life there.

When they leave the train station in Bordeaux, bleary-eyed, it rains in torrents. Again, they cannot find a hotel. Alma accosts a heavily made-up young woman on the street who procures for them – at the price of a thousand francs – a room in a nearby bordello. The next day, they plan to make for Biarritz to escape the advancing Germans and get visas from the consulate to exit into Spain. The taxi costs them six thousand francs, but upon their arrival, all the consulates are closed. A man they chance upon manages to get them a place to stay and claims to be able to obtain all the necessary papers for crossing the border for several thousand francs. They give him the money, and he disappears without a trace.

Franz Werfel then commutes to Bayonne for two whole days in the constant rain to obtain visas there at the administrative bureaus – until he realizes the city is already occupied by the Germans. In horror, he flees with Alma to Hendaye, directly on the Spanish border, but with no papers, the customs officials will not let them pass. Instead, they catch wind of a rumor that the Portuguese consul in St. Jean de Luz is eagerly allocating visas to refugees. When they arrive there, they learn that the consul has suffered a nervous breakdown and thrown all the passports into the sea. By this point, the German occupiers have arrived here as well.

This is too much for Werfel. At the hotel, he throws himself onto the bed in a sobbing fit and is no longer amenable. Luckily, a married couple they befriended on the run is able to scare up a taxi again. At half past eleven at night, the four of them set out for the country's interior, away from the Germans, into the unoccupied zone. In his haste, however, the driver has forgotten to install the headlights on his vehicle. It is pitch black, and the rain is never-ending. At a walking pace, they blindly steer down deserted country roads heading east. They have no concrete destination in mind. The driver recommends Lourdes to them as a refuge, the pilgrimage site of St. Bernadette at the foot of the Pyrenees. They are all beyond weary and acquiesce.

Pontacq, late June 1940

For the time being, Lisa Fittko and her friend Paulette feel safe under the protection of the Pontacq gendarmerie. They have found shelter on a small farm, help with the work there, and explore its surroundings in the evening. On a country road a few days after their arrival, they run into other refugees looking for a place to stay. While they deliberate together, a car pulls up beside them, and a woman rolls down the window and asks where the road leads.

"Why, you're Hertha Pauli," one of the refugees says, recognizing the former actor.

"That's right," the woman replies. "Where are we?"
"In the Basses Pyrénées. Where are you coming from?"
"From the west, from the coast. What direction are we headed?"
"South. Where are you trying to go?"
"Perhaps to Lourdes ...?" The vehicle gives a shudder and drives off.

Saint Nicolas, June 27, 1940

Feuchtwanger and his fellow prisoners are awakened on their fairytale meadow outside Nîmes much too early. The guards order them to ready themselves to march. But then nothing happens for hours, except that the train with which they wandered through all of southern France lurches forward and rolls off slowly – and empty.

Not until the sun is high in the sky does the signal come to head out. Wearily, the approximately fifteen hundred men begin moving. Like a group of hikers, they climb up the slopes, guards and those under guard colorfully intermixed as if together on an outing. Most internees walk completely unencumbered; they have long since left their luggage behind somewhere. Others like Max Ernst or Anton Räderscheidt struggle with large rectangular pasteboards, with pictures they painted in Les Milles sandwiched in between.

No one is in a rush. Feuchtwanger remains off to the side. He takes a seat on a rock, listening carefully to the silence, and attempts to enjoy this moment of solitude as intensively as possible. Ever since arriving in Les Milles over a month ago, he has been constantly surrounded by people. The opportunity to step away for a moment is precious to him. Then he pulls himself together again and follows the others.

His friend Alfred Kantorowicz, by contrast, inconspicuously turns off into a copse of trees and hides. Hailing from a Jewish family, Kantorowicz is a literary scholar with a great deal of battle experience. In the First World War, he was a soldier on the front lines. Before Hitler's seizure of power, he joined the Communist Party of Germany (KPD) and got deeply involved when his party comrades engaged in street battles with the SA and the SS. In the Spanish Civil War, he became an officer in the International Brigades and befriended Ernest Hemingway. Now and again Hemingway still sends him money, knowing that Kantorowicz cannot earn anything in France as a scholar or author.

Kantorowicz has run out of patience for the perilous disorganization of the French internment camp. He crouches in the underbrush, waiting for all the prisoners and guards to march past him. He intends to make his way to the Côte d'Azur, to his wife in Bormes-les-Mimosas, without papers or provisions, but full of confidence that they can manage to escape the country together.

After a few kilometers, the others reach the new camp. It is an old, desolate estate called Saint Nicolas, with a manor house and smaller outbuildings. As ever, nothing is prepared, everything improvised. The guards and their officers quarter in the buildings and distribute tents and barbed wire to the internees. Out in the open, the men must first fence themselves in, then pitch their round, pointed tents, which look like tepees.

As soon as the tents are up, Saint Nicolas looks from a distance like a boy scout camp, and Feuchtwanger is tempted to find a bright side to their renewed internment. But then his fellow prisoners pull him aside. They have gotten their hands on a leaflet from the city of Nîmes, the purpose of which is to provide information to the populace about the terms of the armistice. Every one of the prisoners immediately grasps the implications of Article XIX for exiles, especially for Feuchtwanger. The Nazis have banned and burned his books, they have revoked his citizenship, and Joseph Goebbels has publicly declared him one of the most hated writers in exile. His name ought to be near the top of the Gestapo's wanted lists.

New York, June 27, 1940

Paul Hagen was unable to foresee this invitation. Eleanor Roosevelt, the First Lady, has asked him, an antifascist underground guerrilla who has been living in America for only six months, to a meeting at her New York home.

Over the past several weeks, Hagen and Varian Fry have of course been trying to win over not only potential donors for their new committee, but also politicians. And it was natural to write Eleanor Roosevelt. She is far more than just the woman at the side of President Franklin D. Roosevelt. Never has a First Lady involved herself in the country's politics as confidently as she has. For years, she has been the liberal conscience of her husband's administration. In interviews and her daily column "My Day," which is carried by a host of newspapers, she advocates for strengthening civil rights and supporting the Black population. Because women journalists are only seldom accredited at the White House, she gives press conferences almost weekly to which only women are invited.

In addition, she is an avid reader, and in January 1933, when her husband had already been elected president but had not yet taken office, she met Lion Feuchtwanger on his book-signing tour through America. She was greatly impressed by him and his books. Even so, Fry and Hagen were surprised when they actually received a reply from her to their letter.

Eleanor Roosevelt remembered meeting Feuchtwanger when the head of an American publisher had sent her a stirring photograph three weeks earlier. It is a random snapshot showing Feuchtwanger in tattered clothing and with a sunburned face behind the barbed-wire fence of Les Milles. Ever since she saw this picture, the plight of writers and artists in France has been one of her primary political concerns.

The Roosevelts' New York home is situated in one of the finest districts of Manhattan, between Park Avenue and Madison Avenue, just a few steps from Central Park. Paul Hagen does not have occasion to visit this area often. He describes the exiles' perilous state of affairs to his host and informs her of the founding of the Emergency Rescue Committee, but also of the enormous resistance they encounter when requesting visas from the State Department for these persecuted persons.

To his astonishment, Eleanor Roosevelt picks up the phone in his presence and calls the President. For twenty minutes she attempts to persuade her husband to loosen the entry requirements for refugees from Europe on humanitarian grounds. But Roosevelt declines. Upset, she ends the conversation with one long line: "If Washington refuses to approve these visas immediately, the German and Austrian emigrant leaders will charter a ship with American assistance, bring as many of the endangered refugees in France as possible across the Atlantic Ocean, and, if necessary, cruise along the East Coast until such time as the American people, ashamed and annoyed, force the president and the Congress with demonstrations to allow these victims of political persecution to come ashore in America."

Lion Feuchtwanger in the internment camp Les Milles, 1939

Lourdes, late June 1940

A hundred years ago, Lourdes was still a plain mountain town nestled among gray cliffs and sparse meadows, regularly plagued by the flooding of the Gave. Since then, it has been beautified with ostentatious churches and plazas by the windfall of money pilgrims have poured into the village. On every street, there are hotels and guesthouses for the faithful who flock here to pray to the Blessed Mother in the grotto where she is supposed to have appeared to Saint Bernadette. But even Lourdes, which is used to masses of visitors, is now overrun with refugees.

Alma Mahler-Werfel can no longer stand it. She is at the end of her rope. When she cannot get a room at the Vatican, the second hotel in which she has inquired, she bursts into tears at the reception desk. She looks so miserable that the innkeeper takes away the room from a different, younger couple and gives it to the Werfels.

Of course they are happy to have a roof over their heads; for the first time since their escape from Marseille, they can feel safe. But in Alma's eyes, though, the room is ultimately only a stopgap measure. The bed is too narrow, the room too small, and outside, beneath their window, there is a grubby projecting roof littered with trash. Their suitcases and bags are all lost. They have only their travel funds and the clothes they are wearing.

To reenter civilization, they go out the next morning. Werfel gets a shave, and Alma roves through the bookstores. Each of them offers dozens upon dozens of brochures about Saint Bernadette, the unfortunate daughter of a drunkard and his drunkard wife, who succeeded in convincing the whole world of her encounters with the Blessed Mother. Werfel, the Jew with a predilection for everything Catholic, is immediately taken with the story and buys all of the treatises that recount her tale.

Naturally, he also goes with Alma to visit the grotto where all the faithful are streaming, and they drink from the spring that has its source there. The Werfels could well use a miracle, because now that the armistice has been concluded and the conditions of state are consolidating once more, they are stuck in Lourdes. They are permitted to leave town only with a *sauf-conduit*. Since on their chaotic exodus they arrived in the city illicitly without such a travel permit, however, the authorities refuse to issue one now. They have become prisoners of bureaucracy.

While Werfel again browses a bookstore for literature about the life of Saint Bernadette, he senses movement by the entrance. He looks up, and standing before him are Walter Mehring and Hertha Pauli. The three fall into each other's arms; they know one other well from Vienna's cultural scene. Amid the vast thronging of people, at least one small miracle has occurred and brought them together.

Because Mehring and Pauli are homeless yet again, Werfel takes them along to the Hôtel Vatican. Alma has since gained astonishing influence over the hotelier. For the most part, she keeps him busy with the dubiously auspicious mission of hunting down the twelve suitcases they lost outside Bordeaux. It is now child's play for her to persuade him to let Mehring and Pauli spend the night on the billiard table in the hotel's bar.

It does both couples good to confer together about their messy situation – but the feeling of relief does not last long. Mehring is restless. He hopes to be able to obtain via the American consulate in Toulouse a reply to the telegram they sent in Paris to Thomas Mann, but because hardly any trains have been running since the armistice, he means to set out with Hertha Pauli on foot.

An outrageous plan – a slog of a hundred fifty kilometers with no travel permit, always on the lookout for the police. That is not to the Werfels' taste; they are too old for that. And thus their paths diverge again the following morning. Alma and Franz trek to Bernadette's grotto at an ungodly hour to drink from the spring and continue waiting for miracles. After a passably restful night's sleep on the hard table, Mehring and Pauli, however, entrust their fate once more to the road.

Lourdes, late June 1940

Hannah Arendt has escaped the travails of the road for the time being. She sits across from Walter Benjamin in Lourdes, a table with a chessboard between them. They had played one another a few times in Paris, friendly duels between one thinker and another. At the moment, there is nothing better for them to find calm again after the hardships of their escapes.

Even while in Gurs, Hannah Arendt stayed in touch with Walter Benjamin. For her, particularly in such perilous times, friendships are among those possessions that cannot be replaced. Initially, he wrote to her from Paris. Then later, she learned he escaped to Lourdes together with his sister Dora – carrying in his luggage scarcely more than a few toiletries, a gas mask, and a single, not especially interesting book.

For Dora, it was an absurd journey. She had only just been released from Gurs to Paris because of her back ailment before once again sitting on a train taking her back into the foothills of the Pyrenees.

Here, in Lourdes, the siblings have found cheap accommodations. Walter Benjamin likes the mountainous landscape and the equanimity with which the residents face the surging waves of refugees. By the same token, he is bored, and he longs for libraries and companionship. Hannah Arendt is all the more welcome a sight for him. She plans to continue onward to Montauban in one or two days to begin her search for Heinrich Blücher from there. She trusts that her husband has also escaped from the internment camp by now and was able to flee from the Germans. That will not make it any easier to find him, though. But for now, she enjoys the respite after her imprisonment at the camp, as well as the pleasure of once more feeling the acuity of her mind, while playing chess or in conversations with Benjamin.

Toulouse, late June 1940

Since the authorities do not give her any hope of being able to join her fiancé in Yugoslavia within the next few weeks, Miriam Davenport has no choice but to kill her time in the cafés of Toulouse. Here, she runs into an acquaintance from Paris, Charles Wolff, a skinny man with a large beret. He loves records, owns a huge collection of them – around 18,000 – and writes pieces of music criticism. As a Jew, he was also forced to flee Paris and now does not know where to go. And when Miriam visits young Gussie again at the Cinéma Pax to be cheered up by his sunny disposition, she crosses paths with Walter Mehring, her next-door neighbor from the Hôtel de l'Univers in Paris. He is carrying a bottle of wine under his arm, but he is not in a talking mood.

The following day, Charles Wolff looks around for Miriam and is happy to find her in a café. He tells her a young American woman, Mary Jayne Gold, is arriving on the next train, a friend of friends. He would like to introduce her to her countrywoman.

At the train station, they barge in on a heart-rending familial tableau. Mary Jayne Gold is just now alighting from the train, carrying a little boy in her arms and delivering him to his shaken parents. That this is about more than a reunion after a brief separation – that much is palpable.

As it turns out, Mary Jayne is an unusually attractive woman, a real beauty: tall, blond, athletic. She has been living in France for years now, Miriam is told, and, as the daughter of a father worth many millions, knows no financial woes. Before the war, she earned her pilot's license and bought a plane, a small single-engine aircraft. She flew back and forth across Europe with it to be present in the most beautiful places and for the most thrilling galas at a moment's notice. But that is in the past. When war broke out, she donated the plane to the French army in the hopes it might be of use in battle.

These two young American women quickly take a liking to one another. They spend the afternoon outside a café by the train station, in the shade of the plane trees, and tell each other their tales of escape. Mary Jayne fled from Paris along with the French Bénédite family. She has known them for years; Daniel and Théodora are her closest friends. Together, they were overtaken by the German troops and for a time were in utmost danger. At their time of need, the panicked parents entrusted their baby son to Mary Jayne. It was the most difficult decision of their lives, but with her American passport, Gold had the greater chance of survival. She then tried to reach a ship in Bordeaux bound for England; it was a race that came down to the wire. In the end, she arrived on time, but without the necessary paperwork for the child, she was not allowed aboard. She had no other choice but to go into hiding with the boy for a few days. Fortunately, she managed to get in touch with the Bénédites again and was able to return their son to them.

Miriam meets her new friend at the same café the next morning as well. Mary Jayne must first pick up her dog, a black poodle named Dagobert, at a friend's home, and then she plans to continue onward to Marseille to arrange her return to America at the consulate. Because she is aware of the difficulty of Miriam's circumstances, she gives her money and jots down the name and address of the custodian of her trust in Chicago for her. She will let him know accordingly – if Miriam needs

Mary Jayne Gold

more money, she should turn to this man, who will direct it to be sent to France.

Nîmes, late June to early July 1940

The barbed-wire fence around the camp at Saint Nicolas is barely more than window dressing. The prisoners have had to put it up themselves and have understandably expended little effort while doing so. At several points, the wires are so bent out of shape that you can crouch through beneath them. That may be uncomfortable, but it presents no serious obstacle. The men actively exercise this freedom, and the guards watch them do so without intervening.

Feuchtwanger, too, often leaves the camp in this manner. He goes with the other internees to bathe in a river and eat at a nearby tavern. Still, he finds it to be humiliating to have to squeeze himself beneath the fence, and because any moment of inattention is enough to rip one's clothes on the barbed wire, he would rather use the entrance gate. But as soon as he approaches it, the guards shout to him: "Go no further!"

At some point, Feuchtwanger has had enough and addresses one of the guards. "What would you do if I did keep going? Would you shoot?"

"I'm not crazy," the man replies. "But," he adds, "make it easy on yourself and on me and crawl through the barbed wire."

There is a simple explanation for the guards' cool-headedness. The prisoners, as the camp commandant puts it, are in fact no longer prisoners. Since the signing of the armistice, there is no reason to detain them anymore. They are all to be released just as soon as the chaotic situation in the country has eased. Those who wait that out will receive official release papers. Those who abscond from the camp illegally without papers can be arrested at checkpoints at any time and end up in prison – and they also have no hopes of getting a ration card, a work permit, or an exit visa in the future.

The situation is not quite as simple for the internees as the camp commandant makes it out to be, however. The German occupiers have formed a commission that will gradually survey all French camps. Its primary purpose will be to make sure that Hitler supporters who may still be interned in them are released. But Gestapo investigators searching for Hitler's enemies are also on the commission. Several dozen men have fallen into their clutches in the first few days, so anyone on a Nazi wanted list has to have cleared out before the commission shows up.

As a consequence, a new war of nerves begins. How long can the men in Saint Nicolas wait for their release papers? By when, at the latest, should they flee? Feuchtwanger hesitates for a while. He knows how blundering he is in all practical matters and that any Frenchman will recognize him as a refugee by his German accent. To have a companion who balances out both weaknesses, he joins up with a rugged farmer who speaks simple but accentless French.

It is a Friday at eleven o'clock in the morning when they shimmy beneath the barbed wire. They know that a leisurely lunch is an immutable part of the French daily routine. Police officers also abide by this sacred tradition. Around midday, therefore, the streets will scarcely be monitored. It is hot, but the pair make good headway on foot. To appear like an officer worker, Feuchtwanger is wearing the best suit still in his possession and has stuck a portfolio under his arm. The file folder contains no business documents, to be sure, but a nightshirt, a comb, and a toothbrush.

Just when they are about to board a bus in Nîmes, the driver immediately recognizes that they are refugees from a camp. He warns them that his bus will be searched by the police at the first stop, and so they quickly get out – and are already at their wits' end. Feuchtwanger feels too weak to hike days on end through the woods to his villa in Sanary. But if they want to hitch a ride in a car or buy a train ticket at the station, they will need identification and travel permits they do not have.

And so their escape is over before it even really started. His companion turns around right away, but Feuchtwanger hides for five more days in Nîmes. Then he realizes that he has no chance and likewise returns to Saint Nicolas.

July 1940

Mers-el-Kébir, July 3, 1940

After France's collapse, Great Britain is the only country still battling Hitler. Prime Minister Churchill leaves no doubt about the will to continue the war: "if necessary for years, if necessary alone." The extent of his resolve is immediately evident after France signs the armistice agreement. In no way does he want the French fleet, one of the most powerful in the world, to fall into German hands. A considerable portion of it lies at anchor in Mers-el-Kébir, Algeria. In the early morning hours of July 3, Churchill conveys the demand that these ships either join the Royal Navy or withdraw to one of the French colonies to be disarmed there under British or American supervision.

Negotiations take place all day under extreme tension, but no conclusion is reached. As announced, a British naval unit ultimately opens fire before nightfall on the ships of Frenchmen who, only eleven days earlier, were allies. The shelling lasts around fifteen minutes and is devastating. Several ships sink, and 1,300 French seamen die. Marshal Pétain severs diplomatic relations with Great Britain. From this point on, Churchill views General Charles de Gaulle, who had fled to London, as the legitimate representative of "Free France."

New York, early July 1940

The board of the newly founded Emergency Rescue Committee (ERC) has rented an office in the Chanin Building, right in the heart of Manhattan, at 122 East 42nd Street. This prestigious address pairs nicely with the well-to-do donors the committee needs to fund its work. Connoisseurs who know something of European cultural life have since assembled lists with the names of the writers, scientists, and artists facing the greatest danger. The list of German-language authors who are to be rescued from France comes from Thomas Mann. All in all, there are over two hundred people, many of whom have spouses and children. Gradually, it dawns on the committee the magnitude of the task before it.

Discussions prove tough. Erika Mann's consideration that the ERC will need employees in Marseille has persuaded them all, but no one knows who is able to undertake this risky mission. Paul Hagen has the most experience with underground political work, but the Gestapo knows him too well. As soon as he sets foot on French soil, he would have only minimal chances at survival. Others lack the necessary language proficiency or have no feeling for the complicated political state of affairs in a defeated and divided France.

Varian Fry becomes more impatient by the day; the committee is losing too much time. In the meantime, rumors are circulating that Heinrich Mann has been arrested and Franz Werfel murdered by the Gestapo. No one can say whether the reports are accurate, but from them, an irrefutable truth emerges: the longer the ERC hesitates, the more unlikely it becomes that it can actually get people to safety.

Understandably, Eileen reacts with skepticism when Fry confronts her with the idea that he might be the right man to go to France for the committee. She knows he possesses little knack for diplomacy and tends to become depressed after failures. He also has no experience of any kind with illegal work. He is an idealist and an intellectual, not the strong-nerved guerrilla type it will take for such a scheme. On the other hand, Eileen hopes, the trip to Marseille might also present an opportunity. After nine years of marriage, she and Varian are still childless. Perhaps her husband could adopt a war orphan in France and bring it back to America?

After his wife has abandoned her resistance and the Foreign Policy Association has agreed to release him from his work for a few weeks, Fry has made up his mind. He calls Paul Hagen and informs him that he is willing, "should a more appropriate person not be found," to go to Marseille for the ERC.

Although the committee is very much pressed for time, it still takes two more weeks before the board can bring itself to accept Fry's offer. Paul Hagen has similar scruples to Eileen's; the mission needs a doer, not an aesthete. Still, a good deal speaks for Fry. He is still young, just thirty-two years old, speaks excellent French and rather good German, and he is exceptionally well versed in political matters. Mostly, however, he can trust not to be killed by the Gestapo at the first signs of suspicion. The United States has continued to remain neutral, and the Germans have no interest in drawing America into the war by murdering American citizens in Europe.

Montauban, early July 1940

The route from Lourdes, in the foothill of the Pyrenees, to the plains around Montauban is a slight decline of over a hundred eighty kilometers – a minor advantage for anyone covering the distance on foot, like

Hannah Arendt. After bidding farewell to Dora and Walter Benjamin, she has set out again alone, mindful of standing out as little as possible. It is a long, quiet trek amid a gorgeous landscape. As a precaution, she avoids even the guesthouses, most of which do not have any vacancies anyway. She prefers to sleep in the open air, on bare ground – the summer is warm and dry. When she arrives at her friends' cottage near Montauban, her joints hurt, but otherwise she is doing well.

The house is small: a mere two rooms with a kitchen. Her friends were not interned so that they could take care of their children. Hannah Arendt spends the night with five others in a room with just one bed, but that dims neither her mood, nor her enterprising spirit. Ever since France descended into chaos, new methods of communication have developed among the refugees. Most carry notebooks or accumulated slips of paper with them, and when they meet people who share the same fate, they take down one another's names and destinations. From random conversations like these, important havens for escapees materialize with astonishing speed, and sometimes clues turn up regarding lost friends and relations. In addition, the itinerants post brief search notices on the walls of government buildings, on city halls, prefectures, or postal stations, in the hopes that missing relatives will find them there.

This is how remote Montauban became an important nexus for refugees. The reigning prefect, a socialist, fully expects to be replaced soon by the nationalist administration in Vichy, and so in light of the refugees' misery, he ignores all government decrees and approves vacant buildings to be used as emergency shelters. In addition, the newly consecrated bishop, Pierre-Marie Theás, takes the commandment of Christian charity very seriously and has food distributed, which attracts more and more needy persons, and Hannah Arendt spends a great deal of time in the city center to see whether she might learn something about her husband's whereabouts from those arriving.

For several days, she asks around with no success – until she suddenly has inconceivable luck. Amid the throngs of people, on one of Montauban's main streets, Heinrich Blücher hobbles toward her as though they had arranged to meet there. With unbelievable joy, they fall into each other's arms.

The camp in which Blücher was interned had been dissolved on the day the Germans occupied Paris. The commandant wanted to escape south with the prisoners, but low-flying German aircraft attacked the marching column, so he released the men as if to say: save yourselves if you can. Blücher injured his knee, but was loaded onto a truck and taken out of harm's way. Later, he also contracted an infection of the middle ear. He set out for Montauban because he had heard rumors that even penniless exiles might find medical treatment here.

With the addition of Blücher, the friends' diminutive house has now grown even more cramped. But things fall into place for him and Arendt astonishingly favorably; the prefecture allots them a vacant home. It only has one tiny room and no furniture, but in their view, it represents the height of happiness and luxury: a room for them alone.

Paris, July 13, 1940

Since her return to Paris, Anna Seghers has been living with her children in a small hotel not far from the Jardin du Luxembourg. In order to pay for the tiny room, she has pawned her last piece of jewelry. They cannot go back to their apartment in Meudon. It is quite likely the Gestapo knows their address and is waiting for them there. Seghers has registered her kids for summer school in Paris so that they have something to occupy them during the day and their lives have at least a shred of normalcy.

She knows she now desperately needs people willing to help her. She cannot stay in the hotel too long. She has too little money, and the risk that the Germans will check the hotelier's registration documents is too great. She rides through Paris on the Metro, discreetly trying to find out which friends or acquaintances have remained in town. At the Hôtel de l'Univers, she learns that Walter Mehring and Hertha Pauli departed weeks earlier. The concierge at the Hôtel Trianon in Montparnasse claims Ernst Weiss was evacuated. Later, she learns that Weiss killed himself. "Evacuated," she writes to a friend in New York, "what a peculiar expression for suicide."

Today, she is riding around once again on the Metro when she suddenly feels like she is being watched. She is a level-headed woman, no hysteric, but she cannot shake the impression that clever investigators are hot on her heels. She immediately changes her plans. She absolutely does not want to lead her tails to the friends she was about to visit. She changes trains multiple times and tries to think straight. If the Gestapo is in fact after her, there is only a single safe place for her – the Soviet embassy, exterritorial area. There, people know her. There, they know that she is a communist and an important writer.

When she finally arrives at the embassy, she calms down a bit. The employees kindly listen to her, but then shrug their shoulders. They cannot help her because the Hitler–Stalin Pact made allies out of Germany and the Soviet Union a year ago. The embassy must not and does not want to get involved in the affairs of the German occupying powers.

The gentlemen rise, asking Anna Seghers for her understanding and to please leave the embassy. She is dumbfounded. If she exits the building now, it could be her death sentence, and the country she considered the most humane in the world, the Soviet Union, denies her any protection. On the way out, she serendipitously runs into the subversive Ilya Ehrenburg. They know one another from countless meetings with other communist authors and together organized the Writers Congress at the Maison de la Mutualité five years earlier. Distraught, she tells of the danger she is in. But even Ehrenburg shakes his head. He can do nothing for her, as sorry as he is to admit it. The pact has tied his hands; Anna is on her own. If the Gestapo is waiting for her outside the embassy, no one can help her anymore.

Toulouse – Marseille, mid-July 1940

Walter Mehring and Hertha Pauli admire Toulouse city hall, a castle-like Neoclassical building of rose-colored bricks decorated with white half-columns. Hanging just next to the entrance gate are hundreds of slips of paper with missing persons notices for refugees or for soldiers discharged from the army who have been separated from their relatives. Everyone seems to have lost someone – families torn apart, children gone missing, grandparents left behind. Fates on fluttering leaflets.

Pauli and Mehring also weigh whether or not to chance it and post a note listing where they have come from, where they are going, and at what address they might be reached. Otherwise, they do not have much to do. The American consulate in the city is closed, so they had to abandon Mehring's crazy hope of learning there whether Thomas Mann had answered their Paris telegram. They have no choice but to wait and studiously avoid all Germans and all police officers as they have neither passports nor travel permits.

While the two are studying the papers on the wall of the Capitole, Hertha Pauli suddenly hears her name said aloud, turns around, and Hans Natonek is standing before them. Surprised, they embrace their friend. He escaped from Paris in the Polish officer's car and later caught a ride on a truck with soldiers from the Czech Legion, which ultimately dropped him off here in Toulouse.

This reunion, too, is an almost impossible stroke of luck. Remaining in Toulouse, however, makes little sense. At this point, most emigrants are surging to Marseille, the largest city in the unoccupied zone. Rumors tell of ships sailing from there to North Africa or America which welcome aboard passengers without papers. They are only rumors – that much is clear to the three – but they do not have anything better than rumors.

The train station is so densely mobbed by people that they are able to slip past the checkpoints unnoticed. And the train is so overcrowded that no conductor is able to squeeze through and ask them for tickets or travel permits. In Marseille, however, they are warned, the identification papers of everyone arriving are stringently checked. The police monitor the station exits; no one goes in or out without valid papers.

The closer they get to the city, the more nervous the three of them become. Then the train crawls up one of the hills outside Marseille, moving more and more slowly and finally stopping before a railway switch. With all their might, they shove their way to the door of their car, fling it open, and leap down onto the ballast. Behind them, the train jolts forward and continues its trip. They have no idea where they have ended up, and so they walk down a gentle slope leading to the sea. Before them lies a suburb of Marseille called, they learn, Pointe Rouge.

Saint Nicolas – Marseille, late July 1940

Max Ernst is not yet even fifty years old but is already white-haired, very pale, and gaunt. Life in the camp is literally diminishing him. By coincidence, he is standing at the barbed-wire fence of Saint Nicolas when Marta Feuchtwanger shows up there. She has never met the much-vaunted painter but has seen pictures of him in newspapers and recognizes him immediately, his penetrating gaze and his prominent nose. He smiles at her so kindly that she gathers the nerve to ask him about her husband. "Old Feuchtwanger," Max Ernst replies, "he's in the rear part of the camp." He will look for him and send word for her.

With its fifteen hundred inhabitants, Saint Nicolas is a strange sight. The main path into its center is now flanked by shop stalls, improvised cafés, cookshops, and even a little cabaret stage. The tent city is redolent of a fairground. Farmers and publicans from the vicinity of Nîmes smell good business and have opened their stands here. Prisoners who still have money can have fabulous meals, drink exquisite wines, or hear the music programs of famous cabaret singers from Vienna or Berlin, without leaving the camp.

Nothing about the dangerous unhygienic conditions, however, has changed. Water is strictly rationed, and the state of the latrines is disastrous. The camp commandant responds to protests with a mere shrug. By this point, many of the men suffer from severe diarrhea. Highly contagious bacterial dysentery is making the rounds. Feuchtwanger has caught it, too, and was so weak for days that he was unable to get up from his straw mattress. He had to relieve himself inside the tent in a bucket. Without the aid of several friends, the disease could have been lethal.

Now he is doing better again, but he is so emaciated that Marta does not immediately recognize him when he walks toward her. She is also exhausted and marked by her weeks in the camp. Her lips tremble upon greeting him; her hair has turned gray.

They sit at a table in a cookshop for hours, telling each other how they have fared. All the while, Marta keeps eating and eating, having starved for weeks. Lion must keep to a diet to sort out his bowels again. Initially, Marta was detained near Toulon at a large garage yard, together with former women combatants in Spain. She experienced several bombing attacks there. The guard details took cover in ditches, but for the women, there was no protection. Then she was transferred to Gurs and fled from it not once, but twice. The first time, she had to return to camp because she could not get a ticket for busses or trains without a *sauf-conduit*. Then, one of her fellow prisoners procured for her a poorly forged release certificate. She dug her way underneath the barbed-wire fence and at the nearest train station requested a ticket to Nîmes. The official at the counter hardly looked up and slid her the ticket without casting a glance at the release document.

Marta cannot stay with Lion in Saint Nicolas for long. She must continue on; she plans to go to Marseille to find a way there to free her husband from the camp. Her hope is to be able to persuade the American consulate to put pressure on the French authorities somehow. That is the only rather desperate chance they have. And so she takes her leave of Feuchtwanger and at Nîmes station smuggles herself onto a military train carrying demobilized soldiers toward Marseille.

The consulate is located in the city center, housed in a dignified multi-story old home. A line of people waiting to be admitted bears up outside in the heat. Marta is ashamed, but worry for her husband's life drives her past the queue to the two guards at the entrance. As soon as the door opens, she hands in a slip of paper with her name on it, and shortly thereafter, she is in fact invited in and taken to the two vice consuls, Hiram Bingham IV and Miles Standish.

To her surprise, both are thrilled to see her and obviously seriously concerned about her husband. This unexpected, kind reception robs her of her composure for a moment. She has survived the air raids near Toulon and the Gurs camp without complaint, but now, faced with two Americans who considerately attend to her needs, she bursts into tears.

Indeed, the consulate has been instructed by the very highest levels, by President Roosevelt personally, to support Feuchtwanger with all available means. Bingham and Standish suspect that Eleanor Roosevelt pressured her husband into it. Some State Department officials have already gotten to experience the zeal with which the First Lady advocates for refugees in France. Even Consul General Hugh Fullerton, Bingham's and Standish's boss, assumes that she is behind the president's sudden interest in Feuchtwanger – which, however, rather inhibits Fullerton's willingness to deal with the writer. He is a diplomat; he refuses to get involved in the domestic affairs of Pétain's France. Besides, he is outraged at the First Lady's brazen attempts to dictate instructions to the State Department despite her never having been democratically elected nor ever having held an official government office.

The two vice consuls find it hard to share their boss' professional callousness. Since they have to process the visa applications, they are confronted every single day with the exiles' position. People come to them who are literally trembling in fear, who are facing torture and death if they do not find a country willing to take them in.

Over the past several days, Standish has already secretly tried to set something in motion to rescue Feuchtwanger. He maintains contacts with some gangsters who, like most of the mafiosi in Marseille, are from Corsica. They declared themselves quite ready to do him one or the other illegal favor, no problem. For now, though, they would rather avoid conflict with the German occupiers, whose reactions they cannot even begin to guess.

Now that he knows where Feuchtwanger is being held, however, Standish no longer wishes to stand by. "If no one means to do something," he says to Marta, "I will go myself." Since, as a diplomat, he may move freely throughout the country without a *sauf-conduit*, he plans to go to Saint Nicolas, intercept Feuchtwanger on one of his jaunts outside the camp, and take him to Marseille. What is important is that Feuchtwanger does not hesitate in the moment he meets Standish, but that trust is quickly established. It would be disastrous if Standish first had to bargain with him for a long time and the camp guards thereby discovered the American diplomatic vehicle and could denounce him for abetting an escape.

Marta thus gives him a little note to take with him on which she has written for Lion: "Ask nothing. Say nothing. Go along." She likewise gives Standish the address of a woman in Nîmes with whom Feuchtwanger briefly lodged during his failed escape attempt two weeks earlier.

Standish sets out the very next day, a Sunday. He takes his wife along to make the ride seem like a harmless weekend outing. He is a somewhat eccentric man who attaches great importance to his outward appearance. Because of the heat, he wears a snow-white suit paired with white driving gloves.

First, he picks up the trustworthy woman in Nîmes whom Feuchtwanger knows and gives her the note Marta wrote. Then he drives near the camps and conceals the vehicle between bushes not far from the river where the internees like to bathe. They are in luck. Several minutes later, Feuchtwanger is walking toward them in a short-sleeved shirt and thin linen trousers. The acquaintance from Nîmes approaches him and hands him the note: "I bring you news from your wife."

Feuchtwanger is flabbergasted and offers his thanks. "Read it," the woman urges him, "read it right now," and points out the car to him in which Standish is waiting. Feuchtwanger needs a moment to grasp the situation. Then he climbs into Standish's automobile and finds a lightweight woman's coat, a large pair of sunglasses, and a colorful headscarf on the backseat. He dons the coat and headscarf, puts on the sunglasses, and now, as scrawny as he is, in fact comes across as an older lady.

As he was during his ride there, Standish is stopped on the return journey at several roadblocks and checked by the police. His diplomatic passport, however, spares him all troubles. And to the police officers who ask after the lady in the backseat, he replies that Feuchtwanger is his mother-in-law.

Washington, D.C., July 26, 1940

The representatives of the State Department and the Department of Justice who were instructed by President Roosevelt to find a legally practicable way to rescue threatened exiles from France have settled on an emergency visa program. It goes into effect immediately and is regarded as a compromise between the humanitarian obligations of the United States and its security interests. But viewed in perspective, it is a political curiosity. A personal consultative body of Roosevelt's, the President's Advisory Committee for Political Refugees, is assigned the task of individually assessing each refugee applying for an emergency rescue visa and facilitating entry to the unobjectionable candidates.

The process has three flaws. For one, it is time-consuming and inappropriate as assistance for people in acute mortal danger. Second, the committee has only a few members and so is often utterly overwhelmed by the huge number of visa applications. And finally, the council makes its decisions centrally, in Washington. The consulates abroad that otherwise have a substantial say in issuing immigration visas are thereby disempowered. It is no wonder when a number of consuls view the new program with hostility and do what they can to thwart it.

Brentwood, July 28, 1940

Katia and Thomas Mann have traveled by train across the American continent, from the East Coast to Los Angeles. Thomas Mann does not care for the weather in Princeton, and his teaching responsibilities at the university are becoming bothersome to him as well. The couple wants to take a vacation and has rented a villa for the summer amid the sweep of gentle hills between Beverly Hills and Santa Monica.

The house is bright and spacious. Here, Mann has what he so urgently desires: light, warmth, and the genial roominess he was lacking in Princeton. He enjoys the live oak, cedar, and palm tree vegetation and, most of all, the refreshing walks along the Pacific, which can be reached by car in just a few minutes. He and his wife consider moving to California the following year. Friends of theirs live close by: Liesl and Bruno Frank and the family of Bruno Walter. Arnold Schönberg even lives on the same street, not five hundred paces away, but they hardly have any contact with him.

It could be a glorious summer, but thoughts of the war in Europe weigh on everyone. For weeks now, Thomas Mann has had no credible information about how his brother and Golo are doing. Friends with good connections to France claim Golo is in Marseille. Then, word is he is in a camp or even in a hideout in Le Lavandou. Thomas cannot ascertain anything at all about Heinrich's whereabouts. And it is still unclear whether the State Department will permit Heinrich and Golo to enter the United States if they do succeed in escaping from France at some point. To be safe, Thomas endeavors to obtain visas for them for Brazil or any other South American country.

Appeals for help from fearful exiles reach him almost daily: distressing letters and telegrams beseeching him to fight for them, for it is a matter of life and death. The letter writers do not seem to be mindful of the burden they place on his shoulders by doing this. Added to this are horrible rumors. Two weeks ago, it was said that Feuchtwanger had fallen into Nazi hands and was beheaded in Paris. Four days later, a letter from Feuchtwanger arrived in Los Angeles for his old girlfriend Eva Herrmann in which he told of Walter Hasenclever's suicide and of a five-day train ride in cattle cars. The letter is nevertheless no sure proof that Feuchtwanger is still alive. The mail is slow and sometimes takes weeks to cross the Atlantic from Europe. It may be that Feuchtwanger was arrested and murdered after he sent the letter.

Mann dictates dozens of letters to ministries, embassies, and consulates in which he implores the officials, for heaven's sake, to assist those being persecuted and to interpret visa requirements liberally. Recently,

Klaus, his oldest, was here in Brentwood for a visit. When they spoke of the drama in France, he said the exiles resembled a nation that viewed Thomas Mann as their emissary.

To do more than write the same old petitions, Katia and Thomas have asked Frank Kingdon of the Emergency Rescue Committee to tea this afternoon and have invited some important people from Hollywood as well. Unfortunately, when Kingdon arrives, there is a small accident. Kingdon bumps into a candelabra in the front hall. He begins bleeding and must be bandaged up. After four o'clock in the afternoon, around thirty guests arrive, Bruno Walter among them, as are Charles Boyer, Ernst Lubitsch, and other directors, actors, and film producers. They are all shown into the parlor where Mann gives a brief opening speech and Kingdon, in spite of his injury, delivers the main address.

Apparently, both do their jobs well, as the willingness to give money is great. Around $4,500 is collected, more than was raised from over two hundred guests at the founding of the ERC in New York. Afterward, Thomas mingles with the visitors and makes conversation. He chats for a long while with the charming Charles Boyer and gives him the French edition of his book *Achtung Europa!* [*Europe Beware!*]. Some of the producers offer to give yearlong contracts as scriptwriters to German authors who come to America. The expectation is low that something useful would come of it for their studios. They view the contracts more as a jump start in their new country for those who have fled.

Over the Mountains

August 1940

Lourdes – Marseille, August 4, 1940

Alma Mahler-Werfel now directs the owner of the Hôtel Vatican entirely according to her own designs. Although food in France is becoming increasingly scarce, the man has sumptuous parcels of food tied up for her and Franz Werfel before their departure, with white bread, ham, hard-boiled eggs, and madeleines. What's more, he promises her to continue searching for the suitcases she lost on her flight from Bordeaux. The loss dates back weeks now, and the search has long since been hopeless, but the hotelier is happy to continue to be able to be of service to her.

Yesterday, after they finally received the *sauf-conduit* for the journey to Marseille, Franz Werfel went to the grotto of the faithful again. There he solemnly swore to the Blessed Virgin that he would write a novel in honor of Saint Bernadette if the escape to America is successful. He now knows the girl's fate down to the smallest details: her miserable childhood, the apparitions of Mary, her early death, her canonization. This life story fuels his religious longing as much as it does his literary fantasy.

Six weeks after they set out headlong from Marseille, the Werfels arrive back in Marseille. It is beastly hot, high summer, and as Alma realizes to her annoyance, they have no choice but to walk from the train station to their hotel and carry their own meager luggage. When they arrive back in front of the Hôtel Louvre et Paix, six limousines polished to a high gloss are parked in the driveway, and at reception, they suddenly end up amid a group a German officers. For a month and a half, they have fled through southern France to escape the Nazis. Now they virtually run straight into their arms. Luckily, no one recognizes them, but the bell captain immediately catches on. He does not address them by name and whispers to them which room has been reserved for them. He begs them, for God's sake, not to leave it in the interim; he will inform them as soon as the officers have disappeared.

New York, August 4, 1940

Eileen Fry has come along to LaGuardia airport to say goodbye to Varian. She looks out from the pier with her husband onto the East River, where the Dixie Clipper lies moored at the landing stage. It is a gigantic aircraft, one of the largest airplanes in the world. It looks like a blue whale with two very wide wings attached to its back.

The banquet at the Commodore Hotel at which the Emergency Rescue Committee was launched is now six weeks past. Much time has been lost to discussions about questions of details and to searching for the man the committee will send to Marseille. Now, things are to move all the more quickly.

For Fry, the ERC did not book passage on a ship, but a wastefully expensive plane ticket instead. A regular air connection across the Atlantic has existed for just a few months now – a pioneering feat only made possible because Pan Am had the requisite planes built for it. The Clippers are majestic, silvery gray seaplanes as tall as a two-story house, with a wingspan of just under fifty meters, and with four powerful propeller engines. Their fuel consumption is so enormous that pilots must stop over in the Azores on the way to Europe to refuel, only then to reach Lisbon on the second go. To begin with, they used to take on even more fuel in Portugal and continue the flight to Marseille or Southampton, but ever since the start of the war, airspace over France and England has been closed to commercial flights and they have done without the last leg.

Fry's luggage is already on board. Although he will be on the move for not even four weeks – the return ticket is booked for August 29 – he has packed four suits, ties, and a stack of white dress shirts. He takes his mission for the committee very seriously. He wants to be dressed appropriately at all times.

First, he will scope out the situation in Marseille and may hire dependable employees for the ERC. There is no mention of illegally aiding escapes in his written employment contract. He has not entrusted

A Clipper in flight

the most important cargo to his suitcases, however; he is carrying it directly on his person. The list with the two hundred names of artists and writers in the greatest danger he has taped to his leg along with three thousand dollars in cash, in order to get both past customs in Portugal without being inspected.

Naturally, he is nervous. He and Eileen exchange words of courage one more time before he descends to the landing stage from the pier with the other passengers. They walk beneath the huge wing toward the plane, as though it were a tall metal roof, before crouching through the hatch and vanishing into the gigantic floating belly.

The Clippers are more than spectacular long-haul aircraft. Pan Am has spared no expense to make them palaces in the skies. They are supposed to be advertisements for the luxury of flying. There are only sixty-eight seats on board, the floors are lined with thick carpets, and the windows may be closed with velvet curtains. In a small dining parlor, passengers are served multi-course meals by top New York chefs. For passengers who would like to change clothes before eating or before landing, there are changing rooms available.

Such a glut of ostentation has never sat well with Fry. He has known the superrich of the American East Coast, however, since attending various expensive boarding schools with their children, and they do not overly impress him. The Dixie Clipper casts off and first taxis beneath the gentle arch of the Whitestone Bridge. As soon as the open seas stretch out before them, the pilots let the engines roar up, and the kilometer-long takeoff run they need to heave this colossal airplane from the water into the air begins.

Paris, early August 1940

The evening of her escape from Meudon, Anna Seghers was in a panic. By now she realizes how many important papers – not to mention valuables and clothes – she left in their flat. She herself cannot go to the little suburb; her face is simply too well known. For her son, however, a fourteen-year-old in shorts, the risk is minimal. The Nazis cannot stand watch around the clock at every place where exiles once lived.

Seghers thus asks her son Peter and Justyna, a Polish friend, to pay one more visit to the house, taking the utmost care, and to fetch a few forgotten items. The two set out in the bustle of the morning rush hour on a commuter train. The distance from Meudon's train station to the street on which the family lived only three weeks earlier is just a few hundred meters. Everything seems peaceful. Staid middle-class houses with front yards abut one another in neat rows. To be on the safe side, Peter and Justyna do not head directly for the familiar little garden gate of their home, but first ring the bell at a friendly older neighbor's, a sedate, world-wise retiree who used to run a porcelain factory.

The Gestapo was already there, he says. Two weeks ago. Early that morning, the men came, broke into the house, searched it, took a few things with them, and disappeared again. He does not know if the home is still being watched today. He has not noticed anything.

This they did not expect. Peter and Justyna at first do not know what to do. All of a sudden, the quiet street has a sinister feel. Once they calm down a bit, they take a closer look around and cannot detect anything suspicious, so they pluck up their courage, inconspicuously approach the rear of the house, unlock the back door, and quickly ascend to the apartment on the second floor. In haste, they gather the things they are supposed to take with them: a few pairs of clothes, utensils, official documents. In the course of their search, Justyna opens a drawer, and before her lies the manuscript of a novel Anna Seghers completed a year earlier but reworked again just before they fled. The title on the cover page reads *The Seventh Cross*. Justyna removes the stack of papers right away and runs to the stove. The book, she says, must not under any circumstances fall into Nazi hands, and she begins burning the manuscript.

When he is with his mother again at the hotel that afternoon, Peter tells of the quiet street, the Gestapo's visit to their home, and the manuscript that Justyna burned. As soon as he looks up, he sees, for the first time in his life, his mother unable to hold back tears and begin to cry.

The Seventh Cross is the story of an escape. Seven prisoners break out of a concentration camp near Worms. They immediately part ways and each try to get to safety alone. Six of them are caught within a few days and die. Only the seventh, a young communist named Heisler, reaches safety abroad, making him a symbolic figure of hope and indomitability for all enemies of the Nazis. Heisler's survival proves that even Hitler's police force is not infallible. They can be eluded. Resistance can succeed.

The novel is incredibly suspenseful. Heisler's escape route leads not only across Germany, but across all social classes. Seghers shows that an implacable moral choice is demanded of each individual whom the harried Heisler encounters. Those who aid Heisler put themselves at risk. Those who deny him aid align themselves with the Nazis. Depending on their circumstances and their character, the people react sometimes bravely, sometimes with cowardice. Most are indecisive, but quite a few roll up their sleeves and show great resolve. Each of them is given a choice that touches upon the core of their personality.

Anna Seghers senses that she succeeded in doing something special with this narrative. The book celebrates a humanness that asserts itself even in murderous times. The manuscript had not yet been printed, though. There were seven copies, but their survival seems star-crossed. She sent one copy the previous year to a literary magazine in Moscow. The editorial team was riveted by the novel and immediately began producing a preprint. Then Hitler and Stalin signed their non-aggression pact, and from that moment on, it was no longer permitted to publish a single critical word about the Nazis in the Soviet Union. The printing was canceled, and it is impossible to suss out what happened to the rest of the manuscript: whether the editors kept it or threw it out.

A second copy was kept in the editorial department of the *Pariser Tageszeitung*, where the Gestapo discovered and confiscated it. Seghers delivered the third copy to her publisher Fritz Landshoff in Amsterdam, but after the Germans invaded and occupied the Netherlands, he was no longer able to publish the book. The fourth and fifth copies she sent to friends in the United States who, however, cannot find a publisher for it. She expressed in letters to them how important to her this book was, of all books, but no one in America has yet to show interest in a novel by a German communist woman. The sixth copy is with a French teacher of German who wants to translate the book, but Seghers has lost contact with him entirely. The only copy she still had was the one in the drawer in their flat. She should never ever have left it there. But who lugs around a stack of hundreds of pages of paper when forced to flee in a mad rush? Seven copies of *The Seventh Cross*. One is burned, and six are scattered between Moscow and New York. She herself no longer has one. She can only hope that one copy will be saved – just like one of the seven men fleeing in her novel.

Marseille, early August 1940

Pointe Rouge lies south of Marseille, a genial suburb nestled placidly between the sea and the peaks of the calanque in the backcountry. Walter Mehring and Hertha Pauli have no eyes for scenic beauty, however. This, purely by coincidence, is where they leapt from the idling train. By now they have realized, though, that they have ended up in the best haven they could have found far and wide.

The city center of Marseille is hopelessly overcrowded. It was always cramped and full of life, but the city has never experienced a throng of people like it did this summer. Ever since the division of France, Marseille has been the country's sole international port not controlled by the Nazis. Also located here are the consulates that issue the visas everyone who wants to escape the Nazis needs. And this is where the different aid organizations affiliated with the Red Cross, the unions, the churches, the Jews, the Quakers, and the Unitarians have opened their offices to provide makeshift support in the form of foodstuffs and monetary donations for the refugees wandering the country. All of this exerts an enormous attraction and draws more and more people to the city.

Before the beginning of the war in France, Marseille had 900,000 inhabitants. Now, just three months later, over half a million people have joined them. Refugees from Belgium and the Netherlands, English soldiers who have taken adventuresome routes to escape south from Dunkirk, French colonial troops from Algeria or Indochina, Moroccans with silk sashes, Senegalese with their tall red caps, Foreign Legionnaires with white kepis – including many demobilized soldiers who still have not found a way to return to their homes. Add to that the countless exiles from the internment camps; German, Austrian, Czech, Polish, and Hungarian socialists and communists; Jews and intellectuals; and finally, Spaniards fleeing from Franco, Italians fleeing from Mussolini, and Russians fleeing from Stalin. They are all crowding the city's streets and alleyways in the summer heat. They are all searching for some way out of this country.

The suburbs, of course, are not spared from this mass inrush either, but the conditions in them is less dramatic. In the center, near the Old Port and on the large boulevards, the police patrol at all hours of the day and night, carry out raids, or randomly search cafés and hotels. Those unable to produce a passport or a residence permit are arrested and disappear in jail or one of the countless camps. By comparison, it is almost idyllic in Pointe Rouge.

Hertha Pauli was even able to rustle up a shabby attic room for herself, above Bar Mistral, right on the harbor. And in an even shabbier addition to the bar, Mehring and, a short time later, Hans Natonek have found a place to sleep, too. What's more, it is not far from Pointe Rouge to the most important spot for exiles in Marseille at the moment: the American consulate.

Strictly speaking, there are two American consulates. One is located in the city center, in the dignified old building where Marta Feuchtwanger met Vice Consuls Bingham and Standish. But it is responsible for citizens of the United States. Those wishing to enter America as foreigners must go to the other consulate, which is in Montredon, a suburb adjacent to Pointe Rouge, just a stroll away from Bar Mistral.

The route leads from the port through a park to a veritable small castle, the Château Pastré, which a shipowner had built for himself in the mid-nineteenth century. His descendants have rented it to the consulate. Even with such a large building, however, the Americans are out of their depth with the storm of petitioners. Multitudes of people accumulate on the terrace outside the entrance, and those waiting often must stand for hours in the summer heat before they have shoved their away forward, inch by inch, into the lobby.

The chateau's splendor is grotesquely disproportionate to the refugees' wretchedness. The walls are decorated with precious paintings and hung with tapestries, Baroque stuccowork lines the ceiling, and slender vases as tall as a man occupy the alcoves. Ordinary employees work at mahogany desks in a hall at the rear. The offices of more senior consular officials are located on the second level, reachable by a curved marble staircase.

Pauli, Mehring, and Natonek also fight their way through the masses to submit their application for an entry visa to the United States. That is not enough, though. To receive a visa, they must produce three crucial documents: first, an affidavit that states that an American citizen pledges to vouch for them financially in case of emergency so that they do not under any circumstances become a burden on the public coffers. Further: a morality affidavit, a kind of certificate of good character, confirming that they lead a both morally and politically impeccable lifestyle. There are questions asking explicitly whether they belong to or have ever belonged to an anarchist or communist organization. Those who answer yes can abandon their hopes for a visa; there are no questions about memberships in fascist groups or parties. And third, they must present a biographical sketch that shows the extent of the danger posed to them by the Nazis. All of these declarations must be submitted in triplicate, two copies of which must be notarized. Then the documents are sent to the President's Advisory Committee for Political Refugees for examination, which after a lengthy processing period will either accept or reject them.

That is still not all, though. Ever since war broke out, the large transatlantic ocean liners have only set sail from Lisbon. To get there, however, you need a Spanish and a Portuguese transit visa. Both cost money and are ordinarily granted only once the persons in question are able to prove that they have already booked and paid for passage on a ship to America or to another country of refuge. For, with such a booking, they can credibly attest that they will not remain in Spain or Portugal, but in fact only want to pass through both countries. These visas are only issued for a limited period of validity, though. If

Château Pastré in Marseille

unfortunate delays arise, it might happen that a refugee does not receive the last visa required until the first has already expired, and thus has to start the whole process over again.

The starting point for this obstacle course, however, is always the visa for the United States, Mexico, Brazil, or another country of rescue overseas. Without this document, it is pointless to buy the expensive ticket for the crossing, and without a ticket, in turn, the prospects for the Spanish and Portuguese transit visas are vanishingly small.

Thus, Hertha Pauli makes a habit of first bathing each morning on the beach of Pointe Rouge and then walking through the park to the consulate with Mehring and Natonek to inquire whether there is news from the President's Advisory Committee. At first, they still have to give their names to the porter at the gate outside the chateau so he can check for them on his lists. But after several days, he recognizes them from a distance and waves them off: "Rien pour vous." Nothing for you.

A daily routine the three keep to, if for no other reason than for conviviality. In the park or on the terrace outside the castle, they often run into acquaintances from Berlin or Paris. From afar, they recognize Konrad Heiden, who was editor of the *Frankfurter Zeitung* for a long time and wrote the first large biography about Adolf Hitler, full of debunking facts. He quickly walks over to them. "I'm calling myself Silbermann now," he whispers. Only the people in the consulate know his real name. Like so many others, he, too, fled from an internment camp. If the Nazis should find out that he is still alive, they will demand his extradition, and he knows what awaits him then.

On another day, they meet Leonhard Frank, who already had to go into exile once before, during the First World War, as a pacifist. In the twenties, he earned a small fortune writing as a novelist and screenwriter but lost it all again on the run from Hitler. Soon he will be sixty years old. His face is narrow and gaunt, his hair snow-white. In Brittany, he managed to break out of the internment camp and escape from the Germans only at the very last second and then made it to Marseille with two friends on bicycles.

He, too, lodges with Mehring and Natonek in the derelict annex of Bar Mistral. During the day, he and Mehring often write letters in the bistro to friends or aid organizations in the United States. Then, in the evenings until late at night, everyone crowds into Hertha Pauli's garret room. Through the porthole window, they can hear the surf, and when they are not debating new means of escape, Frank works on a new novel, a love story, and Mehring sits at the table across from him and fine-tunes poems.

At some point, the rumor spreads among the refugees that overseas visas can be had in the city for the Belgian Congo – legal papers for a low price. They might be sufficient for obtaining transit visas to Lisbon from the Spanish and Portuguese consulates. It is nothing more than a crazy hope, Hertha Pauli has no illusions about that. But in her situation, one cannot be choosy. With the streetcar, it does not even take half an hour from Pointe Rouge to the city center.

Right after alighting, she stumbles into a police checkpoint. The situation is dangerous because she has neither a passport nor a residence permit for Marseille. Could she at least produce the confirmation of her release from the internment camp? the policeman asks her.

"No," she says, "I was never in one."

This is nearly inconceivable for the officer. "Why is that?"

"They didn't want me," she bluffs.

The man is impressed and lets her go. A foreign woman who was not sent to the Gurs camp must have special connections, potentially to a more highly placed protector. It is better not to get into trouble with such people.

To avoid further checks, Pauli shoves her way on every street into whichever crowd is the densest and thus makes slow forward progress. Suddenly, she ends up in a line queueing before one of the consulates. Hanging from the portal is a Portuguese flag, and in the middle of the queue, she espies Alma Mahler-Werfel and Franz Werfel. The corpulent Werfel is sweating profusely in the midday sun, bracing himself feebly on his wife's arm.

"Alma, Alma," Pauli calls to her, "How in the world are you both able to stand here in the heat?"

"We need that visa," Alma Mahler-Werfel replies soberly and without any sign of surprise, as though meeting in the middle of the street were a matter of course.

The line is long, and it will take time until the pair reach the shade at the building's entrance. Werfel has a heart problem, that Pauli knows. The temperatures pose a real danger to him. She can hardly believe that a writer like him, whose books are celebrated the world over, does not receive a private audience with the consul immediately.

Alma shakes her head. "We wanted to send in our card," she says, "but the porter won't let anything through. We just have to wait like everyone else."

Werfel is pale. Sweat runs down his brow. His breathing is heavy. It will not be long before he collapses, Pauli thinks. Then she has an idea, leaves the two to wait, and runs to the next café where she looks up the consulate's number in the telephone book and calls. A secretary answers and asks for her name.

"Madame Werfel," she replies. "You know of course, Franz Werfel, the writer ..."

"Oui, Madame Werfel," the secretary is clearly versed in literary matters.

"My husband," Pauli says, "would like to see the consul, please. But the porter will not let us through ..."

"One moment, Madame Werfel." It takes a moment, there is a crackle on the line, and the consul picks up. He, too, knows exactly who Franz Werfel is and would be happy to meet him. Might he invite them to an appointment in his office at four o'clock in the afternoon?

Hertha Pauli accepts with thanks and runs back to the Werfels, who are still standing in the heat. The line has not moved a meter. She pulls the two aside and reveals to them that they have a date with the consul himself. Overjoyed, Alma embraces her, and the three of them proceed back to the café from which Hertha placed the call.

"Garçon, une bouteuille de champagne," Alma shouts. "This calls for a celebration."

Marseille, mid-August 1940

Two months. Feuchtwanger only spent two months in the camps in which other refugees will soon have been detained for a year. On May 21, he got out of the taxi before the gate of Les Milles, and on July 21, he collapsed into the backseat of Miles Standish's vehicle near Saint Nicolas. A manageable period of time: he tried to bear it with stoic composure. The abysmal latrines, the filth, and the constant fear of the Gestapo, however, took him to the edge of a breakdown. He watched Walter Hasenclever die, stood in overcrowded cattle cars until his legs swelled up into sausages, and survived bacterial dysentery.

When he arrived with Standish by car in Marseille, he was exhausted and suffered head- and stomachaches, but all dangers seemed overcome. During the ride, Standish told him they had already been in touch with the Red Cross, which would soon take him out of the country. For now, he would live with one of the vice consuls, with Hiram Bingham, whom everyone calls Harry. There he would be safe; diplomatic protection is accorded the homes of consular members and for the police are nearly untouchable.

When Feuchtwanger climbed out of the vehicle at Bingham's home that evening, Marta came toward him. He realized that without her, without her efforts, he would still be spending his night on filthy straw mattresses in Saint Nicolas. Bingham's house turned out to be a spacious villa with a garden, a swimming pool, and a large library as well as quite a few domestic servants. The time of hardship was over, and everything seemed to be taking a turn for the better.

But since then, nothing concrete has been undertaken in the matter of his rescue. Feuchtwanger lives almost as he did at his villa in Sanary, except that no one must know about his stay with Bingham. The weather is glorious. He reads a great deal, lies by the pool, and practices gymnastics in the garden with Marta to regain his strength. He has also begun working again on *Josephus and the Emperor* [German title: *Der Tag wird kommen*], his new novel. After a few days, he even receives visitors; Lola Sernau, his secretary, and Lilo Dammert, the screenwriter, come from Sanary. Among the women as well, everything seems to be as it once was. Marta inveighs against Lola, and Lola is jealous of Lilo, as though nothing had changed.

In truth, however, the situation is serious. As hard as Standish and Bingham try, they cannot get an exit visa for the Feuchtwangers from the French. For a while now, there has been no talk of the planned escape with the help of the Red Cross. Standish continually has new plans – he wants to obtain forged French papers or persuade a pilot to fly the two out to Lisbon. But it all comes to naught. On top of that, it turns out that Consul Hugh Fullerton is unwilling to lift even a finger for Feuchtwanger despite the president's telegrams.

The actual precarity of his situation becomes clear to Feuchtwanger after Frank Bohn visits him in Bingham's villa. Bohn is a squat fellow of about sixty, an experienced American union leader. Together with some colleagues, he succeeded in extracting an agreement from President Roosevelt in Washington to provide a respectable one hundred thirty blank visas to rescue famous German union members and SPD politicians from the Nazis. He subsequently did not hesitate to come to Marseille himself to somehow get the endangered men and women out. Bohn is an energetic man who gets things done, and in Feuchtwanger he sees a socialist intellectual he immediately views as one of his charges. But even he has not found a way to get his people across the border. His most recent plan is to charter an Italian ship for the escape and attempt it by sea. "I'll get you out, whatever the cost," he asserts as he takes his leave.

Feuchtwanger, of course, does not want to seize this opportunity only for himself and Marta. "We have to get Heinrich Mann out," he declares to Bingham, "and there is another of Thomas Mann's sons as well, Golo. He also needs to be rescued."

To his surprise, however, Bingham responds warily. "I don't know if such a large group is part of the arrangement," he says. "We will probably have to decide which of the two we can take with us. Do you think the younger man should be saved, Golo, or Heinrich Mann, who may be the more notable of the two, but who has already lived his life?"

Feuchtwanger declines to entertain such considerations for a second. He replies: "I cannot make any compromises. Both must be saved."

The remark makes him realize, however, just how horribly long their odds are. If even a fundamentally well-disposed and influential man like Bingham thinks he must weigh the survival of a highly deserving writer against that of his nephew, the prospects for emerging unscathed from this are clearly poor.

Feuchtwanger feels trapped. He senses himself sliding into depression. Bingham was able to procure visas for them for the United States, and Marta stood in line for hours outside the Spanish and Portuguese consulates until they received transit visas for both. But what good are they as long as they cannot leave France?

Marseille, mid-August 1940

By this point, Miriam Davenport has also arrived in Marseille. She dithered for a long time; life in Toulouse was cheap. But now she has nearly used up her reserves, and her passport has expired. She has to visit the consulate to have it renewed.

At first, she is in luck. Although the city is bursting at the seams, she finds a place to sleep in the attic of a barracks – which she must share with several stridently cooing pigeons, though. And very nearby, she discovers a soup kitchen in the side aisle of a church. By chance, she crosses paths with two acquaintances. Walter Mehring, the lanky poet from Berlin, looks like a clochard; fleeing has had a visible effect on him. A short while later, she also runs into Gussie Rosenberg, the young boy from Danzig she met in Toulouse. He is hauling suitcases at the train station and hoping for tips from travelers.

Miriam makes her way to the consulate in Montredon. Dumbfounded, she stands before the little castle where refugees jostle to enter its luxurious reception hall, and she stands just as dumbfounded before a consular official who does not even remove his feet from atop his desk when he tells her he cannot renew her passport. Renewals are only allowed in order to facilitate direct returns to the United States. He is not permitted to issue her a passport for the journey to her fiancé in Yugoslavia. Sorry, but those are the rules.

Only upon leaving the chateau does Miriam understand she has no business there anyway. She is an American, and thus it is not the visa department for foreigners in Montredon that is responsible for her, but the central office of the consulate in the city center. Nevertheless, she has learned something important in Montredon. It is wrong to act like a petitioner. For a petitioner, they will not even remove their feet from their desk. And so she walks past the people waiting and surrounding the consulate in the city center and up to the two soldiers guarding the entrance, and requests to speak to the consul general personally. She is actually taken to him, the man listens to her, and only five minutes later, her passport is renewed, and a letter is en route to the consul in Geneva who, from neutral Switzerland, can procure a visa to Yugoslavia – though, the consul adds, experience has shown that that will take several months.

As she leaves the building, she spots a posting in one of the corridors that rounds out her good fortune for the day. It is a list of Americans looking for options for direct passage back to the United States. Since the armistice, the port of Marseille has been closed. Aside from fishing boats, ships may only leave in exceptional circumstances. Those lacking the appetite for the arduous land route to Lisbon are therefore stuck in the city, even if they possess an American passport with all requisite visas. The name Mary Jayne Gold catches Miriam's eye, along with her address and telephone number. Apparently, her friend from Toulouse has not even left France yet.

Marseille, August 14, 1940

As soon as Varian Fry has heaved his suitcases from the train, a porter collects them. Marseille is built atop hills. The central train station at Saint-Charles lies a good fifteen meters higher than the Boulevard d'Athènes, which leads to the old city and the port. The flight of stairs descending to the street from the station forecourt is an object of architectural interest, but for travelers with luggage it is and remains an ordeal, particularly in high summer. This provides a sound income to the city's professional porters.

The Hôtel Splendide is the very first large building on the right side of the Boulevard d'Athènes. Fry knows that Frank Bohn is staying there, the refugee helper from the trade union federation. For that reason, he would also like to lodge there, but unfortunately, there is no vacancy, and he must temporarily make do in another hotel.

Fry is in a hurry. In Lisbon, he spoke with employees of various aid organizations – with the Unitarians, the Quakers, the Jewish Joint Distribution Committee – to learn more specific details about the war refugees' situation firsthand. That cost him more time than planned. Now he only has two weeks until his return flight on August 29. He thus quickly changes his shirt in his room and sets out for the city's American consulates to introduce himself there as the representative of the ERC. Both, however, are mobbed by refugees, and the office holders are entirely set on defense. No one lets him in, and no one is willing to have a conversation. Irritated, he makes his way back after hours of waiting. He has little patience with authorities, particularly when he feels rebuffed by them.

But Fry absolutely intends to make use of the day. In Lisbon, he met with the sister of Franz Werfel, who is near the top of the list of people whose rescue he is supposed to arrange. She disclosed to him that Werfel is staying at the Hôtel Louvre et Paix, right on the Boulevard La Canebière, the city's magnificent mile.

Initially, the concierge at the Louvre et Paix hesitates and keeps Fry waiting a while before announcing him to the Werfels and allowing him up to their room. Naturally, the couple is surprised to hear that an American has made his way across the Atlantic to aid them in their escape from Europe. But they are quite willing to accept Fry as their personal guardian angel. Werfel has already made himself comfortable for the evening – he is wearing slippers and a dressing gown. He is mostly worried that the Nazis might learn at which hotel he is staying. Alma Mahler-Werfel, by contrast, appears more composed. She offers wine as a welcome and pours it into water glasses.

Already at this first meeting, Fry grasps how important it is for an escape agent to meet in person the people he plans to help. Werfel makes a sickly impression; he is pale and limp and comes across, Fry thinks, like a half-full sack of flour. He is likely not up to any physical stresses. His wife, on the other hand, is alert and energetic.

The Werfels invite Fry to dine at Basso, one of the city's most elegant restaurants. It is located right on the Old Port and, for one evening, can easily make one forget how terrible things are in the country. The view from here overlooks the two forts, St. Jean and St. Nicolas, that safeguard port access to the right and left. Before them, a ninety-meter-tall steel construction spans the port, the *pont transbordeur*, the transporter bridge, the city's modern landmark. A capacious gondola hangs from the bridge by steel cables, connecting the two sides of the port like a floating ferry just overtop the water.

Over dinner, the couple report that they have assembled all necessary documents for their escape: the entry visa for the United States, the transit visas for Spain and Portugal – they lack only the exit permit for France. Neither of them know what awaits them in Spain if they illegally cross the border. Werfel fears being arrested and handed over to the Germans. His wife, who is in less danger than he, makes the case for risking it.

"You must save us, Mr. Fry," Werfel says.

"Oh, yes," his wife repeats. "You must save us."

Back at the hotel, Alma Mahler-Werfel orders another bottle of champagne and continues importuning Fry to help them out of the country. But Fry has to ask them to be patient. He only arrived a few hours earlier and still lacks reliable information. He promises to find out everything necessary and keep them both updated. For the moment, he cannot do more.

Marseille, mid-August 1940

Lisa Fittko and her husband Hans have been in Marseille for two weeks now. In Toulouse, with a French uniform and forged papers, Hans Fittko blended in among the soldiers being demobilized on orders from the Vichy government. He never served in the French army but, in exchange for his fake military identification papers, received a real discharge certificate and, like the other soldiers, a temporary allowance of one thousand francs.

It is to be the seed capital for their escape from France. As always, the two have joined forces with comrades from communist resistance groups, too. First, they all purchase tickets for the crossing from Lisbon

The transporter bridge in the Old Port of Marseille, with the Basilica Notre-Dame de la Garde in the background

to New York at the English travel agency Cook. The promised ships, that much is clear to them, will never leave the port of Lisbon; they may not even exist. The seller is a crook, but his tickets look real and only cost two hundred francs.

With the fake tickets, they can now get the necessary transit visas at the Portuguese and Spanish consulates. At the Portuguese one, they queue up in the evening, stand in line overnight, and have their turn the following day. The crowd outside the Spanish consulate is larger. For three days and nights, they hold out in the queue until they are allowed inside. As a precaution, they refrain from trying to apply for a French exit visa. For one thing, they do not delude themselves; they hear from all the exiles that each and every application is rejected these days. For another, they fear drawing the attention of German investigators to their group. There is only one way for them; they must illegally cross the border to Spain in the Pyrenees.

Because there are also women with small children in their group, they need a safe, easily manageable crossing, perhaps an old smuggling trail. As is their custom, all possibilities are discussed in the group with pointed objectivity. The most rational course of action is to send a scout to the Spanish border in advance to identify an appropriate route and to make contact with people in the region willing to help them. Naturally, the risk for this scout is especially high because the person not only has to cross the border in this unknown territory, but also return. And later, he or she shall lead everyone else over the mountains as their guide.

They will need someone who is young and strong, someone with steady nerves, and, if possible, with experience smuggling other people across borders.

"Lisa," someone from the group says.

"We'll handle raising the money for the journey," another concurs, as though the price of the train ticket were the biggest problem. "So, Lisa, do you agree?"

"I can give it a try," Lisa Fittko replies.

Marseille, August 15, 1940

The next morning, Fry heads to the Hôtel Splendide to meet Frank Bohn. The latter is overjoyed to find in Fry a comrade-in-arms. Until now, he was almost entirely left to fend for himself in Marseille. He invites Fry up to his room and introduces him to two guests, both SPD operatives who have been living in exile for years.

The three of them are able to give Fry an initial survey of the situation, which is confusing enough. Ever since the armistice, Marshal Pétain has been preparing unoccupied France to collaborate with Hitler. But by no means everyone agrees with the new regime in Vichy. Many officials and policemen are sympathetic to the refugees and help them, as long as in doing so they do not endanger themselves. In Spain, it is similar. Most customs agents have no problem if a refugee enters illegally and crosses the French border without an exit visa. What is important is that the person accepts a Spanish entry stamp.

"If this is all so simple," Fry asks, "why hasn't everyone left already?"

"For various reasons," Bohn replies. "First, many of them are still waiting on overseas visas. Many are still in internment camps. And finally, there are a lot of famous exiles who don't dare enter Spain. They're afraid of being arrested there and deported to Germany."

Not least among the latter group are the fleeing politicians Bohn is trying to help. Rudolf Breitscheid and Rudolf Hilferding, for instance, for years belonged to the senior leadership of the SPD. Breitscheid was the party whip in the Reichstag, and Hilferding was the finance minister. Both are convinced they will be recognized in Spain and handed over to the Gestapo. The only chance of getting people like them out of the country is by sea, Bohn thinks. He adds, whispering, that he is already working on a concrete plan, but at the moment cannot yet reveal anything about it.

There are thousands of exiles in Marseille who want to leave the country. In order to be able to assist as many of them as possible and not stir up competition with one another, Bohn and Fry settle on a division of labor. Bohn will handle the political refugees, and Fry primarily the writers, artists, and intellectuals.

When he is about to say goodbye, Fry asks whether Bohn knows where Lion Feuchtwanger is staying. His rescue is an especially high priority for the ERC. Bohn hesitates a moment with his reply, then invites Fry to go into the bathroom with him so they are able to speak in private. When the door behind them is closed, he tells Fry of his visit with Feuchtwanger at Bingham's villa. "I promised Harry Bingham not to breathe even a single word about this to anyone. But I am sure he would have nothing against it if I told you."

"Do you have any plans for how to get him out of France?" Fry asks.

"No," Bohn replies, "I don't. He is your responsibility, not mine. But you can put him on my ship if you want."

"Good," says Fry. "I'll put the Werfels and the Feuchtwangers on your ship."

Back at his hotel, Fry writes letters to the people on his rescue list whose addresses he knows. Paul Hagen advised him to do so in New York. He is convinced that Fry's name will get around rapidly as soon as he even faintly suggests wanting to aid escape from France. Then he will be utterly swamped with people seeking help.

Provincetown, August 16, 1940

Eileen Fry has fled from the New York heat to her little garden on the Atlantic coast. She has heard nothing from her husband since he boarded the Clipper at LaGuardia. But a telegram from him just arrived at the ERC office with his address in Marseille, so she writes a first letter to him: "You seem to have disappeared into a vacuum."

Varian Fry wrote to her four days earlier from Lisbon that he was continuing onward by plane to Madrid – and in a ramshackle Spanish aircraft at that, for which reason he jokingly wished himself luck: "Bonne chance." Letters, however, take up to three weeks to cross the Atlantic. Telegrams are faster, though they are not a good means of communication for intimate messages between spouses.

Marseille, mid-August 1940

For Hertha Pauli, Walter Mehring, and Leonhard Frank, the battle for the salvific visas is even more difficult than for other refugees. By bureaucratic standards, they are considered stateless ever since the Nazis officially expatriated them.

Now, though, an unforeseen opportunity presents itself to get valid passports. Franz Werfel, whom Hertha Pauli helped obtain a private appointment with the Portuguese consul, is on friendly terms with the Czech consul in Marseille. The man's name is Vladimir Vochoč, and, from a political perspective, he plays an odd role. In March 1939, Nazi Germany occupied the Czech portion of Czechoslovakia and declared it the "Protectorate of Bohemia and Moravia." Since then, the nation for which Vochoč works as consul de facto no longer exists. The government in Vichy, however, still recognizes him as the legitimate representative of this nation.

In his role as consul of a vanished land, Vochoč is now doing everything he can to help as many people in danger as possible get out of France. He especially enjoys aiding men fit for military service in the hopes that they join the fight against Hitler in England.

Equipped with Werfel's reference, Pauli, Mehring, and Frank seek out the Czech consulate, which consists of only a single room now. Chaotic mayhem reigns; crates and suitcases are stacked along the walls, signs of disintegration are everywhere. The three must each fill out a form and submit their photos. Soon thereafter, their names are called, and they receive their brand-new passports. Unfortunately, these passports have a pink cover, and the regular Czech passes have a greenish-brown one. There are no other differences, however. They are genuine documents of a non-existent state.

Leonhard Frank is still skeptical whether these passports could protect them from an extradition to Germany while transiting through Spain.

Mehring, too, distrusts them. When he stumbles into a raid a short while later, he disappears into a bathroom, tears his new passport to shreds, and flushes the scraps down the toilet. He would rather wriggle his way out of an arrest with some sort of excuse than be caught with papers he considers phony.

Only Hertha Pauli is undeterred. She obtains the necessary transit visas to Lisbon and for a small price – from obviously corrupt employees at the Chinese consulate – an entry permit for China. The Chinese stamp takes up an entire page, though the beautiful characters are illegible to her. Mehring pores over them for a long while and finally claims to have deciphered them: "Entry to China forbidden under penalty of death."

Naturally, Pauli also goes to the American consulate with her new identification papers. Whenever she steps out of the park's summery sunlight into the gloom of the front hall at Château Pastré, she is blinded at first. Suddenly, she hears her name. "Miss Pauli ... Consul Bingham wants to see you."

A secretary emerges from behind her desk and accompanies her to the elegantly curved marble staircase leading to the upper level. "Up here ..."

Upstairs, a tall, slender gentleman receives her, introduces himself as Hiram Bingham, and invites her to have a seat in his office.

"Miss Pauli," he says, "your visa has arrived."

Hertha Pauli is flustered. She does not speak English well and hardly understands Bingham. She has received, he explains to her, only a visitor's visa. Normally, someone who enters with such a visa must also exit the United States within a certain time period. In this case, however, the exit requirement was waived. It is, Bingham says, "as emergency rescue visa."

Hertha Pauli understands the word "rescue." It means she is saved.

Marseille, late August 1940

The Continental is a mid-range hotel near the Old Port, clean and comfortable, but not luxurious. When she arrived in Marseille, Mary Jayne Gold was lucky to finagle an ensuite room here. The city's fancy addresses, the Louvre et Paix, or the Dieu, which sits enthroned above the old city like a castle, were fully booked. She and her poodle Dagobert were tired from the train journey so she took what she could get. She has grown happy with her choice; the Continental is centrally located but still quiet, and the hotelier has a soft spot for dogs.

Miriam Davenport sees the room with different eyes; for her, it is a patch of paradise. Upon her very first visit, she asked her friend if she might use the bathroom. Soap, warm water, a bathtub – for someone spending nights among pigeons in an attic, it is like a dream. From this point on, Miriam is also no longer dependent on free meals at the city's soup kitchens. Mary Jayne loves good restaurants and takes care of every bill without uttering a word about it.

For the time being, the young women have no obligations. Gold cannot expect direct passage from Marseille to America any time soon, nor Davenport her visa to Yugoslavia for several months yet. So as not to be idle amid the distress of the refugees, the pair have inquired with Frank Bohn, the director of the aid organization of American unions, whether they can help him as volunteers. For Gold, this is a somewhat foreign notion; she has never worked in her life. But Bohn does not trust the two anyway. According to his standards, they are too young, too pretty, too independent. He would rather put them off.

They both often spend the afternoon at Café Pelikan near the American consulate in the city center. It is a kind of news exchange for exiles who frequently sit for hours on the terrace beneath the shady marquise over a single cup of espresso. Walter Mehring, too, occasionally ventures this way. Conversations mostly revolve around which overseas countries are generous in issuing entry visas. Besides China and the Belgian Congo, Mexico, Siam, and Panama are now in great demand among refugees.

The friends also enjoy meeting up with three young men, three Foreign Legionnaires. Two of them are Americans who fought for France and now, after its defeat, want to leave the country as quickly as possible. The third is a Frenchman, and he seems shadowy. Apparently, he has a criminal past and went to ground with the Legion to evade the police and other pursuers. Tall and slender, he calls himself Claude and is handsome in a grim sort of way. He tells them he fought in Norway against the Germans and killed several of them with considerable pleasure.

Not just for that reason, but also because he unscrupulously does violence to English grammar with his clumsy language skills, the two women give him the nickname "Killer." The distance between the world in which Killer Claude operates and the world in which Mary Jayne Gold grew up could not be greater. Nonetheless, or perhaps precisely because of that, a tremendous attraction develops between the two. On the first several days, Miriam and Mary Jayne spend afternoons and evenings together with the three others. But at some point, Claude whispers to Mary Jayne as they say goodbye that he will visit her at the Continental the next morning before the others arrive. Since then, they have been two of the city's most unusual lovers.

Marseille, late August 1940

Varian Fry has moved to room 307 at the Hôtel Splendide. It is not very large but offers a fabulous view of the Basilica Notre-Dame de la Garde, Marseille's landmark. The gleaming-white church is perched on a hill above the city, its tower crowned by a golden statue of the Madonna. But Fry does not have time to enjoy the view.

Just a day after he sent letters to refugees, the first visitors line up in the hallway outside his room to be admitted. His name and his intention to help with money and papers to exit France get around with inconceivable speed. In his room, there is only one small desk. He invites those waiting inside one by one, has them sit at the desk, and takes his own seat on the edge of the bed. In short conversations, he tries to figure out whether the visitors are among the people for whom the ERC feels responsible.

The majority of those who come to him are nervous wrecks at the end of their tether. They have spent months in internment camps, are hiding in some hole somewhere under appalling conditions, own only what they are wearing, and do not know how to make ends meet. Whenever someone knocks on the door to Fry's room, they start because they think they are about to be arrested and handed over to the Gestapo. Many are convinced that German troops will invade the unoccupied zone next week at the latest, and perhaps even tomorrow, to round up all enemies of the Nazis and cart them off to concentration camps.

All of them claim to be artists, journalists, or writers, but Fry hardly knows any of their names, and very few are on his list. He guesses how easy it would be for a spy to fool him by impersonating an exile and initially reveals as little as possible about his intentions. First and

The Hôtel Splendide in Marseille

foremost, however, he realizes how arbitrary the selection of people is whom the ERC wants to help escape. In the end, each of these weary people sitting across from him has the same right to be rescued.

Luckily, among the first men to come to Fry are members of Paul Hagen's resistance group Neu Beginnen who have experience with underground work. They merely ask him for money for the train ride to Lisbon. They do not lack for courage and resolve to get there by illegal means. One of them is carrying a hand-drawn map with a mountain path sketched out leading from the border town of Cerbère into Spain. Even the French police stations to be avoided are marked on it. The men plan to take this route and then forge their way onward toward Portugal. Fry gives them the necessary travel money and may keep a copy of the map.

At first, the map causes him quite the headache. If it were to be found during a search of his room, it would be absolute proof that he is an escape agent. In the end, he unscrews the mirror from his wardrobe, attaches the map to its reverse, and remounts the mirror. With this hiding place, he feels somewhat safe.

On one of the first days, an Austrian actor and writer also shows up to see Fry. Her name is Hertha Pauli. The concierge called up from the lobby to ask whether he might send her upstairs. When she knocks timidly and enters the room, Fry at first barely looks up. It is hot, and he is sitting by the open window in shirtsleeves, looking for her name on his lists. When he finally locates it, he welcomes Pauli, straight-faced.

As always, he exercises restraint during the first conversation and concentrates primarily on going through the other names on his lists with her. Far from everyone has established contact with him, and he searches for clues about where he might reach them. In the case of Hans Natonek, Walter Mehring, and Leonhard Frank, it is easy. Hertha Pauli gives the address of the Mistral in Pointe Rouge. When Fry inquires about Ernst Weiss and Walter Hasenclever, however, she must break it to him that the two are beyond anyone's help.

At this, Fry picks up a pencil and crosses out both names. It lands like a very matter-of-fact, heartless gesture. "Now," he says, his face dispassionate, "I have two free spots for others on my list …" Then he bids Hertha Pauli goodbye, who is to call again the following day. "Bring Mehring with you tomorrow. Au revoir."

Marseille, August 27, 1940

Nelly and Heinrich Mann have also received a message from Fry in Nice and have come to Marseille by train. They take a room at the Hôtel Normandie, just across the street from the Splendide.

Fry's time is running out. Things are developing more slowly than anticipated. At this point, he has been able to locate several of the authors on his list, but not rescue any of them. If he were intending to fly back to New York from Lisbon with the Clipper on August 29 as planned, he should have long since set out for Portugal by now. In the interim, however, he has aroused great hope with the Feuchtwangers, the Werfels, and now also with Heinrich Mann and his wife. He does not want to disappoint them, so he has canceled his return flight and asked the ERC in New York, his boss at the Foreign Policy Association, and most of all Eileen for patience.

Heinrich Mann is sixty-nine years old and, like Werfel, does not seem especially able to withstand physical stresses. For that reason, Fry decides to tell him about the ship Frank Bohn has chartered to take refugees to Lisbon by sea. Heinrich Mann agrees right away but asks to bring aboard his nephew Golo, too, who is lying low in Le Lavandou, a seaside resort halfway between Marseille and Nice.

Fry does not want Heinrich Mann to be under any illusions. The escape may not be strenuous but does entail risks. Since they will be traveling illegally, every Italian or French warship they encounter at sea will pose a threat. Should their ship be captured, everyone on board would be arrested and transferred to camps.

But Mann's decision stands firm, if only for a lack of alternatives. Still, he takes Fry's warning seriously and invites a notary to the Hôtel Normandie to draft his will. He would not long survive life in a camp – of that he is aware. He leaves all property that belongs to him at the time of his death to Nelly. The royalties on his books are to be split equally between his daughter Leonie and Nelly.

After that there is nothing to do but wait for the departure of the escape ship. It would be advisable not to leave the hotel since neither Nelly nor he himself have a residence permit for Marseille. But when he learns that Feuchtwanger is in hiding at Bingham's villa, he cannot be deterred from a visit. The two know one another well from Munich and Berlin. To avoid the summer heat, Mann sets out from the hotel at the crack of dawn, makes good time, and is soon sitting with Feuchtwanger in the shady yard at Bingham's home to chat.

Marseille, late August 1940

The first unknown person Varian Fry learns to trust in Marseille is named Albert Hermant. At least that is the name on his French identification papers, in his pay book, and on the discharge certificate from the army. Hermant is very proud of these documents because they are all fake.

One does not encounter people like him frequently. He only just turned twenty-five but is clever and wise to the world as only few men of his age are. He speaks four languages, is bubbling with energy and wit, and still looks radiant to boot, like a younger brother of Cary Grant.

Hermant also quickly gains confidence in Fry and lays his cards on the table. His real name is Otto-Albert Hirschmann. He is Jewish and grew up in Berlin. Because he belonged to the Young Socialist Workers, he had to flee Germany right after Hitler's seizure of power – at age eighteen. He went to Paris and enrolled at one of the venerable French elite universities. Learning was fun for him; every form of knowledge came naturally to him. Just two years later, he had his degree in hand and transferred to the London School of Economics, where a stellar career as a scholar was predicted for him.

University achievements alone did not satisfy him, however. Politics preyed on his thoughts. When the International Brigades recruited soldiers for the fight against Franco's fascists, he quit his studies and went to Spain. Afterward, he joined a cousin in Italy leading a resistance cell against Mussolini and earned his doctorate on the side at the University of Trieste, as though it were a trifle. Then, when France declared war on Hitler, he joined the French army and can thank his lucky stars he escaped to Marseille after its rapid defeat by the *Wehrmacht*. Had he ended up in German captivity, he would have been court-martialed and shot dead as a traitor to his country and a Jew.

Hirschmann is an astonishing blend of exceptionally gifted intellectual, resistance fighter, and bon vivant. This is precisely what makes him an ideal partner for Fry. His steadfast optimism is salutary for Fry's depressive moods, and from his Italian cousin, Hirschmann has learned a great deal about the ground rules of underground activity, about which Fry has no clue. Hirschmann safeguards him from all possible indiscretions by which he would otherwise have swiftly given himself away to the police.

It is only a matter of days before Fry can no longer imagine his work without Hirschmann. He calls him Beamish and entrusts him primarily with all manner of illegal tasks that he, as a representative of the ERC, ought not to know about. Hirschmann establishes contacts with the city's underworld, procures fake passports, changes dollars on the black market, and secures hiding places for refugees in extreme danger.

Fry's second associate is also an experienced pro, but in another field. Franz von Hildebrand has already worked in Paris for an Austrian refugee committee and knows how to build up and lead an aid organization. In contrast to Hirschmann, he is a conservative man through and through, a father, and a strictly observant Catholic. Because the ERC does not espouse a political policy, Fry views the pair as an ideal team. Hirschmann knows his way around the leftwing milieu, Hildebrand around the right. The risk of being fooled by a police informant disguised as a refugee is thus starkly reduced.

Nevertheless, quarters are tight in Fry's hotel room when the three of them work. Fry unscrews the mirror from the low-sitting dressing table in the room and thus gains a second workspace aside from the desk. Hirschmann and Hildebrand conduct interviews with the refugees at both tables; Fry must conduct his while standing. Over the course of the day, it becomes unbearably hot in the small room, and they can never shake the fear of their conversations being overheard in the adjacent room. As it is, they speak of secret matters only in the bathroom with the door closed and the taps on. All of these things, however, are makeshift solutions. If Fry means to cope with the increasing crush of refugees, he must come up with some other solution.

Marseille, late August 1940

Something inconceivable has happened. Franz Werfel asked Saint Bernadette in Lourdes for a miracle, and now a small miracle has occurred. His and Alma's luggage – the twelve suitcases that were lost on their train ride to Bordeaux months earlier – has been found.

The owner of the Hôtel Vatican in Lourdes is a miracle worker. The man pestered the stationmaster in Bordeaux with letters until he began a search, in fact tracked down the luggage in some storeroom, and restored it to its owners. The stationmaster could not have imagined the value of the scores by Mahler and Bruckner tucked away in one of the suitcases. The Werfels are happy. In one stroke, the prospects for their future life in America have improved significantly.

Marseille, August 29, 1940

Fry gets up early to have breakfast in his room in peace. At around eight o'clock in the morning, his two associates arrive, and the first people seeking help line up in the hallway outside his room. At around eight o'clock at night, he sees off the last of them and sits down with

Hirschmann and Hildebrand to decide which of the refugees are in the greatest danger. Then, at night, Fry sends their names and personal information by cable to the New York office of the ERC to request emergency rescue visas for them. From time to time, he visits the Werfels at their hotel or Feuchtwanger at Bingham's house and keeps them abreast of the developments vis-à-vis their escape. It is foreseeable that he will not be able to sustain this rhythm for long. He must look around for other associates, for reliable people who can assume his duties when he returns to America.

Today, though, he is disturbed first thing in the morning at breakfast. The knocking at his door is so intense that he initially expects a police raid. But it is Frank Bohn who flings open the door and bursts into the room. He is extremely agitated and shouts: "They've got it."

"What do they have?" Fry asks.

"The ship," Bohn blurts out.

Bohn underestimated how rigorously the port would be monitored. Because around thirty people are to be taken to safety on his ship, the captain had to bring aboard provisions and drinking water in considerable quantities. While loading up, however, his people attracted the attention of Italian occupation officers, at which point the police confiscated the foodstuffs and posted guards on the ship.

There is more to it than that, though. Bohn and Fry must reckon with the possibility that the authorities will quickly figure out who chartered the ship and for what purpose. The police could detain them any minute now, and an unpleasant interrogation would then be the least of their worries. They may be Americans, but if they violate the laws of the Vichy regime, their consulate can do little to help them. It is entirely possible that they might have to spend a few weeks, or months, even, in a French prison before being deported. Bohn paces nervously, hardly able to think clearly. In the end, he races out of the room without having worked out with Fry which equivocations they will want to employ in a potential interrogation.

But what happens to them then is – nothing. For Fry, it amounts to an important lesson. Naturally, the police will adhere to its government's laws, and quite a few officials are very scrupulous about that. Others, however, are amazingly generous when it comes to exiles and escape agents. They overlook obvious clues, fail to pursue all leads, and ultimately close the case. In the end, whether one ends up with a supporter of Pétain or someone who sympathizes with the adversaries of the Nazis is a matter of luck.

Because he and Bohn have been neither arrested nor summoned to police headquarters by evening, Fry makes his way to Bingham's home to tell Feuchtwanger about the escape plan's failure. But Feuchtwanger already knows all about it. That very morning, Heinrich Mann overheard at the Hôtel Splendide what happened and reported it on his daily visit. As a result, Feuchtwanger reacts calmly to the bad news, hardly speaks of the setback over dinner, and instead chats and jokes as if nothing had happened.

His calm and equanimity impress Fry, who is used to a different reaction from most of the exiles who turn to him. He finally pulls himself together and tells of refugees who cross the Spanish border in the Pyrenees without a French exit visa. Somewhat reluctantly, he asks Feuchtwanger if he would be willing to go that route. He responds right away: "If you accompany me, of course."

Marseille, late August 1940

Hirschmann learns more and more about the shadowy side of Marseille in his work. Whoever looks behind the curtain of this glorious city will learn how powerful its mafia is. There are two large gangs and several small ones. All the key players are from Corsica. The two most important men, Paul Carbone and his partner François Spirito, are involved with everything that brings in money: prostitution, drugs, gambling. At the outbreak of the Spanish Civil War, they also got into the arms trade and supplied Franco's fascists with almost everything they needed to defeat the Republican government. Ever since the two dispatched a politician of their choosing to the mayor's office, they need no longer fear the police. They are the real rulers of the city, and it is better for one's health not to make enemies of them.

Their adversaries are the brothers Antoine and Barthélemy Guérini, also Corsicans and also closely connected to the mayor. They have commanded respect ever since they did away with an Arab pimp ring in a murderous gang war and took over its bordellos. Carbone and Spirito tolerate them but keep a close eye on them.

As Hirschmann has learned, included within the Guérinis' sphere of influence is the restaurant La Dorade. The venue's manager is a strikingly calm, taciturn man named Charles who sits behind the register every night, leerily watches his waiters' every move, and never drinks anything but mineral water. In contrast to Carbone and Spirito, who openly brag about their good contacts among the Pétain regime, the Guérini brothers and their accomplice Charles are regarded as enemies of the Germans. It might, therefore, be useful, Hirschmann thinks, to go out to eat more often at La Dorade and make contact with the quiet man at the register.

Marseille, August 31, 1940

It is Alma Mahler-Werfel's birthday, but she is in a very bad mood. Two weeks earlier, this American named Fry came to Marseille to save her and her husband, but so far he has nothing to show for it except a failed plan to escape by sea.

Over the last several days, she and Werfel have persuaded old Heinrich Mann to move to the Hôtel Louvre et Paix as well. An upscale address, they explained to him, is much safer than a cheap train station hotel like the one at which he has been staying. But by now, Heinrich Mann is getting on Alma's nerves. Now and then he says something clever, which flummoxes her, because most of the time he comes across to her as completely senile.

Today, Golo Mann has arrived from Le Lavandou and has gone straight to check in with his uncle. He is to stay in Vice Consul Bingham's villa with the Feuchtwangers. To Alma's horror, Nelly Mann has also returned from Nice, where she liquidated hers and Heinrich's apartment. Alma cannot understand how Heinrich Mann, a writer known the world over, has tethered himself to such a woman. In her eyes, she is a washing woman and constantly piss-drunk. When Nelly learns that nothing will come of the planned escape because the police have confiscated the ship, she goes into a fit of hysterics. She leaps up, runs onto the balcony of her room, and is about to throw herself over the balustrade. Luckily, Werfel and Golo Mann grab hold of her, but she tries to tear herself loose and brutally pommels the two of them. She is large and heavy; they only narrowly succeed in subduing her.

September 1940

Marseille, early September 1940

Walter Mehring stands on the terrace of Café Pelikan and looks around, searching. It is a hot afternoon, and tables in the shade are in demand. Mehring seems distraught. As soon as he locates Miriam Davenport, he makes for her and asks to pull her aside to be able to speak with her undisturbed.

He was, he says, at the Splendide this morning with this American Varian Fry whom all the exiles are talking about lately. Fry found Mehring's name on the list which Thomas Mann compiled for the ERC and now intends to do everything to rescue him. Mehring is to bring photos by tomorrow so that Fry can have a fake passport made for him. But after Mehring had left, he was arrested right in the hotel lobby. A raid. In short order, the police rounded up all the foreigners heading to or coming from Fry, took them to the station, and interrogated them for hours.

Never again, Mehring curses, will he set foot in that hotel. Could she, he implores Miriam, go to Fry in his stead and request a meeting tomorrow outside the Splendide at some remote café?

Miriam Davenport does not hesitate; she can rely on the protection of her American passport. It is not far to the Splendide. She takes the elevator to the third floor and must first join the queue outside room 307. She recognizes many of the faces of those waiting from Café Pelikan, almost all of whom are talking about the morning's raid, but the prospect of Fry's assistance has driven them back here. When Miriam is finally ushered in, she is standing in a much too warm, overcrowded room. Two exiles are questioned at small tables. A man with dark hair and horn-rimmed glasses offers his hand and introduces himself as Varian Fry. He listens to the story of Mehring's arrest, but then asks more questions: how Miriam got to Marseille, why she wants to go to Ljubljana, and what she has planned in the time before her departure.

Then he says: "Would you like a job?"

Miriam is stunned, at first unable to believe her ears. She needs money and has no work. Of course she wants a job.

"Very good," Fry says. "Would you be willing to act as the general secretary of an aid organization that we want to found? A good American name like Davenport could prove quite useful for it."

Essentially, Fry explains, she must do nothing more than sign the yearly report. But he is also seeking people to conduct initial interviews with the refugees, the purpose of which is to figure out whether and how the Emergency Rescue Committee can help them. Is she willing to do that?

Miriam agrees straightaway. When Fry then adds that he can pay her a good salary, 750 francs a week, she is thrilled. A host of her problems are solved in one go.

Marseille, early September 1940

It is not just Killer Claude's naughty, youthful smile that fascinates Mary Jayne Gold. It is his spontaneous gestures and his bleak stories. One evening, when they are crossing one of the boulevards together, Claude leans down to Dagobert mid-stride and unclips the leash from his collar.

"Heel," he commands the dog, "heel." Dagobert looks up at him and obeys him willingly. All the way to the hotel, he does not budge an inch from his side. "I can't stand seeing my friends in chains," Claude says to Gold. "This way also works."

Another time – they are strolling through the city at night with Miriam and the other two Legionnaires – a rat startles Dagobert. Claude reacts with lightning speed, laying into the rat with a kick as it races off, flinging it into the darkness.

The evenings are warm, and the friends mostly sit in cafés until the wee hours, talking about the course of the war. The rage at the German troops is so intense that it even seems to carry over to the poodle. Whenever Hitler's name is uttered during their conversations, Dagobert begins barking.

One evening, they ask Claude probing questions about his past until he is forced to admit that his name is actually Raymond – and that he was not discharged from the Foreign Legion but deserted. For that reason alone, he is reluctant to use his real name. Mary Jayne is horrified because she knows which punishment awaits deserters. But Raymond reassures her that if he is caught, they will probably not have him shot, but rather sent to an Algerian penal company that builds roads across the Sahara.

Naturally, the friends want to know more. His father was a sailor, Killer Raymond recalls, and only seldom came home. At some point, he vanished without a trace. Before the war, Raymond himself went to sea: not as a sailor, but by himself with a small boat. Even on long hauls, he says, he got by without help. Once, he took twelve prostitutes from France across the Mediterranean Sea to Oran.

Again, Mary Jayne is appalled, this time, however, with indignation. Trafficking in girls is no trivial offense in her book. But Raymond immediately invokes mitigating circumstances. The prostitutes, he reassures her, were ferried over to Algeria of their own volition because they would make more money there. And, to protect them from their pimps, who were already waiting for them in Oran, he set them ashore in a small neighboring port. The pimps were so upset about this, though, that he joined the Legion to go off the grid for a while.

Raymond's latest scheme is to smuggle ten to twelve Legionnaires who want to join the British army to fight against Hitler to Gibraltar by ship. He knows, so he says, the waters around Marseille exactly. He will leave port by himself at night as a fisherman, and he knows which stretch of coastline he can land on in the dark to take the companions on board. The only thing he lacks in order to carry out his escapade is a ship. It could be a worn-out, cheap barge, good only for its final voyage.

A short time later, Raymond calls Mary Jayne at her hotel and invites her on a sightseeing tour of the port. He has found an appropriate ship for his plan. When they arrive at the docks, he presents her with a trawler, rusty and battered, the once blue paint of which has largely flaked off. The name on the prow is *Marie Josette*.

"She doesn't look great," he says, "but her engine runs, and she has a compass." He requires nothing more.

Mary Jayne is skeptical. Can he, she asks, actually steer a ship like this by himself? Raymond shrugs. Two of his crew, he says with the tone of a captain, are experienced sailors. They can lend him a hand. Everything is thought through. He only needs the money to buy the ship. "Are you sure," he asks her, "that you want to pay for it?"

"Oh, I wish I could go with you," Gold whispers.

Raymond turns to her and laughs: "That is impossible, darling."

The next day, Mary Jayne has an appointment at the prefecture with Miriam and their three friends. She needs to have her residence permit renewed: for an American, not a big issue. When she has taken care of everything and is waiting by the building entrance on the other, she sees one of Raymond's two comrades approaching. He is running. He looks agitated.

As soon as he is standing before her, he pants: "Killer has been arrested."

Marseille, early September 1940

The round-up in the Splendide's lobby during which Mehring was detained finally had made Fry realize that he needs to put his work on more sound footing. If he continues on as he has been, he will endanger refugees instead of helping them. He is like the hunk of bacon in a mouse trap; he attracts so many people seeking help that the hotel is constantly under siege. Understandably, this arouses the curiosity of the police, who have arrested and interrogated his visitors if for no other reason than to figure out what is going on in room 307.

If Fry wants to work in peace, he must satisfy the officials' curiosity. And so he registers the founding of an aid committee at the prefecture: the Centre Américain de Secours, officially headed by General Secretary Miriam Davenport. It is a welfare organization like any other, aiming to support refugees stuck in the city with money and donations in kind. The onrush of people can thus be credibly explained. About the rest – about procuring fake passports or real affidavits and, above all, about concrete aid in escape – Fry says not a single word to the prefect. With the Centre Secours, he means to establish a legal façade behind which his illegal activities might disappear from the sight of these lawmen.

In addition, Fry takes over the business premises of a Jewish leather goods dealer on the Rue Grignan. It is a narrow commercial street, not two hundred meters from the Old Port. The tradesman has read the signs of the time and plans to leave France as quickly as possible. While he is still clearing out his store, Fry is already opening up the future headquarters of the Centre Secours there. Now he can divert the stream of visitors causing such a stir at the hotel to an unsuspicious place. A subtle scent of leather will fill the rooms for a long while.

With this move, Fry transforms his improvised aid initiative into a respectable institution with offices and letterhead. From the street, the way leads through a dark courtyard driveway to the rear of the building, and from there up a stairwell to the second level. Until the stock has been cleared out, Fry only has two rooms available. In the larger of the two, he places tables along the front windows where associates will receive and question those seeking help. He himself works in the smaller back room, which contains a desk as well as a few battered filing cabinets. Fry has begun calling the people who come to him his clients. For each person who needs an emergency rescue visa, he has an index card drawn up on which his team notes down what steps were already taken to rescue them.

The bureaucratic hassle is enormous. The ERC in New York must be informed by cable of all clients so that it can take care of the requisite affidavits for entry. For each individual, moreover, passage on a ship must be booked, transit visas applied for, the validity of all documents checked, and, if necessary, forged identification papers procured. There is no way Fry could handle this all by himself, and the new office finally gives him the opportunity to hire even more people besides Hildebrand, Davenport, and Hirschmann.

The first two, Lena Fischmann and Heinz Ernst Oppenheimer, have already worked with other anti-Hitler aid committees. Lena Fischmann hails from Poland and is a language genius. She can not only take shorthand in English, French, and German, but can also speak Russian, Polish, Spanish, and Yiddish. Oppenheimer, a Jewish-German engineer, takes on the bookkeeping. It is a delicate task that requires creativity, for he must not only make the expenditures for forged papers vanish from the balance sheet, but also plausibly disguise the revenues Hirschmann makes with his illegal exchange business on the black market. At Davenport's urging, Fry also hires Gussie Rosenberg. He is employed primarily as a courier who personally delivers messages that cannot be entrusted to the postal service.

In addition, Fry also takes on two Americans, Charles Fawcett and Dick Ball. Both served in Paris as volunteers for the American ambulance unit. Ball is from Montana, led a small French lard company before the war, and on his travels to his customers got to know the remotest corners of the country. Fawcett, on the other hand, is an adventurer blessed with an athletic body and a cheerful disposition. In Paris, he studied art and

A Spanish soldier above the French border town of Cerbère, March 1939

worked as a trumpeter in jazz clubs. He earned his money, however, as a wrestler in exhibition matches, during which there was a lot of yelling, threatening, and arm-waving, without anyone ever being injured. Fry uses him as a doorman who maintains order with a steady hand among the queue of people now forming every day outside number 60, Rue Grignan. One by one, Fawcett sends people upstairs to the office.

Among those seeking help from them are some who already have an American visa and, until now, have hesitated to set off for Spain out of trepidation. Fry furnishes them with the necessary travel money and reasons with them. So far, it has been incredibly simple to get over the border without a French exit visa. A railroad tunnel leads from Cerbère, the final border town in France, to Portbou, the first one in Spain. In front of the tunnel is a gigantic train station where all travelers must transfer from French trains with the narrower European track gauge to Spanish trains with the larger Iberian track gauge. All freight must be transferred as well.

Quite a few refugees are fortunate because some French officials turn a blind eye during passport checks and wave everyone through who wants to leave the country. Then they need only transfer from the French train into the waiting Spanish one and continue their journey without any trouble. Those who are turned away by an official who is a slave to the rules, however, can continue their escape on foot. For everyone he sends to Spain, Fry retrieves the rough map he hid behind his wardrobe mirror to show them where the correct mountain trail may be found. Although the route is steep, it is not long. At three hundred meters of altitude, it leads over a pass called Col de Belitres and soon thereafter descends to Portbou on the Spanish side. Albert Hirschmann and Dick Ball have traveled to Cerbère and familiarized themselves with the route. Ball, in particular, who knows the Rocky Mountains from Montana, was unable to identify any difficulties worth mentioning anywhere.

Among the first Fry dispatches is Hitler biographer Konrad Heiden. As a sign that he has arrived safely in Lisbon, he sends a telegram to the Centre Secours with the agreed-upon text: "Thanks, David." Fry's relief is considerable when the message arrives. After all, it could have happened that the Spanish police intercept the refugees and hand them over to the Germans.

Shortly thereafter, Leonhard Frank and the legendary theater critic Alfred Polgar follow, crossing over Col de Belitres with an American journalist. They, too, arrive in Lisbon without any problems.

Fry's record is nothing to sneeze at. After just three weeks in Marseille, he has created a contact office for refugees with the Centre Secours, hired trustworthy associates, located a usable escape route, and already sent the first authors and artists on his lists to safety. His Underground Railroad from Marseille to Lisbon is gathering speed.

For Fry, however, it is more difficult than anticipated to stay in contact with the ERC in New York. He must count on the fact that everything he conveys in writing through official channels, in letters or cables, will be read by French and German security services. If he does not want to jeopardize his disguise as an employee of a harmless welfare organization, he also cannot employ any codes; they would make him all the more suspicious. In cases of emergency, he has called the New York office by long-wave radio, but that is, for all intents and purposes, too laborious. Every conversation must be booked hours ahead of time and is horribly expensive. There is also no conversation with another person, just shouting, because the line hisses with static and crackles as though an eternal hurricane were raging over the Atlantic. Besides, the Gestapo is listening in.

Fry and Hirschmann thus switch over to passing along confidential information to the clients setting out for Lisbon, with the request that they send it to the committee from Portugal. To safely conceal their messages for transport, they have developed a special procedure. They write their messages on very narrow slips of paper cut to shape and pack them in a condom. Then they cut open a new tube of toothpaste from the back end, stuff the condom into the paste, and roll it up from the bottom in the usual way until it looks like a normal, half-empty tube of toothpaste.

The concealment is fairly secure, yet a number of refugees are so afraid of searches that they dispose of the prepared tubes before border checks. Clandestine contact with New York also continues getting out of step. Messages fail to materialize, replies do not arrive, misunderstandings arise.

Marseille, early September 1940

Killer Raymond had always swept aside any qualms about his desertion. But when Mary Jayne Gold heard about his arrest, she realized the severity of his circumstances. She has obtained a first-rate attorney for him – for now, there is nothing else she can do. Raymond has since been in the military prison at the St. Nicolas fort right on the Old Port, almost within view of her hotel. It will take months, the lawyer thinks, to make it to trial.

Mary Jayne has difficulty waiting. Her concern for Raymond upsets her. Miriam Davenport therefore attempts to take her mind off things. She tells her about the Centre Secours, the rapidly growing number of her clients, the enormous paper war they wage daily. She becomes taciturn, however, once Mary Jayne offers to help her and to donate to Fry the money she intended for Raymond's ship purchase, a not inconsiderable half million francs.

Ultimately, Miriam confesses to her friend that she has already told Fry a great deal about her, about the time before the war, about her sweet life between Paris, Rome, and St. Moritz, about her own plane, which she gave to the French army, and her gigantic fortune. This, though, raised Fry's concerns. He considers money frivolous and not especially confidence-inspiring. To his way of thinking, she might be a shill for the police assigned to the Center in order to scope it out.

"Fine, I'll …" Mary Jayne says. "Miriam, I have to meet him."

"That's exactly what I told him," Miriam replies. But Fry's mistrust is so great that he would rather keep Mary Jayne at a distance.

In the end, Hirschmann and Davenport arrange a coincidental encounter with Fry in broad daylight. Hirschmann acts as if he were surprised to run into Gold and suggests lunch together. Miriam immediately agrees, and Fry cannot easily evade his associates' unanimity. He begins a perfunctory interrogation of Gold while they are still on the aperitif. He has her tell him what she experienced while fleeing from Paris, and by the time the plates are cleared, he has hired her as an interviewer.

Marseille, early September 1940

Activity on Fry's refugee trail quickly grows heavier. To make the route safer, Fry has taken to sending Dick Ball to the border several times a week with two or three charges. Ball gives everyone a sense of security. He leads them up to the Col de Belitres, shows them the way to Portbou, and then turns back. Hans Natonek reaches Spain by this route without a hitch. Hertha Pauli, however, contracts a high fever shortly before departing for the mountains, a severe cold. She only gets one night to convalesce before she stumbles along the trail the following day, half unconscious, and reaches Portbou, completely finished. Walter Mehring wants to travel alone, without a guide, which he considers safer – though that proves to be a mistake.

Fry obtained a Czech passport for him with a fake name; Mehring is plagued by the notion that he is so well known as a writer in Spain, too, that the police are just waiting to arrest him. In addition, he is carrying an American rescue visa issued in his real name so that he does not encounter any trouble with American immigration authorities.

Unfortunately, Mehring, who has never put much stock in his outward appearance, now looks so unkempt that he is detained on the journey to the border by the police as a vagrant. For all intents and purposes, not a huge problem: he can prove his identity after all. But Mehring panics, fearing a strip search during which the inconsistencies between his documents will come to light, and destroys the passport in the bathroom in an unattended moment. As a foreigner with no identification, he is transported by the police to the next best internment camp – and Fry must hire an attorney to free him from the camp and bring him back to Marseille.

This is not the only incident on Fry's escape route. In Spain, five men are said to have been arrested, though no one knows why. Fry still has much too little information about the legs of his Underground Railroad outside France. His promise to accompany the Feuchtwangers on their escape provides him with the opportunity to change this. When he travels with them, as well as with the Manns and the Werfels, via Barcelona and Madrid to Lisbon, he can familiarize himself with the entire escape route and eliminate potential security risks.

Marseille, early September 1940

Among the many people seeking help whom Albert Hirschmann interviews at the Centre, a wiry little Austrian man with substantial talents stands out to him. He is a Jew named Bil Spira but has recently begun calling himself Bil Freier. With almost spellbinding speed, he dashes off brilliant portraits and caricatures on paper and, before having to evacuate from Paris, was one of the Viennese newspapers' most popular sketch artists. He is not on Fry's rescue lists; ERC advisors forgot him, perhaps because he is still so very young, just twenty-seven. But that is irrelevant to Hirschmann. He brings up Bil with Fry in conversation; they are responsible for an artist like him, regardless what the lists say.

And Fry has an idea. Might someone who can draw so well not also be able to forge? The Centre is occasionally offered passports for sale without the requisite stamps and signatures from sinister sources. And a *carte d'identité* can be purchased from any kiosk, preprinted but not yet filled out. Such means of identification are only valid after being furnished with a photo and personal information, and authenticated and stamped by the police. All refugees dream of having such a card, which would transform them into officially accredited French citizens.

Freier has never worked as a forger. But after only a few days, he draws stamps and signatures that even experts cannot distinguish from the real thing. Fry is delighted. He buys the finished documents from him and cables New York to request a rescue visa for Freier and his girlfriend.

Marseille, early September 1940

Walter Benjamin's favorite refuge is still literature. He long hesitated to leave Lourdes, not least out of consideration for his ailing sister. But after Dora found a hideout on a farm and news reached him that travel papers were ready and waiting for him at the American consulate in Marseille, he finally hit the road.

Max Horkheimer, the director of the Institute for Social Research, was able to procure a rescue visa for him in the United States. At this point, Benjamin has received the Spanish and Portuguese transit visas as well. It is only the French exit permit he has failed to get, like all the other exiles. He has had himself added to the list of people seeking assistance at the Centre Secours but was never able to pull himself together to speak with Fry himself.

Benjamin is not doing well. He is only thirty-eight years old, but his heart is causing him trouble, and he senses himself sinking into a deeper and deeper depression. So as not to be altogether powerlessly at the mercy of his fate, he has acquired morphine, fifty tablets, enough to kill a horse. Fortunately, there are a few old acquaintances in the city with whom he can meet to take his mind off things. All of them are in the same situation as he, all of them searching for some loophole to escape abroad. He meets fairly frequently with Siegfried Kracauer, formerly the editor of the *Frankfurter Zeitung*, for which Benjamin wrote book reviews, and occasionally, too, with Soma Morgenstern, who once worked on the editorial staff at the *Frankfurter Zeitung* as well.

It is not just Benjamin's erudition that is phenomenal, but also his memory. As soon as he starts talking about literature, he can liberate himself, at least mentally, from the wretched predicament he is in. Only too seldom, though, does he find interlocutors who are a match for him. When he visits a restaurant with Morgenstern and the two study the menu, Benjamin looks up as though waiting for him to utter some obligatory remark.

"Anything catch your eye?" he asks.

Morgenstern is puzzled. They have not yet eaten or drunk anything. "What should have caught my eye?"

Benjamin hands him the menu again. "Didn't you notice anything?"

Morgenstern again checks the dishes and drinks on offer but remains clueless.

"Didn't you notice the name of the tavern?" Benjamin gradually becomes impatient.

The restaurant is named after the owner, and he is called Arnoux. Morgenstern shrugs. Benjamin asks questions like a teacher does of his examinee: "Well? Does that still not ring a bell?"

Morgenstern senses that he will probably not pass this exam.

"Don't you remember who is named Arnoux?" Benjamin can hardly believe it. "Arnoux is the name of the lover of Frédéric, the protagonist in *L'Éducation sentimentale*!"

Morgenstern missed a random allusion to one of Gustave Flaubert's most important novels. Inexcusable. As atonement for this sin, he has no choice but to follow Benjamin's impromptu lecture on Flaubert, shamefaced, and contribute to the literary table talk to the best of his modest ability.

Marseille, mid-September 1940

Mehring is so diminutive and often behaves so helplessly and hysterically that Fry and his people have given him the nickname "Baby." The attorney Fry engaged for him after his bungled attempt to flee was admittedly able to get him out of the internment camp, but in the meantime, his residence permit for Marseille has expired. Mehring would have to have it renewed.

But he is at the end of his tether. After his stay in the camp, he declares himself unable ever to set foot inside a French administrative office again. Fry, therefore, asks for an appointment with the head of the immigration office – and meets him at an extremely favorable moment. The day before, he had been visited by two Gestapo agents who behaved in his office like the true rulers of France, rifling through his filing cabinets and pumping his colleagues for his political views. He is furious beyond measure and for that reason quite willing to help Fry. Mehring, he says, would only need to produce a doctor's attestation that he was too sick to apply for a renewal of his residence permit in a timely manner, and all problems would be solved. He passes along the address of a sympathetic physician then and there.

Consequently, Fry rents a room for Mehring at the Splendide and sends him to bed. The doctor comes, casts a fleeting glance at the patient, and then drafts a note that Mehring will be healthy enough to be able to leave his room in two months at the earliest.

Mehring is thus out of harm's way for the time being. Fry has a new problem, though, because his baby now in fact no longer intends to leave the room – or the hotel, at least – and must have all his needs provided for by the Centre. Mehring enjoys hotel life. Most of the time, he sits in his room fully clothed and leaps into bed only when the chambermaid knocks on the door to bring his meals. Oftentimes, he pulls the bedspread so far up toward his neck that his shoes stick out from beneath the blanket at the other end.

Marseille, September 11, 1940

Since August, food conditions in France have rapidly gotten worse. The German military administration has begun either confiscating available foodstuffs for the *Wehrmacht* or exporting them to Germany. Marshall Pétain's regime is compelled to announce drastic rationing, including its attempt to enforce a ban on serving any alcohol in public on Tuesdays, Thursdays, and Saturdays – a highly controversial measure. Still, resourceful chefs and restauranteurs succeed for a time in providing their diners with astonishingly good, sometimes sublime fare from secret sources. Yesterday, Franz Werfel celebrated his fiftieth birthday in one of the fancy restaurants on the Old Port. It was a Tuesday, but Alma Mahler-Werfel still made certain that they wanted for nothing.

Heinrich Mann and Alfred Kantorowicz have arranged to meet for lunch today. It is not a pleasant day. Although the sky is deep blue and clear, the mistral sweeps through the streets and puts everyone on edge. Fry has also informed Heinrich Mann that they are to set out for the Spanish border in the early hours of the morning tomorrow in order to leave France – yet another reason to be nervous.

Kantorowicz and Mann have known one another for years. In Berlin, they were both among the leftist intellectuals who issued warnings about the Nazis early on. Since his escape from internment, Kantorowicz has gone underground with his wife in Bormes-les-Mimosas, a small neighboring town of Le Lavandou. Out of an abundance of caution, he agreed to meet Mann in a suburb of Marseille to evade the police checks in the city center.

Mann is shaken by the news that his farewell from France is imminent. The country's way of life and culture mean a great deal to him; from his perspective, they are among the highpoints of European civilization. With weariness in his voice, he greets Kantorowicz and suggests that they celebrate his involuntary departure by visiting an especially classy restaurant they can reach via quiet side streets.

Along the way, both of them must brace themselves against the mistral. Mann is conspicuously taciturn. From the outside, the restaurant appears plain, almost shabby. But in the dining area, the perfect atmosphere of high-end French gastronomy prevails. The menu features around two hundred sophisticated dishes, and after Heinrich Mann has carefully perused the wine list, he selects for Kantorowicz and himself, first, a light rosé and, with the main course, a 1912 Burgundy. He celebrates the rituals of exclusive culinary art with complete abandon, as though it were for the last time.

After the pair have ordered cheese and dessert, Heinrich Mann leans back in his plush armchair, looks around the dining room, and, in his Northern German accent, says: "Well, and now I'm off to America … There'll probably only be fast-food restaurants there."

Marseille, September 11, 1940

Fry is nervous. The group that is to set out for the border tomorrow – the Manns, Werfels, Feuchtwangers, and Thomas Mann's son Golo – is by far the most famous he has organized thus far. Nothing must go wrong. All refugees are important to him, of course, but with these seven now departing, the reputation of the Emergency Rescue Committee is on the line. Should one of these authors or their wives be arrested or come to grief, it would have global repercussions. For that reason alone, it is good that he accompany the group together with Dick Ball.

But on today of all days, the rumor is circulating that the Spanish border authorities have begun turning away refugees who cannot produce a valid passport. In prior weeks, that has never been an issue. Those in possession of a United States rescue visa and the Spanish and Portuguese transit visas had nothing to fear from the Spanish customs agents. Fry need not worry about the Werfels or the Manns either because all four have lawful Czech papers from Consul Vochoč. The Manns' are issued under the surname Ludwig because they are afraid of being recognized under their real name, but that should not present any difficulties. Marta and Lion Feuchtwanger, on the other hand, are stateless ever since being expatriated from Germany by the National Socialists; they have no passports.

This morning, Fry has expressly confirmed to all involved that they will set out the following morning. He finds it all the more difficult to admit to the Feuchtwangers that an unexpected problem has arisen at the last minute after all. Toward evening, he goes to Bingham's home and at their dinner together seems undecided – one minute he wants to leave with their group the next morning, the next he is toying with the idea of postponing everyone's departure.

When Fry leaves Bingham's home after dinner, he promises to call by eleven o'clock at the latest and let Feuchtwanger know his decision. But the call does not come. Around one in the morning, Golo Mann returns to Bingham's from a final meeting with Fry and reports that the group will travel, though without the Feuchtwangers. The risk that they will be turned away by the Spaniards and have to return to Marseille alone without papers seems too great to Fry. He will inquire at the border whether and how stateless persons are able to enter the country and plans to send the Feuchtwangers at another date.

Marseille – Portbou, September 12, 1940

Golo Mann is altogether bleary-eyed when Marta Feuchtwanger brings him breakfast bright and early. He needs a while to clear his head. Fry has decided the group will meet at the Gare Saint-Charles at four thirty because the very first train to Spain is generally not inspected by the police. Even officers do not enjoy leaving their beds before dawn.

In contrast to his otherwise quite composed demeanor, Fry is jittery and uptight this morning, continuously pacing the train platform. He has urged all of them to behave as inconspicuously as possible but is himself too nervous to contain himself. Alma Mahler-Werfel has several porters carry her entire set of luggage, lost for so long, to the train. It is a performance worthy of a film diva. Fry counts twelve suitcases and bags, plus four suitcases belonging to the Manns.

Fortunately, they are traveling first class, which spares them any dangerous hassles. In Nîmes, two gendarmes board the train to check the passengers' *sauf-conduits*. In the first-class cars, however, they only say a polite hello and check no one. Apparently, they think it impossible that passengers sitting there with such a mountain of luggage could be traveling illegally.

Only after nightfall do they arrive in Cerbère. The tiny border town lies wedged between the Pyrenees and the sea. The train station is the largest structure and seems to have shoved all other buildings against the cliff face or down to the beach. Dick Ball collects their passports and takes his place in line before the office of the border police. By this point, he knows some of the officials and intends to persuade them to allow the entire group to continue their journey with the Spanish train although only Fry has an exit visa. In previous weeks, that has occasionally worked for him.

The others wait on the platform and try to conceal their nervousness. When Ball returns, Fry can tell from afar that he does not bear good news. The inspector on duty was friendly and knows exactly what awaits refugees if they fall into the hands of the German police. Still, he is unwilling to make any concessions. He has strict orders to follow the rules to the letter. In the end, Ball had no choice but to ask the man to keep the passports overnight and reconsider the matter. He does not, however, harbor great hope.

The next day, nothing about the situation has changed. The inspector remains unyielding; his superiors are keeping a sharp eye on him. Nevertheless, he is forthcoming and advises Ball to cross the Col de Belitres in the mountains with his people, today if possible. Pressure from the Germans to keep better watch over the border grows by the day, he says, and soon the old smuggling trail will just be teeming with patrols.

Ball and Fry are alarmed. This is the worst news imaginable for their Underground Railroad. They also have doubts about whether they can reasonably expect their group of famous refugees to handle the path over the summit. They gather everyone together to deliberate and explain the circumstances to them. The five are understandably not thrilled. Heinrich Mann is sixty-nine years old and has not climbed a mountain in years. Werfel is overweight and has a heart condition. When looking up at the cliffs, he realizes that today of all days is Friday the thirteenth. He begins trembling. "Today is an unlucky day," he protests. "Shouldn't we wait until tomorrow instead?"

"That is nonsense, Franz," Alma says, interrupting him. At the moment, she has no patience whatsoever with his notorious superstition. She agrees to the hike, on behalf of her husband as well; it is best not to delay and to set out at once.

The path also seems too risky to Nelly Mann. She tries to persuade her husband in German: "Mr. Fry is a very nice young man. He says he wants to help us. But how do we know he isn't just a spy trying to lure us into a trap?"

Fry chimes in: "Pardon, Frau Mann, perhaps you don't know that I understand German." While that is not an argument that could allay her suspicion – and certainly no proof of the mountain route's safety – Nelly Mann feels caught, turns red, and does not say another word.

To make matters worse, it is an oppressively hot day. Dick Ball procures water for the whole group. Since Fry is the only one to have an exit visa, he is to take the train over the border with the luggage. Before saying goodbye to the others, he buys them a dozen packs of cigarettes, Gitanes and Gauloises, which they can slip to the Spanish customs agents as soon as they reach the border posts.

Strictly speaking, the trail to Portbou is not far, all in all just around eight kilometers. From the train station, Fry is able to observe the little group slowly making the ascent for a while yet. Werfel takes the lead, supported by Dick Ball and his wife. Alma is also carrying her bag containing the manuscripts of Mahler and Bruckner. She has sworn to herself never under any circumstances to part with it again. Following behind, at a rapidly increasing remove, is Heinrich Mann. He walks unsteadily and hunched over, with Nelly and Golo looking after him. At first, the six are able to find a little shade beneath the trees, but the higher they get, the barer the landscape becomes – until Fry finally loses sight of them.

For the younger people, the terrain is not difficult. Golo Mann occasionally becomes impatient and climbs a few meters ahead, but then must wait for his uncle or climb back a bit to him. Everyone is quickly covered in dust and sweat. There are only bare rocks, scree, and a few thistles. At several places, they come perilously close to the precipice, at which point Heinrich Mann gropes his way forward, centimeter by centimeter. Because the women are wearing dresses, their stockings are soon tattered and their calves bruised.

Once Dick Ball has reached the summit with the Werfels at Col de Belitres, he shows them which way they must descend to Portbou. Then he does an about-face to help Heinrich Mann. Not all too far ahead of them, the Werfels find a customs shack. Painstakingly, they climb down and knock. The soldier who answers the door only understands Spanish, not a word of French or English, but as soon as they slip him one of the packs of cigarettes, his face brightens. He motions for them to follow him, leads them to a small road on which they advance more easily, and takes them to another, larger shack – the French border post! Apparently, he believes they had gotten lost and were looking for a way back to France.

The head of the French post, however, immediately grasps the intended destination of these two people so inappropriately dressed for the mountains. But he hesitates, regards the exhausted, sweaty couple, and then cannot help but smile and explain to them which path to take to reach Portbou. Across the small road hangs an iron chain separating France from Spain. The Werfels are permitted to climb over it, offer their thanks, and can continue their descent. A short while later, they find half a horseshoe by the wayside, and even though Alma responded indignantly to her husband's superstitious misgivings that morning, she pockets this halved lucky charm for good measure anyway.

Before they reach Portbou, they are overtaken by the three Manns. Ball had also taken them as far as the summit. As he was about to bid them farewell to return to Marseille, however, a French patrol suddenly appeared. Eluding them was impossible; the soldiers were armed and could have fired. They walked toward the refugees, doubtless to arrest them – but then saluted them politely, asked whether they were headed to Spain, and eagerly provided information about which path down to Portbou was most favorable.

By now, all are dead-tired but enormously relieved. Together, they make for the Spanish border station to obtain their entry stamps. The officials check their identification papers meticulously, but hardly bother themselves with the Werfels or the couple supposedly called the Ludwigs. Golo Mann, on the other hand, interests them greatly. He was not given a passport by the American consulate in Marseille, but a kind of sworn statement, an affidavit in lieu of a passport. Such documents are normally readily accepted by the Spanish and the bearers of them treated with great respect as Americans. In this case, however, the consular staff have additionally made a note that Golo Mann intends to join his father Thomas Mann in the United States – and his name means something, even in the Portbou guard shack.

"So you are the son of Thomas Mann?" the border officer asks.

Golo Mann has little desire to deny it, even at the risk of being handed over to the Nazis.

"Yes," he says. "Does that displease you?"

"On the contrary," the officer replies, shaking his hand. "I feel honored to meet the son of such an important man."

Portbou – Barcelona – Madrid – Lisbon, September 14–19, 1940

Seen from a sober perspective, yesterday's escape was a fiasco. Fry, who was comfortably able to travel by train to Portbou, knows this. All of his famous charges were apprehended by French border agents halfway there. Only because these men were brave enough to ignore their orders did no one end up in a camp, or handed over to the Germans. Obviously, the mountains between Cerbère and Portbou are now much better guarded than they were in prior weeks.

Tiny Portbou lies in serious ruins. Franco's air force bombed the town multiple times during the civil war. So far, little has been rebuilt; all that remains of several stretches of roads is rubble. Smashed pieces of furniture lie amid the wreckage, entire exterior walls of buildings have been blown off, and from the faded spots on the wallpaper, one can tell how the inhabitants had set up their lives, where a picture once hung, or where in the kitchen the oven was located.

There is good news, too, however. Counter to what rumors in Marseille would have people believe, the Spanish authorities have not issued any new rules for stateless persons. Refugees without passports may still enter as long as they can produce a visa for the United States. Fry, therefore, sends a telegram to Marta and Lion Feuchtwanger that they may begin their journey but must count on stricter checks in the mountains.

Heinrich and Nelly Mann upon their arrival in the United States, 1940

The next problem awaits them in Barcelona. There are only two more plane tickets to Madrid. Which of his five clients are to get them, and which are to start the journey by train, which is more intensively monitored?

Fry chooses Nelly and Heinrich Mann, not because Mann is more famous than Franz Werfel, but because his body and mind have been more detrimentally affected. When Mann spots a portrait of Adolf Hitler on the wall in the Spanish airline office, he loses his composure for a moment and loudly proclaims: "We find ourselves in the clutches of the enemy."

Fry responds swiftly, shepherding Mann to a café, and calming him with a brandy before a bigger commotion can arise.

Luckily, all remaining legs of the journey are without incident. Together with the Werfels and Golo Mann, Fry first takes a train to Madrid, which takes fifteen hours all the same. There, he can arrange five plane tickets to Lisbon.

Nevertheless, the escapees have still not surmounted all obstacles. Each and every ship headed overseas from Portugal is sold out, as are the few Clippers. It will take days, if not weeks, until they are finally able to put Europe behind them.

Brentwood, September 20, 1940

It is a warm, late-summer day with a cloudless sky. Katia and Thomas Mann are sitting in the backyard of their villa having breakfast when a telegram arrives. It is from Portugal, from Heinrich and Golo. Both have been saved, having crossed the French border in the mountains, and are now waiting in Lisbon for passage to New York. The first reliable sign of life in weeks! Katia and Thomas are immeasurably relieved. A tremendous joy.

Shortly thereafter, further telegrams arrive: from the Emergency Rescue Committee, from a Unitarian aid organization taking care of Golo and Heinrich in Lisbon, from the editor Hermann Kesten, who maintains contact from New York to refugees in Europe. They all relay the same happy news. Heinrich and Golo are safe! However, Thomas Mann writes in his diary that evening, his joy in this is tarnished a bit by the fact that Nelly Mann is also among those saved.

Madrid, September 20, 1940

Varian Fry has made a stop at the British embassy in Madrid already on his outbound journey. He knows that in Marseille a considerable number of British soldiers are stuck who escaped the pocket of Dunkirk and want to return to their units in England. Fry has suggested the ambassador send a Royal Navy ship from Gibraltar to Marseille so that under cover of darkness it can take aboard not just the soldiers, but also Fry's clients, and bring them to safety. Fry has offered to arrange the operation from the mainland and, with his people, to locate an appropriate landing spot for the ship.

Now, on his way back from Lisbon, he has another appointment at the embassy to hear what the Navy thinks of his plan. The admirals, the ambassador discloses, have rejected it brusquely. They subscribe to the doctrine of never separating individual ships from a naval unit in wartimes – especially not for a suicide mission like the one Fry suggests.

But this does not settle the matter for the ambassador. He offers Fry ten thousand dollars if he helps British soldiers get across the border to Spain by land. For Fry, this is risky. He has hitherto limited his work to helping civilians escape from France. If he accepts the ambassador's offer, he will become a paid British agent. In French courts, he could be indicted on a charge of espionage for that, and in German courts be sentenced to death.

Fry nevertheless agrees because the ambassador promises to keep an eye out for a Spanish fishing vessel he can send to Marseille. If Fry wants to get overly anxious clients like Walter Mehring or well-known politicians like Hilferding and Breitscheid to safety, he is dependent on a sea route. He absolutely needs a ship; it is the only chance these men have.

Marseille, September 20, 1940

Back in August, Walter Benjamin told Hannah Arendt in a letter how great the fear is that overcomes him at the thought of his manuscripts' fate. They are the most important things he owns. Among them is unpublished material, including his theses "On the Concept of History," which he worked on earlier in the year. It is not a long essay, but it must not be lost under any circumstances.

Fortunately, Benjamin has learned that Hannah Arendt is in Marseille today. And he managed to get a message to her to arrange a time to meet. She and her husband have to negotiate with the American consulate and the Centre Américain de Secours. There, they appear on the list of clients with prospects for an emergency visa as Madame Hannah Blücher and Monsieur Heinrich Blücher.

During their meeting, Benjamin asks Hannah Arendt to take a carbon copy of the essay for safekeeping. He knows that his manuscript will be in the most reliable hands imaginable with this pugnacious woman. In the coming days, he plans to leave France at any cost. Whether he will succeed is unclear; the risk of falling into the hands of the Gestapo cannot be ruled out. Under these circumstances, he at least would like to give his essay an additional chance at survival.

Paris – Moulins, September 20, 1940

Anna Seghers has chosen to flee via the small town of Moulins in central France. Here, the demarcation line between the occupied and unoccupied zones takes a strange sharp turn. Coming from the north, the border first runs down the middle of the Allier, a tributary of the

Loire. The bridges are strictly monitored by the Germans; Anna Seghers has no chance there. But a bit to the south of the municipal area, the borderline pivots eastward from the river and runs through fields and small wooded areas. It might work here.

In Paris, circumstances have become untenable for Seghers. The hotels are now regularly checked, sometimes by the French and sometimes by the German police. Remaining in their hotel would have been wanton recklessness. Consequently, she has asked friends to take in her children. Ruth has found shelter with Jeanne Stern, a German Studies scholar and combatant in Spain who has translated several books by Anna Seghers. Peter is staying with a very self-confident young woman who has been dubbed Pony ever since she served for Erich Kästner as the inspiration for the figure of Pony Hütchen in *Emil and the Detectives*. Seghers herself is spending most nights at the home of the daughter of a prominent feminist, Gabrielle Duchêne, near the Eiffel Tower.

But it cannot go on like this. As illegal Jewish houseguests, they pose a constant danger to the friends with whom they are hiding. Seghers has, therefore, decided to cross over with her children to the unoccupied zone. She plans to head to Pamiers, a town near the internment camp Le Vernet, where her husband Rodi is incarcerated. She cannot, however, do it without Jeanne Stern's help. Anna speaks French brilliantly, but her German accent is unmistakable. If she does not want to stand out near the demarcation line, she will need someone who can speak for her.

They take the train from the Gare d'Austerlitz early one morning. Anna finds a seat by the window in a compartment and begins knitting with her head bowed. She wants to avoid being talked to and forced to reply by other passengers. Jeanne Stern sits across from her and chats with the children, whose French has for a while now been as good as if they had been born in Paris. They alight in Moulins, cross the street outside the train station, and find lodging in the first available hotel. Then, Jeanne Stern heads out to find someone who can help them cross the border.

At the commandant's office, as a huge swastika flag flutters from its roof, the Germans issue travel passes for the demarcation line. All applicants are screened thoroughly beforehand, though. Stern sits down between those waiting and enters into conversation with a peasant woman who owns fields on both sides of the border. For the harvest, she must move back and forth between the zones. The Germans' bureaucracy gets on her nerves; instead of working, she is forced to waste her time at the commandant's office.

The woman seems trustworthy – serious and taciturn, but not unfriendly. To tug at her heartstrings, Stern tells her only about the two children. For three months now, they have been separated from their mother, who was forcibly evacuated to the south with her business in June. The peasant woman immediately understands, hesitates for a moment, then whispers to Jeanne Stern to come to a village south of Moulins at nine o'clock the next morning. "The first house on the left is a tavern. I'll pick them up there."

The next day, Jeanne Stern and Anna Seghers set out with the children at dawn. A deserted country road leads to the hamlet between endless rows of poplar trees. Initially, the two women have planned that Jeanne will take the children over the border with the peasant woman and then return to the tavern. Anna will wait for her there and then, led by Jeanne, follow the children.

When they arrive in the village, the tavern door stands open. The publican busies himself in silence behind the counter and does not say a word when they enter and sit down at one of the tables. He watches the street through the open door until he suddenly says: "Your acquaintance has just walked past. You must follow her. Right now." Jeanne Stern and the children immediately stand up and walk into the street. Anna Seghers does not move a muscle.

The peasant woman does not stop; she walks ahead of them without turning around. She briskly turns off the road and crosses one of the stubble fields. The countryside is flat, a treeless plain with hardly any cover, just a few bushes here and there. Stern looks around for patrols, but there is no one to be seen. Beyond a small copse, they reach a sandy path and just after that a boom barrier, guarded by two French soldiers in squalid uniforms.

At this point, the peasant woman turns around for the first time. "Across, quickly," she says to the children.

"Does the free zone begin here?" Jeanne Stern asks.

"I s'pose," one of the soldiers replies.

The children must continue following the sandy path straight to the nearest village. It also has a tavern, which is where they are to wait for their mother.

Jeanne Stern thanks the peasant woman and gives her a few francs – she does not have much. When she has reached the narrow copse on the way back, she glances back again toward the children, seeing them walking through the open field with their rucksacks. Amid the vast cropland, they seem very small and very alone.

The children encounter no one until they reach the village. The agreed-upon bar is fairly ramshackle, but the landlady welcomes them amiably, waves them to a table, and brings them two plates of soup.

When Jeanne Stern returns to the tavern in the occupied zone, Anna Seghers is no longer there. Jeanne's rucksack lies abandoned beside a table. Jeanne is so frightened that she collapses into a chair beside the rucksack, her knees weak. The publican exits the kitchen: "You can rest easy. Your friend found a safe escort; I know him well. *Au revoir.*"

Stern believes him. She knows how difficult it must have been for Anna to let her children proceed ahead alone across this unfamiliar frontier. If she found someone with whom she could follow after the two right away without having to wait for her friend's return, then she did not hesitate. Jeanne picks up the rucksack, tosses it over her shoulders, and makes her way home to Paris.

Anna Seghers also crosses the endless stubble field with her unknown escort, unprotected and easily visible to potential patrols, then reaches the copse and the barrier. The two soldiers let her through. She hastily follows the sandy path to the appointed village. Tracking down the bar is not difficult. She hurries toward it, then stops when she glimpses her children through one of the windows. They are sitting at a table, slumped over their plates and spooning soup.

Cerbère – Portbou, September 21, 1940

Marta and Lion Feuchtwanger remain undaunted at the sight of the mountains above Cerbère. Marta is an experienced skier. Before the war, she would often leave her husband alone in the wintertime with his manuscripts and lovers so she could frolic about on Alpine slopes much higher than the Col de Belitres. Lion also retains his composure; for years now, he has been completing a daily program of gymnastics to counteract his deskwork and even today, at fifty-six, is still in good shape.

Both feel up for a lengthy mountain hike at any time. They have come to the border with a clergyman, an American named Waitstill Sharp. He is a Unitarian, a sturdy, hands-on sort of man who, with his wife, heads a small, efficient aid organization. In Prague, they managed to save several hundred persecuted persons from the Nazis, including quite a few Jews. Nowadays, they work from Lisbon and provide money, food, and lodging to exiles coming from France. It was there that Sharp recently received a telegram from Eleanor Roosevelt in which she congratulated him on his successes and asked him to give his all in rescuing Feuchtwanger.

Sharp is a man of God, a minister as the Unitarians call their clergy, and not someone who hesitates for long. He promptly made his way to Marseille. When he was getting off the train in Gare Saint-Charles, Fry had only just left for the border with the Manns and the Werfels. Within the span of a few hours, Sharp learned from the American consulate where Feuchtwanger was in hiding and headed to him. Feuchtwanger was sitting in the garden of Bingham's villa, working on his manuscript, when this brawny man in a dark suit approached, delivered greetings from Eleanor Roosevelt, and said: "I have been sent here just for you."

Then, things began proceeding apace. From Dick Ball, Sharp obtained the necessary information about the current conditions at the border. Then he guided Marta and Lion – who were not permitted even to set foot in the train station in Marseille without passports – past all police checkpoints into a train and without further incident to Cerbère.

Here, however, even Sharp runs up against a wall. He has tried to bribe the border guards – he is skilled at such things – but the officers shake their heads. And so, like Fry, he must take the train through the tunnel to Portbou alone while Marta and Lion take the route over the mountains.

The pair do not keep to the old smuggling trail, instead climbing up the slopes as steeply as possible. From her skiing vacations, Marta is used to orienting herself in unknown terrain. After a lengthy ascent, they hear voices, and behind a boulder, they spot a Spanish border post.

From Bingham, Lion received an American entry visa issued under the name of James Wetcheek, a pseudonym he has also used before as a writer. Bingham could not for the life of him get a visa for Marta, however, and she possesses merely makeshift papers under the name

Feuchtwanger – which in Spain is presumably on the wanted lists. For safety's sake, the two split up so she does not endanger her husband with her bad papers. Lion proceeds ahead, while Marta watches him enter the hut, come out again a short while later, and climb down the mountain to Portbou, unmolested.

Marta waits a bit longer to give him a head start so that he is definitely out of harm's way. Then she gets up and likewise heads to the post. She knocks at the door and tries to appear as calm as possible. Luckily for her, one of the officers speaks French. She unloads a pile of packs of cigarettes on the table before him, saying she had heard the duties on them were so high it was not worth importing them. She would therefore rather give the packs to the friendly officers than pay even more money for them. At this, such bustling and shoving arises among the border guards that none of them shows any further interest in her papers and someone blindly puts an entry stamp on the document. She gets on with her descent straightaway.

In Portbou, she has arranged to meet Sharp and Lion at the Cook travel agency. It is housed in one of the town's undamaged buildings. Sharp is waiting for her there, but there is no trace of her husband. Marta is instantly terribly worried something might have happened to Lion on the descent. Sharp, they agree, will keep waiting for Lion at the travel agency; Marta will scour the town for him. She runs from café to café, from tavern to tavern – all of which are full – but Feuchtwanger is nowhere to be found. Only at the end does she stop at the city's finest and most expensive restaurant. There is Feuchtwanger, sitting over a meal and glad at her arrival: "Sit down and eat with me." He had completely forgotten the rendezvous point at the travel agency.

Marseille, late September 1940

Fry is still bargaining in Spain with the British ambassador when Miriam Davenport receives a tip at the Centre that the police plan to arrest Breitscheid, Hilferding, and Walter Mehring. She rushes to the Splendide, up to Mehring's room. Mehring is lying in bed, trembling from head to toe. He, too, has learned that he is to be taken away. Hastily, she warns Hiram Bingham at the consulate: an emergency, he must come at once, it is a matter of minutes. Then she runs downstairs to the lobby where half a dozen detectives are inquiring about Mehring's room number.

She is a diminutive and cheery young woman, just twenty-five years old, but, as she reminds herself, she is now also the secretary general of the Centre Américain de Secours, to which people entrust their lives. Miriam walks right up to the detectives, introduces herself by name and title, and declares Mehring's arrest absolutely impossible.

She intends to buy time, hoping for a miracle, so she digresses with a long speech, touching upon Mehring the writer, his international fame, and his serious illness, the influential women and men in the United States who have taken an active interest in his fate and well-being, including not least Eleanor Roosevelt, wife of President Franklin D. Roosevelt, and the damage it would do to France's reputation around the world were something to happen to this ailing poet, damage that would seriously compromise the hitherto friendly relations between the United States and the officers' so severely tested fatherland.

After a few minutes, the detectives lose patience, interrupting Miriam with the usual justifications. It is not they, workaday officers, who ordered Mehring's arrest, but their superiors, and they had issued them strict instructions that left them no leeway of any kind in decision-making. And so they were going to arrest Mehring now and take him away – by force if necessary. Right then, by the hotel entrance, Miriam spots the tall, always somewhat stiff, but very dignified frame of Hiram Bingham just entering the lobby, and so she, in turn, cuts the officers short and warns them very sternly to think long and hard about their next steps, because everything they do from this point onward would occur, in a sense, in view of the world public. "If you, messieurs, still have any doubts about my remarks, I ask you to turn your attention over there, where the American consul is personally watching these proceedings, since America takes great interest in them."

This changes everything. None of the officers had reckoned with this. They balk. They are rattled. They deliberate. One of them heads to the telephone and calls a superior. A long conversation ensues. Finally, he replaces the receiver and declares that they require an attestation. If Mehring presents a doctor's note saying that it is impossible for him to leave his bed, the arrest warrant will be suspended. Miriam immediately phones Mehring's physician. A few minutes later, the attestation has arrived, and the policemen depart.

Hilferding and Breitscheid are more adversely affected. They are arrested, though not handed over to the Germans for now. The police force them to move to a hotel in Arles, about a hundred kilometers from Marseille, where they will be detained under guard. Apparently, the authorities want to be sure they are available to them at all times.

Marseille, September 23, 1940

Fry returns from Madrid on the night train. Early in the morning, Lena Fischmann and Albert Hirschmann fetch him from the station and walk with him to the Hôtel Splendide for breakfast. The three are facing a huge catastrophe. The escape route over the Col de Belitres has become too unsafe; they have no other choice but to temporarily decommission their Underground Railroad. In addition, the police are now looking over the shoulder of the Czech ambassador, Vladimir Vochoč, so closely that he can no longer supply any fake passports. And then, what's more, a few days ago, the prefect of the *département* summoned the American consul and complained about "the activities of Dr. Bohn and Mr. Fry." He lacks proof, but the man is not stupid. He suspects that aid from the Centre Secours is not limited to handing its clients money or donations of clothing.

Fry books an appointment for the very next day with Consul Fullerton to speak with him about how they might appease the Frenchmen. The refugees' situation is much too serious to take the prefect's objections into account. They must look for ways they can enhance the Centre's cover.

But the conversation goes differently than Fry expected it to. Fullerton is an old-school diplomat. He sees it as his primary task to protect the interests of the United States; everything else he views as secondary. From his perspective, the situation is clear. The United States is not under any obligation to the refugees, and it does not consider conflicts with Pétain's regime worthwhile. If, therefore, Fry's and Bohn's activities constitute an annoyance to the French, Fullerton wants nothing to do with them. He forwarded the prefect's complaint at once to his superiors in Washington and received a crystal-clear reply. Fullerton slides the cable across the desk to Fry; he can read it for himself.

> THIS GOVERNMENT CANNOT REPEAT NOT COUNTENANCE THE ACTIVITIES AS REPORTED OF DR. BOHN AND MR. FRY AND OTHER PERSONS IN THEIR EFFORTS IN EVADING THE LAWS OF COUNTRIES WITH WHICH THE UNITED STATES MAINTAIN FRIENDLY RELATIONS

Fry is stunned. He feels betrayed. Never would he have expected Fullerton to stab him in the back. Since his arrival in Marseille, far more than a hundred refugees have been taken to safety already under his direction, among them several of the most famous to be stranded in France: Franz Werfel, Alma Mahler-Werfel, Lion Feuchtwanger, Heinrich and Golo Mann – giants of culture, admired the world over, who faced mortal danger. He had counted on appreciation for these successes. But all that occurs to the bureaucrats at the State Department is that they do "not countenance [his] activities."

To be sure, Fry knows from speaking with Hiram Bingham that the rescue visa program is a thorn in Fullerton's side. Although Fullerton is the consul in charge, he is allowed no say in allocating the emergency visas. Still, Fry would have expected his protection from the allegations of the French; after all, he and his people take serious risks. Most of them are Americans – Miriam Davenport, Mary Jayne Gold, Dick Ball, Charles Fawcett – all of whom could comfortably be following the war from America. But they are here, putting a great deal on the line to save people, people whose only offense is being a Jew or taking a stand against Hitler and his brutal regime.

Fullerton knows this, but in his view, it makes things not better, but rather even worse. The situation here in Marseille is quite unclear; professionalism and experience are necessary not to get caught in the middle. Fullerton has no use for good Samaritans who, intoxicated by their own kindheartedness, rush into dangerous situations out of which he, their consul, is supposed to extricate them in a pinch. Right now, the main political task is to keep America out of a war that costs the lives of hundreds of people in Europe each day. American soldiers are not supposed to have to die, too. And compared to this danger, Fry's rescue operations count for little. The Germans are dangerous and militarily horrifyingly successful; Fullerton is quite convinced they will win the war. "Why," he asks, "should we do something that upsets them?" Better not to make enemies of them.

For Fry, the conversation gets more and more insufferable. He is furious; only with great difficulty is he able to curb his anger. His whole life he has hated when authority figures demonstrate their power so impassively, when they do not ask whether something is right or wrong, but only what advantage it has. Politics without consideration for morality and humanity is, to him, pure cynicism. In the face of such accusations, however, Fullerton can spare little more than a shrug. Instead, he issues Fry an emphatic warning. The prefect will arrest him in the coming days and have him deported – an unpleasant procedure during which Fry will certainly have to spend several days or weeks in prison. Better for him to preempt that and return voluntarily to the United States.

Banyuls – Portbou, September 24–28, 1940

Lisa Fittko has found a room a few kilometers from the border, a tiny attic room, just big enough for a bed and a chair. She came here to fulfill her promise to scout out a safe escape route to Spain for herself and her friends. In the past few weeks, the mountain path near Cerbère served well, but ever since soldiers have patrolled regularly on the Col de Belitres, it has become an incalculable risk. She has thus asked around with people in Marseille who hail from this border region, communists like her whom she trusts. They have advised her to confer with Vincent Azéma, the mayor of Banyuls-sur-Mer. He is a socialist with a great deal of sympathy for the exiles.

The day before yesterday, she met Azéma, a short, broad-shouldered man with dark hair and a long, sharply profiled nose. She did not need to offer him much by way of explanation. He understood immediately what she was looking for and mentioned a way he called *la route Líster*. This trail is more difficult than the path over the Col de Belitres, leading farther away from the sea, deeper into the hinterlands, and higher up into the mountains. It is also considerably longer: fifteen kilometers, all told. In exchange, though, there are almost never police checks there. After Franco's victory, Enrique Líster, a commanding officer for the Spanish Republicans, led his soldiers to safety in France via this route.

Azéma dictated instructions to Lisa Fittko by heart for how to gain access to the *route Líster* between the vineyards of Banyuls, the points of orientation she must follow, and where the descent to Portbou begins. It would be best, he said in parting, if someone could stay for a while in Banyuls to take the many refugees still to come over the mountains.

This morning, Lisa Fittko wakes with a start when someone knocks at the door to her garret room. She blinks for a moment into the pale morning light, then there is another knock, and she gets up and answers the door. Standing outside is Walter Benjamin, a somewhat quirky friend she knows from Paris and with whom her husband spent several weeks in the Vernuche internment camp. To her, he is a typical scholar: erudite and perceptive, but clumsy in all practical matters. In her mind, she likes to call him "old Benjamin" even though he is not even fifty years old.

"Madame," Benjamin greets her, "please excuse the disturbance. Hopefully, I do not come at an inopportune time."

Benjamin's elaborate politeness, retained from his upper-class childhood around 1900, sounds like a personal protest against the vulgarization caused by the war.

"Your kind husband," he says, "told me how to find you. He said you would take me across the border to Spain."

She has only just arrived in Banyuls, and already her husband is sending her the first candidate to help. Lisa Fittko does not know whether she ought to view this as an excessive hardship or a compliment; her husband seems to think her capable of a great deal.

Because her room is too small for a second person, she arranges to meet Benjamin for a stroll through town. Yes, she then confirms to him, she knows of a secret route to Spain, but she must warn him that she has never walked the trail and only knows it from an oral account.

Benjamin's mind is made up, however; he has his back against the wall. His transit visas he so arduously acquired in Marseille are in danger of expiring in the next few days, so he must put the border behind him as quickly as possible, preferably today. Besides, he is not alone. He has brought along two acquaintances from Marseille, the photographer Henny Gurland and her seventeen-year-old son Joseph. When Fittko realizes he will brook no objections, she would at least like to share the responsibility with Benjamin. She visits Azéma once more with him so that Benjamin can be given the description of the *route Líster* firsthand.

Azéma advises them to familiarize themselves with the first segment of the route that afternoon in daylight. It leads into the vineyards above

Banyuls to a clearing about an hour's distance away. There they should turn around and go back to town to walk the entire route to the border and Portbou the next day. It is important to know the beginning part of the route well so that they can find their way even in darkness. This part is the only section monitored by the police. But if they blend in with the countryfolk headed to work in the vineyards in the morning before sunrise and dress inconspicuously in a beret or headscarf, then no gendarme will be able to distinguish them from the locals.

Benjamin fetches the Gurlands from the inn where he is staying and brings along a black briefcase he does not under any circumstances want to leave unattended in his room.

"My new manuscript is inside," he explains.

"But why have you brought it with you on this reconnaissance errand?" Fittko asks.

"This briefcase is the most important thing to me, you see," he replies. "I mustn't lose it. The manuscript must be saved. It is more important than my person."

With Benjamin in tow, the group makes only slow progress. The ascent causes him great difficulty, but he does not complain. The directions Azéma gave them are reliable. Still, they reach the clearing Azéma mentioned not after one hour, but after three. Benjamin lies down in the grass immediately and closes his eyes, so greatly did the route exhaust him.

When after resting Lisa Fittko urges them to leave so they are back in Banyuls in time before dark, Benjamin does not stand up. "I'm staying here. I'll spend the night here, and you'll join me again tomorrow morning."

Fittko does not want to accept this. Benjamin has no blanket for the night with him, no provisions, not even water. Again, however, he is not to be deterred in his decision. If he descends now along with Lisa and the others, he says, there is no way he will manage the entire route tomorrow. This first part alone – according to Azéma about a third of the whole distance – has taken a lot out of him. He must pace himself. Only then will he be able to handle the remaining two thirds tomorrow.

In the end, Lisa Fittko concedes, and when she arrives back at the clearing the next day along with the Gurlands, Benjamin has indeed made it through the night. The second ascent from Banyuls presented no problems; Azéma's advice has stood the test. They had to observe ironclad silence while still in town so as not to give themselves away with their German accents. Otherwise, they looked exactly like the winegrowers in the dark. And then, outside town, where it gradually grew lighter, there were no more checks to be feared.

After they have left the clearing, hardly anything like a trail can be made out. The path is overgrown on both sides by chest-high bushes and interrupted by low rocks that must be scrambled over painstakingly. The ground is covered with flat, rough-edged chunks of stone; each step demands one's full attention so that one does not start sliding. But with Azéma's outline of the route, they are able to orient themselves well even here. A portion of the trail leads right past a mountain road, where they must be quiet, lest they be heard by patrols. Still, they cannot be seen from the road as their path is concealed by a mountain ridge.

Benjamin seems unagitated and calm. He walks slowly but at a steady tempo, stopping every ten minutes and resting for around a minute. "With this method," he says, "I will make it to the end. I stop at regular intervals – I must take the break *before* becoming exhausted. One mustn't ever wear oneself out completely."

Because he has enough to carry already with his person, Lisa Fittko and young Gurland alternate in relieving him of his briefcase. Benjamin sweats and breathes heavily. Finally, they come to an upland vineyard that is very steep, and there is no way for them to go around it. They must climb up between the rows of vine stocks. That, however, lies beyond Benjamin's powers. Joseph Gurland and Lisa Fittko place him between themselves, he puts his arms on their shoulders, and they practically pull him up the slope step by step.

After that come only minor inclines; the worst is behind them. When they reach the summit, and thus the border to Spain, Fittko walks a few paces ahead. She wants to gain an overview of the coming section of the route. When she lifts her gaze on the pass, a dazzling panorama opens up before her. Far below lies the sea, smooth as a mirror and dark blue, and before it the foothills of the mountains, sloping downward ever more, overgrown by scrub and vineyards in every hue of green and brown – a vista so overwhelmingly beautiful that for a few moments she is speechless.

At this point, she really ought to take her leave of Benjamin and the Gurlands. The route no longer presents any major difficulties, gently descending down into Portbou, and the three have the necessary identification and visas they need for entry. Lisa Fittko, by contrast, is carrying no papers whatsoever. She would certainly be arrested if she were to run into a police officer. Yet she just cannot part ways and accompanies the others until the first buildings in Portbou are within sight. Only then does she turn around. She has been on her feet now for ten hours and must see to it that she returns to Banyuls. Now, however, she has gained the certainty of having found a passable escape route.

Before Benjamin reaches the tiny customs office of Portbou with the Gurlands, they stumble upon another group of refugees: four women, including the attorney Carina Birman, who worked for the Austrian embassy in Paris. They walk the last stretch together. The seven of them ultimately sit before the border agents to receive the entry stamp without which the continuing journey to Lisbon is not possible.

They are forced to wait for a long while and gradually become nervous. Then, it is suddenly as if they had walked straight into a trap. The officers arrest all of them. Today of all days, the directive came from Madrid to immediately deport back to France all refugees who enter the country illegally without a French exit visa. Perhaps, though it remains unclear, they are even to be handed over to the German occupiers.

There are no exceptions. All protests are futile. Since it is now evening and no more trains are running through the tunnel to Cerbère today, all seven are led under guard to a simple hotel and quartered there for the night.

The state of the arrestees is abysmal. They try to call the American consulate in Barcelona to arrange help, but at such a late hour, they are unable to reach anyone there. The final hope is not to be delivered up to the Germans, but to the French. Even then, however, they must reckon with ending up in an internment camp. Benjamin knows the conditions in the camps; only with a great deal of luck did he survive the two months he spent in Vernuche a year earlier.

After Carina Birman has moved into the room assigned to her, she hears a loud rattling from one of the neighboring rooms, and when she goes to look, she discovers a despondent, physically completely exhausted Benjamin. He is lying on his bed half naked and keeps staring at an opened gold pocket watch. There is no way, he declares to the attorney, that he will allow himself to be transported to the border, and what's more, he is unwilling to leave the hotel. Birman replies that there may well be no other choice. Benjamin shakes his head. On the contrary, he says, there is an alternative for him; he is carrying pills with him that contain a poison sure to work.

Later, Benjamin calls out for Henny Gurland. Worried, she enters his room. He lies in bed feebly, his breathing shallow and labored, and asks her to pass off his condition as a sudden illness. He hands her two letters, one addressed to her and one to his friend Theodor W. Adorno, then loses consciousness. Gurland immediately calls for a doctor, but when one finally arrives at the hotel, it is already too late. Benjamin dies shortly thereafter.

News of the death of a refugee who was to be deported spreads quickly in tiny Portbou. A priest and around twenty monks are summoned from a nearby monastery. Carina Birman is sitting in the hotel's dining room when the clerics pass by her holding candles, as if in a procession, to sing a requiem at the death bed. Then the police interrogate the witnesses to record the events of the night. A magistrate examines the body and seizes Benjamin's personal effects. In the course of the official record keeping, however, inconsistencies creep in. The doctor lists the cause of death as a cerebral hemorrhage, probably to conceal the suicide, and claims to have visited Benjamin four times during the night. Since Benjamin is a common first name in Spain but unusual as a surname, the deceased is recorded and buried under the name "Dr. Benjamin Walter."

Henny Gurland burns the pair of letters Benjamin gave her in the morning so as not to be even more deeply entangled in the matter and potentially detained in Portbou. For Benjamin's death provides the others with a new, unexpected opportunity. The Spanish officials are shaken and temporarily refrain from carrying out the announced deportation. Then, the day after, the disastrous directive to only allow refugees with a French exit visa through to Portugal, is officially lifted again. As a result, everyone wants to get to the train station as quickly as possible to catch the train to Barcelona.

The only thing of Benjamin's left in Portbou are his belongings. In the magistrate's notes, there is mention of "a leather briefcase such as businessmen use, a men's watch, a pipe, six photographs, an x-ray image,

The last known photograph of Walter Benjamin, from the official death registry of Portbou

a pair of spectacles, various letters, periodicals, and a handful of other papers of unknown content, as well as some money."

None of this ever comes to light again. All of it goes missing. Whether the manuscript Benjamin considered more important than his own person was among the "papers of unknown content," no one knows.

Paris, September 27, 1940

The German authorities order a census of Jews in the occupied zone. Everyone must have their names and addresses registered, and Jewish businesspeople are forced to install signs in their stores that read "Entreprise juive – Jewish business." The suspicion is that future arrest lists are being prepared from the registration lists of the Jews.

Pamiers, late September 1940

Anna Seghers and her children are now living with a fortune teller. She goes by the name Madame Jeanne and reads tarot cards for superstitious citizens of Pamiers. Seghers gets along well with her. Madame Jeanne does not demand much for the two small rooms she has ceded to her, and, aside from her affinity for clairvoyance, she is an intelligent and agreeable woman.

Except for three medieval towers and an austere cathedral, Pamiers does not have much to offer. It is a small town like hundreds of others. But there is a *lycée* for Peter and Ruth, and from here it is only ten kilometers to Le Vernet, where Rodi has been incarcerated for half a year. Le Vernet is the nastiest of the French internment camps: a double barbed-wire fence, violent and abusive guards, unheated barracks, thirty grams of bread per day, a watery soup for dinner. It strongly resembles a prison camp, even if the inmates have done nothing wrong except be undesirable foreigners.

Once a week, Anna and the children get up before sunrise, take the train one stop north, and arrive at the camp gate at dawn. Usually, a throng of people has already gathered there to visit the prisoners. Guards search their bags, help themselves to the bread Anna and the children set aside from their rations during the week for Rodi, and lead them to the visitors' barracks.

Rodi is severely emaciated. His clothes have turned to rags over these six months. That he has nevertheless remained somewhat healthy is due not least to his fellow prisoners. They treat him with great respect and deliver him, wherever possible, from many of the camps' travails. Rodi studied sociology and philosophy and is a passionate teacher. After the First World War, he fled from Hungary to Germany as a young communist. In Berlin, the KPD [Communist Party of Germany] tasked him with establishing the Marxist Workers' School. After Hitler's seizure of power, he founded the Freie Deutsche Hochschule [Free German University] for communist exiles in Paris. In the camp, he has run into many of his Paris students again, and even here he continues his lectures on dialectical and historical materialism; he is not easy to hold back in his compulsion to spread Marxist thought.

Over the summer, the camp commandant occasionally allowed individual internees who were to receive visas for the United States to be transferred to Les Milles camp near Aix-en-Provence. There the men receive parole to go to Marseille to apply for the necessary transit visas and the French exit visa. At this point, however, stricter rules are in effect. For weeks now, the commandant has not allowed anyone else to go to Les Milles. Anna Seghers' greatest concern is the winter. Here, at the edge of the Pyrenees, it gets bitterly cold. The wind coming down out of the mountains is icy. How the men are to survive this in barracks without stoves is a mystery to her.

October 1940

Marseille, early October 1940

The leather goods trader has now completely emptied out his warehouse in the Rue Grignan. This way, Fry gains more space for the Centre's offices and can hire additional people. He reorganizes their work. Interviews with refugees are now to take place only in the morning. In the afternoon, he sits down with his closest confidants to decide whom they can help and whom they have to turn away. The lists he has brought with him from America do not always play the main role in this choice. Naturally, everyone whose name is on them is to be rescued, but so are others, aside from them, who are at risk. By this stage, Fry no longer feels beholden to the stipulations of the ERC. He is convinced he can better judge the state of things from Marseille than the committee can in New York.

Franz von Hildebrand is the first of his people to leave the Centre. The American consulate obtained visas for him and his family, and he does not want to pass up the opportunity to get his wife and children out of France. In his place, Fry has hired an archconservative Berliner, Marcel Chaminade, a short, rotund man with a bald head who once worked in the press office of the French foreign ministry, as well as Marcel Verzeano, a young Romanian doctor who shall tend to their clients' frayed nerves. In addition, Fry adds two Frenchmen to his team, Daniel Bénédite and Jean Gemähling. Bénédite and his wife Théodora were recommended to him by Mary Jayne Gold; they are the friends who in desperation entrusted Gold with their small son Pierre while fleeing the Germans. Daniel once worked as secretary for the prefect of the Paris police and knows the organizational structure and methods of the French security services in detail. Jean Gemähling, a chemist, is a friend of Bénédite's; they got to know one another in the military. He is from the Alsace, yet seems like he comes from Normandy: tall, blond, and blue-eyed. Originally, he sought a way to join de Gaulle's troops in England, but then he got stuck in Marseille.

In addition to them comes Hans Sahl, a German film and literary critic, a Jew and a socialist. Among other things, he wrote songs and sketches for Erika Mann's cabaret *Die Pfeffermühle*. Most writers loyal to Moscow avoid him, including Bertolt Brecht and Anna Seghers, because he publicly condemns Stalin's crimes as forcefully as he does Hitler's. For that reason, he feels even more deeply isolated than other refugees. He lives, he says, in an exile within exile – he is ostracized by the ostracized.

The first time he heard from Fry and visited him at the Hôtel Splendide, Sahl could not even believe that someone had assumed the risks of the journey to France to help people like him. Fry, who as always was afraid his room might be bugged, drew him to the window and whispered that he would send his name to America by wire so as to apply for a rescue visa for him. Sahl was overwhelmed by this unexpected goodwill. Tears streamed down his face when Fry also disbursed a small sum of money as a first round of support.

Since Fry now knows all too well how long it can take for the President's Advisory Committee in Washington to approve a visa, he summarily hired Sahl as an advisor and procured a room for him at the Splendide. Sahl possesses a profound knowledge about German literature and the artists forced to flee from the Nazis. He is the perfect information bureau for when they are sitting down together in the afternoon and need information about unfamiliar clients who claim to be writers, theater folk, screenwriters, or journalists.

Vichy, October 3, 1940

Marshal Pétain's government passes a "Law on the Status of the Jews." Jews are to be removed from France's public life. They may no longer assume any political roles or upper-level posts in the administration and may no longer work in the field of diplomacy, for the police, in law, for the press, or in the education sector. The next day, the prefects are accorded by decree the right to place "foreign citizens of the Jewish race" under house arrest at their discretion without a trial or commit them to a camp.

Justus "Gussie" Rosenberg above the Marseille harbor

Marseille, early October 1940

Gussie Rosenberg is the ideal courier. He speaks French without any accent, looks like he is only sixteen, and is blond on top of that. No policeman in Marseille would suspect he was a Jewish escape agent.

Over the first few weeks Gussie worked for the Centre, he shuttled mostly between the offices on the Rue Grignan and the post office to send telegrams to New York. Now, for the first time, however, Fry gives him an illegal mission. Gussie knows Bil Freier, the Centre's forger. He observed him weeks ago at the Old Port sketching portraits for passersby or customers of the cafés for a few francs. Without his ever having to correct a line, likenesses came to life under this man's delicate fingers at a frenzied pace, as on a conveyor belt. Gussie could not tear himself away from the spectacle.

Now he is supposed to take several still unmarked *cartes d'identité* along with passport photos to Freier and pick up from him completed identification papers furnished with forged stamps and signatures. Gussie is so insouciant that it only occurs to him on the way back from Freier's hotel the danger he is in if the police catch him with a batch of forgeries in his jacket pocket. Instinctively, he glances over his shoulder to see if he is being followed and tries to throw off potential pursuers like he has seen gangsters do in the movies. He strolls calmly into a large department store, but swiftly leaves it again by a different entrance, then springs into a departing bus, and transfers at the next station. Only after that does he feel safe again and returns to the office.

Marseille, early October 1940

Albert Hirschmann has his ear to the ground. He maintains contacts among the authorities, in the black market, in the mafia, and, not least, in the various ideologically quarreling groups of exiles. Now he has been informed that the honorary consul of Lithuania in Aix-en-Provence is selling passports to his country for reasonable prices. They are even a bit better than the passports the Centre used to get from the Czech consul Vochoč, because Lithuania disappeared from the map not a year ago, but a mere two months ago, subsumed by the Soviet Union. This would solve their Underground Railroad's first problem.

Hirschmann has heard from another source that two Germans recently succeeded in getting refugees to Spain via a secret route through the Pyrenees. Apparently, a married couple, the Fittkos, are involved, leftist resistance fighters from Berlin who are currently staying in Marseille. Such people are extremely careful and difficult to track down. If they were not, they would not have survived the period since 1933. But Hirschmann himself comes from Berlin and was active there in the Young Socialist Workers. He has a feel for people like the Fittkos and here, too, finds middlemen who can pass them a message. He asks them to meet with him, Fry, and Bohn in a run-down bistro near the Old Port. The Centre Secours needs their help.

The locale is poorly chosen. Hans and Lisa Fittko realize that at once. The two Americans to whom Hirschmann introduces them look far too healthy, unjaded, and neat. They do not suit the joint. They stand out.

But without waiting for the Fittkos' commentary, Fry gets right to the point. It has gotten around, he says, that they know a new route across the border to Spain. The Centre has many refugees outfitted with the necessary passports and visas, but ever since the police began monitoring the route near Cerbère, these people cannot get out of France. Would the two be willing to help them?

"Yes, of course," says Lisa Fittko. "I can write down the route and describe it to you."

Fry hesitates, then explains to her that he and Bohn are not talking about some handful of people, but about hundreds they want to smuggle out of the country in the next few weeks – including British soldiers and pilots stuck in Marseille. The Centre needs a well-organized point of contact near the border for this, and guides with local knowhow and steady nerves to help the refugees on the route over the mountains.

Fry clears his throat. "Money will not be a problem," he says. "It is a question of finding the right person with experience at the border, someone willing to do this and who can be relied upon." He clears his throat again. "We've been told," he continues, "that you both have taken anti-Nazi literature and people across the German border. For a few months, would you …"

"Us?" says Hans Fittko. "No, that won't work."

"No," his wife adds, "we can't afford that. Now that we finally have our papers together, we need to figure out how we'll be able to get out."

Their lives in recent years were dangerous enough. There was no doubt the Germans would kill them immediately if they got their hands on them. They escaped the Gestapo's investigators often enough only by some coincidence. Now they finally have all the documentation and visas they need to go to ground abroad. The door is wide open for them. They just have to walk through it.

But Fry stands his ground. He absolutely needs them for his scheme. "I promise you," he says, "that if you get stuck here because of working the border, we will help you out."

Hans and Lisa set little store by such assurances. They have already experienced too much to get involved in such a matter. Even if Fry is serious about every word, his situation might already have changed tomorrow such that he is no longer in a position to keep his commitment.

Whatever they do, they do on their own account. They alone must bear the consequences. They must not count on help.

Hirschmann also tries to persuade them. The two Americans, he says quickly in German, are not especially seasoned, but they take the matter very seriously, and they have something rare in illegal work: money.

While Fry can speak some German, he has only picked up the word for "money."

"*Combien*?" he asks. "How much?"

"What does he mean?" Hans Fittko asks in irritation. "*Combien* what?"

There are in fact bands of smugglers in the Pyrenees who funnel refugees to Spain for exorbitant sums. But money was never the incentive for Hans and his wife.

Those who take men of an age fit for military service across the border, he says to Fry – British soldiers, for instance – will also be punished with death by the French. "And you offer us money? We'd have to be insane. Do you even know what an antifascist is? Do you understand the word 'conviction'?"

Fry apologizes, a misunderstanding, his question was not meant in this way. He quickly brings the conversation back to the many people whom the Centre wants to help and also, with its financial means, is able to help.

Hans Fittko ponders for a moment, and then it is he who raises the subject of money again. "Whoever is stationed at the border," he says, "will need enough money to live there. It doesn't have to be much, but it needs to be enough so that everything goes smoothly. They should also have a cushion for emergencies in case something doesn't work out with the refugees."

Fry agrees with him. It is best, he says, if the Centre restricts itself to paying for expenses and apart from that gives the people at the new border station completely free rein.

Hans Fittko hesitates. "My wife and I will have to think this over carefully," he says. Then they get up and leave.

Marseille, early October 1940

The man who takes a seat in front of Miriam Davenport's desk looks like an armchair academic: pale, around fifty, receding hairline, rimless glasses. In the course of her work for the Centre, Miriam has heard many stories of escape, all of which resemble one another. They involve people whose worlds have been turned upside down, breathless tales full of drama and panicked fear. There are many recurring motifs. The terrifying speed of German tanks. The convoys wedged in on the country roads. Fear of not crossing the Loire in time. Hedgehoppers. French soldiers throwing down their weapons.

But with this man, a chain smoker who literally lights one cigarette from the other, the stories sound different. Miriam conducts the first customary interview to find out whether he is among the artists or intellectuals for whom the Centre feels responsible. His reports of escape are tinged with an undercurrent of curiosity and expectation. You can be in a good mood while living in a tent in the rain, he says. You can sleep well and deeply in a slaughterhouse. You can watch people throw aside their belongings because they become burdensome. Where everything collapses, space is created for new things. Destruction does not scare this man. He possesses a rich wealth of experience in dealing with political cabals, chaotic coups d'état, and sudden changes of government.

The man's name is Victor Serge. His own parents were Russian revolutionaries by vocation who fled the tsar's regime into Belgian exile. He himself has also devoted the majority of his life to revolutions. He first served time in prison in his early twenties in France because he had held up banks with a gang of anarchists. As soon as he was released, he joined a socialist uprising in Spain. In the wake of the Russian Revolution, he fought first for the Bolsheviks in 1919, then against them in the Kronstadt Rebellion. In the German annus horribilis 1923, he failed in his attempt to instigate a communist revolution in Hamburg. Back in the Soviet Union, he opposed Stalin's politics of terror, writing articles and books until the secret police made him disappear to a penal colony in the Urals.

In 1935 at the great Writers Congress in Paris, opinions about him and his arrest were divided between independent leftist authors and Stalinists loyal to Moscow. At the time, in the brutally hot hall of the Maison de la Mutualité, the organizers of the congress used all possible means to try to quash a debate about his fate. Serge had become a symbolic figure of communist protest against communist dictatorship. Since he had fought for revolutions in France, Spain, Russia, and Germany, many politically involved intellectuals in Europe knew him and trusted his judgment when it came to the murderous dictatorship in the Soviet Union. The media campaign for his redemption ultimately became so dangerous for the regime's reputation that Stalin actually let him emigrate in the year after the congress.

Miriam is riveted by this man. To her, he seems like a living monument to the century's European revolutions. At this point, he has broken with his belief in Marxism and advocates for democratic socialism. The chaos of the exodus of millions in the face of German troops was unable to affect him adversely. He is homeless, he says, living in Marseille with his son and girlfriend with neither money nor a roof over his head, but compared to any Nazi, he feels splendidly superior.

Marseille, early October 1940

Ever since his argument with Consul Fullerton, Fry has been regularly summoned to the consulate and urged to leave France. Frank Bohn fares similarly. He has been in Marseille since late July, has obtained rescue visas for around a hundred SPD politicians and union leaders, and has taken them to Spain. But Fullerton's stratagem of attrition demoralizes him; he wants to return to America. The night before his departure, he asks Fry to take care of his remaining clients, especially Breitscheid and Hilferding. Then he shakes his hand one last time and boards the train for the border.

The State Department has also gotten actively involved now. It informs Frank Kingdon, the head of the ERC, that Fry has violated French laws and must be withdrawn from Marseille immediately before the French arrest him. Kingdon believes the officials, yet also suspects that it will not be easy to induce Fry to return. To avoid time-consuming arguments with him, he asks Eileen to formulate the message to her husband. For his decision, Kingdon also loops in Paul Hagen, the co-founder of the committee, and Mildred Adams, with whom Fry very closely collaborates in his day-to-day work. Eileen lists these three ERC people most important for Fry at the very beginning and adopts a very personal, very worried tone in the cable:

> MILDRED FRANK PAUL ALL BELIEVE YOU MUST RETURN IMMEDIATELY STOP SITUATION SERIOUS YOUR PEOPLE

ENDANGERED STOP SUCCESSOR WILL LEAVE EARLIEST POSSIBLE DATE STOP

Fry does not respond at first. He maintains silence and lets the warning come to nothing. His closest confidant, Albert Hirschmann, is convinced the French police will close the Centre Secours the same day Fry leaves the country. That would be the end of all hope for his clients. Within the span of a few weeks in Marseille, he has accrued humanitarian commitments, the scope of which obviously no one in the ERC envisioned. People like Mehring, Breitscheid, or Hilferding have no chance of survival without him. He has just made promises to the Fittkos, who are to risk their lives for the Centre, that he cannot keep from America.

Fry's mind is quickly made up. He will not leave France only because the State Department wishes it. If the French want to be rid of him, they ought to throw him in jail or expel him. He will not go voluntarily.

Only when he cannot keep Eileen waiting any longer does Fry send her a response. But strictly speaking, this letter is not even addressed to her, but to the French postal censor. "It appears," Fry writes, "that the prefecture had got the absurd idea that some members of my staff had been conducting persons illegally over the border. Actually no member of my staff had been near the border or has been since. … The only trouble we have is with certain members of the American Foreign Service [...], who evidently busy themselves with slandering and libeling our organization and the Americans active in it."

Marseille, early October 1940

Charles Fawcett speaks only a little French. Nevertheless, there could be no better doorman for the office on the Rue Grignan than him. He is tall with a very solid build, a pro-wrestler who maintains his calm and through his very body language defuses potential conflicts early on. In addition, he speaks such a warm, sincere Southern American English that people like doing what he says even if they do not understand him.

Without Fry's knowledge, Fawcett sets up his own little refugee program. One of the attorneys who work for the Centre seeks an American willing to marry a Jewish woman being detained in an internment camp. Fawcett agrees, and following a brief ceremony at the civil registry office, she is regarded as an American, thereby solving all of her problems as if by magic. She is immediately released from the camp, receives a French exit visa, and is able to flee to Lisbon.

As soon as the woman has left France, the attorney prosecutes the divorce – and procures for Fawcett, once more single, the next camp inmate who wants to get married. Fawcett rarely sees his wives for more than a few minutes, and since the attorney selects the right marriage registrars, everything runs smoothly with the French authorities as well. Things settle into a bizarre rhythm; just about every two weeks, Fawcett leaves his work for one or two hours, says 'I do' to some anonymous bride, and returns at once to the Rue Grignan to continue guarding the entrance to the Centre.

Marseille – Le Vernet, early October 1940

Gradually, autumn arrives. The wind snatches the leaves from the trees, yet the street cafés along the Old Port are still bustling with life. Mary Jayne Gold looks for a table on the terrace of the Basso. She has arranged to meet Miriam Davenport and Albert Hirschmann, but both are running late. Located directly in the line of sight from the Basso is Fort St. Nicolas, where Killer Raymond is serving time in prison. Mary Jayne was allowed to visit him twice and brought him more food than she could carry. Miriam and Gussie had to help her haul it.

When the two friends finally arrive, Albert orders cognac for everyone and tells of four Germans stuck in Le Vernet. The four men once belonged to Paul Hagen's organization Neu Beginnen, and Hagen has received rescue visas for them. For weeks now, however, they have been denied permission to leave the camp to pick up the visas in Marseille. Fry has written the camp commandant multiple times on behalf of the Centre and asked him to send along the four under guard but has not received a word in reply. Even letters from Bingham, who advocates for the men as the representative of the American consulate, prompted no response. Hagen is gravely concerned that the Gestapo will find out where the men are and demand they be handed over. They are all at risk of death by guillotine.

"Why are you telling me this?" Mary Jayne asks.

"Because we'd like you to go to Le Vernet and persuade the commandant to let the four of them come to Marseille."

"Me?" Mary Jayne is dismayed. "I can't do that. I haven't the faintest idea how to do that."

Albert does not acknowledge her in the least. "As soon as the four are in Marseille, they'll give the guards the slip. They're experienced people. Then we'll take care of everything else."

"Yeah, fine. But I can't do that."

She only has to go there, Albert explains to her, and claim that their wives are horribly worried – that they sent Mary Jayne to ask the commandant personally to let the men travel to the consulate.

"Sure, but I'm a very bad liar," Mary Jayne says. "Others are better at it. What about you, Miriam?"

"Miriam shakes her head. "You've got to do it."

"Why me?"

"Because," Albert says, looking into her eyes, "with your face people will simply believe anything."

"What's that supposed to mean? With my face?"

"Mary Jayne, you have the most innocent face I've ever seen. People believe everything you say."

"That's ridiculous," she protests.

"You're our last shot," Albert says. "The heads of four men are at risk."

It is the image of these four heads ending up beneath the guillotine that changes Mary Jayne's mind. She hesitates, then finally gives in. "Fine, okay, Albert. I'll try."

That same evening, Miriam helps her pack. She only needs one bag since she will not stay longer than one night. Her colleagues from the Centre think she must look as attractive and rich as possible; her appearance should literally dazzle the commandant. On Miriam's advice, she wears a deep-blue dress by Parisian couturier Robert Pigeut, the color of which terrifically complements her blonde hair, as well as a diamond brooch and a diamond ring. So as not to stand out too much on the train ride, she wears a beige raincoat over the top.

Mary Jayne must change in Toulouse and take a regional train toward Le Vernet. She is nervous and smokes too much. Naturally, she mulls over whether she ought to sleep with the commandant so that he will let the men travel to Marseille. Albert spoke of her innocent face, which can sell people any lie. That was thoughtful of him, but illogical. After all, this is not about lying to the commandant, but about asking him for something, inducing him to a bit more generosity. But if she goes to bed with him, what guarantees does she have that he will actually release the four men afterward?

Le Vernet is a miserable cesspool at the edge of the Pyrenees. There is a café right by the train station. Mary Jayne orders the most expensive cognac they serve there and asks the man behind the counter to mind her bag. Then she removes her raincoat, places it with the bag, and heads out.

It is only two hundred meters to the camp entrance. The two military guards open the boom gate, and one of them takes her to the administrative building. It is a hideously ugly box resembling a warehouse with high walls, into which windows that are much too small were installed as an afterthought. Two watchtowers outfitted with searchlights jut up behind it.

In the orderly room, Gold asks for the commandant. An officer around forty years of age approaches her. He seems serious and stiff but is graying at the temples congenially.

"What can I do for you, madame?" He pauses. "You have your husband or beau here at the camp?"

"Mademoiselle," Mary Jayne corrects him, "not madame." And, she goes on, it is not a husband she has at the camp, but four friends. The commandant cannot help but smile, pauses again for a moment, then invites her into his office.

It is only a tiny room with a plain desk and a narrow window, which Mary Jayne walks over to immediately. "What a wonderful view you have of the mountains."

The officer agrees, listing the names of several peaks, but then returns to his businesslike tone. "Mademoiselle, what can I do for you? You have four friends here. Their names, please."

Mary Jayne does not respond immediately. She wants to play for time. She notices the commandant eyeing her closely. She is a pleasant surprise for him, a diversion amid the quotidian monotony. Seduction requires time, though, so she first tells of the four wives of her friends, of their delightful children and the horrible worries the wives have for their husbands, as well as of the consul in Marseille who has American visas for all four families.

The commandant sits down behind his desk and begins observing her. What she recounts about the wives' anguish he has heard a dozen times before. "Please, mademoiselle," he interrupts her, "what is the purpose of your visit? What are the names of the four?"

"Of course," Mary Jayne says, "it's just that some people are so … unfriendly."

"It's not a crime," the commandant replies, "to have American visas."

Mary Jayne pulls herself together. "Franz Bögler, Hans Tittel, Fritz Lamm, Siegfried Pfeffer."

The commandant passes their names along to his adjutant and has their files brought to him. As soon as they are on his desk, he arranges them in alphabetical order and begins paging through. From Bögler's dossier, he pulls one of Fry's letters.

He holds it up and look inquisitively at Mary Jayne. "The Centre Américain de Secours?"

"We are," she replies, "a welfare committee and travel agency." She sheepishly fingers the uppermost button on her blouse, which pops open as if by accident. "I'd be so very happy if you could give the men permission to travel to Marseille – under guard of course." She places her hand with the diamond ring on the side of his desk and slowly strokes along its edge.

"That is possible on occasion," the commandant says.

"I thought it'd be better," she says, "to come here and meet you in person. Better than sending a letter or a telegram."

"Much better, much better," he agrees. "So you work for a welfare organization. What would you think of cheering up an old soldier a bit? There is damn little amusement in this godforsaken place. Would you be so kind as to go to dinner with me this evening?"

"Oh," Mary Jayne says, "how nice. What an excellent idea."

There are, he apologizes, precious few good restaurants in this remote area, alas. The best one is in Pamiers, a town ten kilometers south of the camp. Might he pick her up at six thirty at the café Les Platanes?

Before Mary Jayne leaves the camp, she asks to be allowed to meet briefly with her friends. All four have shaved heads; the skin stretches over their gaunt faces. They stand before her marveling like children before a Christmas tree. She gives her name and says that Varian Fry has sent her to find a way to get them to Marseille. Then she asks how they are faring in the camp. The men's report comes off as matter-of-fact. There is no organized sadism. Some guards treat them brutally, others do not. Filth, cold, and deficient hygiene cause them the greatest trouble. "Dachau was much cleaner, there's no comparison." While saying goodbye, Mary Jayne whispers to them: "Until soon in Marseille."

She catches the last bus to Pamiers. Luckily, a hotel is part of Les Platanes café, and it has a vacant room for her.

At six thirty on the dot, she takes a seat on the terrace and orders a dry vermouth as an aperitif. Sitting at the other tables are merchants or wealthy farmers from the region talking business. The commandant is a bit late. For Mary Jayne, this is no problem. She is in no hurry. She orders a second vermouth. Little by little, the terrace empties out until, finally, she is the last one there. At nine o'clock, she gets up and goes to her room. The commandant has stood her up.

The next morning, she realizes she cannot simply leave. She has to go back to the camp to find out what went wrong yesterday. Everything inside her bristles at doing so, but she has no other choice if she intends to do anything for the four men in spite of it all.

She is in luck and finds a truck to drop her at the camp entrance. When she enters the orderly room, the commandant walks over to her immediately and leads her into his office.

"Well," she asks, "what happened to our little rendezvous?"

"Mademoiselle, I assure you I would have preferred to dine with you yesterday."

"And?"

"I had to go out to eat with the Gestapo last night."

"My God."

"I would much rather have eaten with you."

"I believe it." Mary Jayne pauses a moment. "And ... what will happen to my friends?"

"Your friends will travel to Marseille. Under guard."

"Really? Do you promise?"

"I give you my word as a French officer."

"So I can rest easy and travel back?"

"The next train leaves in half an hour," the commandant replies. "Your friends will arrive in Marseille tomorrow."

"I owe you a great deal of thanks," Mary Jayne says. "I'll never be able to make it up to you."

Relieved, she starts back to the train station. Things have taken the best possible turn for her. What luck, she thinks. Perhaps it would have been a good idea, even if she had had to sleep with the commandant, always to tell the story like this and never differently.

Marseille, October 7, 1940

Hiram Bingham phones the Centre and asks Fry to come to the consulate right away if possible. In his office, he shows him information that was wired overnight from Washington. Although Lion Feuchtwanger arrived in Lisbon a week after the Werfels and the Manns, he got a ticket for passage to America a few days before they did. The day before yesterday, he landed ashore in New Jersey on the luxury ocean liner SS *Excalibur*. On the pier, a reporter for the *New York Times* was waiting for him and asked to interview him.

Naturally, Feuchtwanger realized he would put Fry's organization in extreme danger if he divulged details of his escape in the newspaper. He thus put on a very secretive act, but was still incautious enough to speak of "American friends" who procured fake papers for him and got him out of France on "a smuggler's pass over the Pyrenees."

Bingham and Fry are speechless. They impress upon all their clients never to let anything get out about the activities of the Centre Secours. But Feuchtwanger pays no heed and in his loquacity furnishes the Gestapo with valuable clues. The information alone that "American friends" helped him fuels suspicion about Fry and his people. And the tip about the route over the Pyrenees is virtually an invitation to monitor the frontier near Cerbère even more closely.

Marseille, early October 1940

The commandant of Le Vernet kept his word. He actually sent Bögler, Tittel, Lamm, and Pfeffer to Marseille, together with two guards. The men arrive in the afternoon. Since Bingham has prepared everything at the consulate, there are no delays, and he can hand them their visas that same day.

No one expected this. Usually, visa matters drag on for weeks. Neither the four prisoners nor their two chaperones are expected back in the camp for a while. There is thus no reason why they should not stay on in Marseille for a few more days – a short vacation from camp life.

It quickly becomes apparent that the guards are much more interested in prostitutes and wine than in their supervisory obligations. To nurture their passions, the internees pass them money they received from the Centre. That very first evening, the two soldiers become so thoroughly inebriated that there can be no more talk of supervision. They arrange a meeting place with the four prisoners for the next day and stagger into their quarters to sleep off their intoxication.

The guards' gamble is not very big. If the four of them were on their own, they would have little hope of escape. Aside from their visas, they have no papers, the network of checks on the street and in trains is tight, and the border is still closed. Over the past several weeks, however, a surprising opportunity to flee by sea has presented itself to Albert Hirschmann. It is a risky endeavor, but he and Fry want to at least tell their protégés about it.

They meet the four men in a bordello because they feel safe from informers there. A few Frenchmen who want to join de Gaulle's troops in London have purchased an old sailing yacht that has been grounded in the docks for years. They have taken on the former owner as skipper to bring the ship out of the harbor at night and to Gibraltar. The yacht is admittedly already overladen, but for a horrendous sum, the captain would take the German refugees aboard.

While Fry and Hirschmann negotiate with the men, the women who work in the bordello attempt to flirt with them all. They sit in their laps, caress their cheeks or their hair, and wonder why these guests are only interested in their conversation and not in sex. So that they do not become even more mistrustful, Hirschmann finally gets up and announces: "I will sacrifice myself." He quickly strikes a deal with one of the women and vanishes into a room with her. The prospect of returning to Le Vernet is not enticing for the four men, so they declare themselves in agreement with the escape plan.

On the night they are in fact to board the yacht, their guards are again lying drunk in their beds. From the shore, Hirschmann watches the ship gliding out of the strictly monitored docks north of the Old Port. He suspects it is the riskiest maneuver of their journey. Evidently, the skipper bribed the port supervisor; no one sounds the alarm. Around two in the morning, Hirschmann arrives at Fry's place in the Hôtel Splendide, and together they once more make all suspicious documents vanish from Fry's room; as soon as the two guards from Le Vernet realize that their prisoners have disappeared from the city, Fry and Hirschmann can expect a visit from the police.

At first, however, nothing happens – until Dick Ball returns a few days later from one of his trips to the Spanish border and reports that he saw the four in handcuffs under close guard at the Narbonne train station. Fry at once retains an attorney who enquires about the men and learns that their flight failed. Their yacht ran into a storm that very first night, became disabled, and was seized by the coast guard. In the meantime, they have been convicted of attempted escape by a court in Aix-en-Provence and returned to Le Vernet camp.

Banyuls-sur-Mer, October 13, 1940

Mayor Azéma has found a fabulous house for Hans and Lisa Fittko. It is located right on the sea, a narrow, three-story residence not far from the harbor. It belongs to a doctor who vanished abroad after war broke out. Azéma has confiscated it on behalf of the town. All rooms are paneled in wood and have built-in closets and fireplaces – although there is no running water in the entire house and no bathrooms. This downside can be overcome, however, because right across the street are the town's public toilets.

Lisa and Hans select the house's most beautiful room; it is on the third floor, gets lots of sun, and has an unobstructed view of the sea. When the two are standing at the window, they feel as if they could touch the waves with their hands. The room is empty. They carry over a large bed, a table, and two chairs from the other rooms. In one of the wall cabinets, they find blankets and bed linen. Even after the bed is made, however, Lisa still finds the room quite bare, so she removes her headscarf, spreads it out on the table, smooths it out, and places a bowl on top.

Fry had Bil Freier craft for them perfectly forged papers which they can use any time to identify themselves as French citizens from the north who were expelled by the Germans. Azéma also helps them assimilate into the city's day-to-day life as inconspicuously as possible. He advises them to wear espadrilles like everyone else in town. One does not find enough purchase with leather shoes while climbing in the vineyards. When the peasants head out to work at dawn, many toss their spade over their shoulder and hang a bag from it containing bread and wine for lunch. Perhaps Hans might also buy a spade for himself? They are by no means to use rucksacks; among the locals, a rucksack is regarded as the unmistakable trademark of a typical German hiker.

From this point forward, the Centre will send the Fittkos small groups of refugees two to three times a week – never more than three or four persons. Anything else would attract too much attention. To keep from being infiltrated by informants, the Centre sends a letter to Lisa and Hans in advance containing a torn sheet of paper with a random number written on it. The refugees from Marseille bring the other half of the paper. If both pieces fit together at the tear perfectly, they form the ticket for the Underground Railroad to Spain, which can now, finally, restart its operations.

Marseille, October 15, 1940

This morning, Hiram Bingham once again gets bad news in his diplomatic pouch. Two days earlier, the Manns and Werfels arrived in New York with the Greek steamship *Nea Hellas*. Journalists were waiting for them at the harbor, too, and pumped them for details about their escape. Unlike Feuchtwanger, they provide no information whatsoever. "It would be very dangerous," Werfel says, fending off the questions, "to speak about it. Many of my friends are still in the camps."

This time, the telltale information is in the lede of the article in the *New York Times*. The writers, it reads there, were greeted at the harbor by "Frank Kingdon, chairman of the Emergency Rescue Committee, which has helped many intellectuals in their flight from Europe."

Incredible. It is as if the newspaper had served the French police the escape agents' calling card on a silver platter. But as if that were not enough: Fry knows that Frank Kingdon is no idiot. Could it be that Kingdon attended the reception for the two famous authors so that his name would be printed in the newspaper? Together with the name of the

ERC? To expose Fry in Marseille like this once and for all and force him to return to America?

Or does his mistrust go too far? Fry knows that he has trouble dealing with people in positions of authority – Eileen has reproached him for this often enough. In any case, monkey wrenches like this one cause his willingness to return to New York not to increase, but rather to decrease. His defiance has been aroused. He will not leave France so long as he is not expelled.

For the evening, Fry invites all employees of the Centre to the Hôtel Splendide. It is his birthday; he has turned thirty-three. He wants to celebrate this day with the people he can trust completely. The constant tension in their work has prompted them to grow together into a tight-knit fellowship – with him as its ringleader. He, the perpetual loner, has never played such a role in his life. He senses how much the others feel emotionally connected to him. He told Eileen in a letter that his people do not work for him for the money and not just to help refugees, but because they love him and he loves them.

Today is the first evening in weeks they do not work. Miriam Davenport has decorated the table at the Splendide with dahlias, their blossoms almost as large as dinner plates. Fry selects wine, good old vintages. The menu they are served comes off as stingy. Even for the city's hotels and restaurants, it is becoming more and more difficult to source food. After the meal, Fry is rather exhausted and drunk. Although he normally sets so much store by proper attire and chilly distance, he now loosens his collar and tie, stretches out at the table over two or three chairs, and rests his head in Miriam's lap.

He can be satisfied with his work from his first two months in Marseille. With his people, he has so far gotten around two hundred people over the border. In addition, he has taken on the tricky task of getting scattered British soldiers back to their outfits in England. The work for the Centre is the most important work he has ever undertaken, and, he wrote to Eileen, it will likely remain the most important. It gives his life meaning. To be sure, he must not complain if the French police try to thwart him in everything he does. That is part of his work. But he did not anticipate the machinations of the State Department and the consulate – and certainly not that it would be the Emergency Rescue Committee now putting obstacles in his way, to boot. When writers like

Werfel, Feuchtwanger, and Heinrich Mann step off their ships in New York, they send him not cables of congratulations, but the order to abort everything and return. Is it wrong to see treachery in that?

Saint-Gilles, October 19, 1940

Fry feels burned out. It is not solely the pressure from work that wears him down. For two months, he has no longer had a place to withdraw to. Far too many exiles throughout southern France now know room 307 in the Splendide and seem to view him as their personal rescue commissioner.

He needs a reprieve and needs to learn how to unwind. Last weekend, he invited Miriam Davenport to travel with him to Arles to visit Breitscheid and Hilferding in their house arrest, but also to see the scenery and locales where van Gogh and Gauguin painted some of their most famous pictures. At the Gare Saint-Charles, they happened upon a young man, a friend of Miriam's, who until recently served as an officer in the French army but who now ekes out his living as a newspaper salesman. Stéphane Hessel grew up in Berlin and Paris, having essentially been born into the cultural life of both metropolises as the son of writer Franz Hessel and journalist Helene Grund.

For Fry, this encounter was something like a friendship at first sight. Stéphane Hessel's calm familiarity with the world of literature, art, history, and architecture makes him an ideal conversation partner and travel companion. This weekend, Fry has invited him on an excursion to Saint-Gilles, a neighboring town to Arles, where they visit a medieval abbey. Finally, Fry is able to discover the beauties of Provence for himself. Subsequent weekends are also scheduled full of joint side trips to Nîmes, Uzès, or Saint-Rémy. Precisely because Hessel is not part of the Centre, he provides Fry the opportunity to cast off, temporarily, the tension caused by his work.

Pamiers – Marseille, late October 1940

Anna Seghers does not like leaving her children alone in Pamiers with Madame Jeanne, even if only for a few days. She must, however, go to Marseille. She does not want to let this opportunity pass her by. In

Marseille, she has learned, there is a Centre Américain de Secours, which helps writers leave the country.

When she descends the flight of stairs outside the Gare Saint-Charles to the city center, she is downright floored after weeks in sleepy Pamiers. The throngs of people, the innumerable cafés, the hubbub on the Boulevard Canebière – she likes Marseille, it is a glorious city. On the Rue Grignan, however, she must first join the queue outside number 60. Yet after the burly American overseeing access at the gate has let her into the Centre's offices, everything proceeds quite quickly. Seghers is greeted and questioned with practiced courtesy. She is a Jew and has been in exile with her family since 1933. She can report that her home in Meudon was searched by the Gestapo, can list various books she has published, and mention the Kleist Prize awarded to her. No doubt: she is one of the imperiled writers whom the Emergency Rescue Committee was founded to save.

Her interlocutor refers her on to the director of the bureau, an American journalist in his early thirties with horn-rimmed glasses and an expressionless face. The man's name is Fry, and he enumerates for Anna Seghers what conditions she must fulfill and which affidavits she must procure to obtain entry visas to the United States for herself and her family – but as soon as he asks her whether she or her husband were ever members of a communist party, it is clear that they will never receive American visas.

On this point, Fry is personally more easygoing than the State Department. He adds her to the list of authors who will receive regular financial support from the Centre going forward and advises her to try for Mexican visas. Gilberto Bosques, Mexico's consul in Marseille, is known throughout the city for pulling out all the stops to rescue mostly communist exiles and former Spanish combatants from the Nazis.

The street outside the Mexican consulate looks similar to the one outside the American consulate in Château Pastré. People seeking assistance pile up at the entrance, holding papers and petitions in their hands. As soon as an employee appears at the door or at a window, those waiting shout as though afraid of being forgotten out on the street. Here, too, Anna Seghers must join the queue and wait. She has a few friends in America; she knows almost nothing about Mexico. She and Rodi know no one there. Should they ever arrive there, her family would be wholly on its own. And yet, from one day to the next, Mexico has become Seghers' dream destination.

Hendaye, October 23, 1940

Adolf Hitler meets with Franco in Hendaye, at the border between Spain and occupied France. Both have arrived on special trains. Hitler hopes to induce Franco to enter the war against England. For nine hours, the dictators deliberate in Hitler's lounge car. Franco cannot be persuaded, declaring Spain "unfit for war" on account of the massive destruction from its civil war. But he indicates his willingness to cooperate more closely with the German police.

Montoire, October 24, 1940

On the return journey from Hendaye, Hitler meets with Marshal Pétain. Their encounter takes place at the train station of Montoire, a small town north of Tours. Pétain fully expects a German victory, and that Hitler will draw new borders in Europe after the war. Through close collaboration with Germany, he intends to win Hitler over to restoring France's unity at that stage. In a radio address one week after the meeting, Pétain announces his "policy of collaboration," which, needless to say, shall also encompass a close cooperation with the German police.

Montauban, late October 1940

Paper is in short supply. Newspapers often consist of only a single sheet with tiny print. Hannah Arendt and Heinrich Blücher, however, read them very intently. The laws against the Jews that have been passed in both zones of France speak plainly enough. Any day now, Arendt expects concrete antisemitic measures. Open season on Jews has not yet been declared, but it will not be much longer.

About the conduct of the people of Montauban, though, the two cannot complain. It is astonishing how greatly influenced the populace is by the model set by personages like the prefect or the city's bishop. Their commitment to refugees focuses public attention on how they can be helped, not on how they can be gotten rid of as quickly as possible.

At the moment, Arendt and Blücher are mainly concerned with the search for food. Fruits and vegetables are still available – probably because gasoline is so scarce that the Germans are unable to ship them out of their areas of cultivation. Apart from that, however, there is hardly anything else to be had in the stores. Lines queue long everywhere outside the shops. There are no more croissants or brioches, no cooking oil, no coffee, no fat, and no cheese after meals – virtually a sacrilege in France! Meat is available on occasion; Arendt suspects that many animals are slaughtered so that they no longer consume any more feed.

Arendt's mother has since joined them in Montauban. For a long while, she was in hiding in Paris, but the food situation in large cities is even worse than it is in the countryside. They have applied by mail for emergency visas from the American consulate in Marseille. Günther Stern, Hannah Arendt's first husband, who uses the nom de plume Günther Anders, has been living in the United States now for three years and got them the requisite affidavits in New York.

At the moment, they would rather not leave Montauban, though they will soon have to travel to Marseille to pick up their visas at the consulate. The Centre Américain de Secours, their point of contact there, has proven surprisingly active and helpful. A rich American woman involved with the Centre has made three thousand dollars available specifically for the refugees in Montauban. An enormous sum – exchanged at the usual black market rate, that amounts to around 200,000 francs. The woman's name is Mary Jayne Gold.

Vichy, October 27, 1940

Pétain's government decrees by law that every French citizen over sixteen years of age must carry a personal identity card with them, the *carte d'identité de français*. According to a resolution by the German military governor of France, a red stamp that reads "Juif" or "Juive" shall be added to the personal identity cards for people of the Jewish faith in the occupied zone.

Marseille, October 27, 1940

Albert Hirschmann wants Fry to disappear from Marseille for two days. The mission the Centre has planned for this weekend is very dangerous.

If something goes wrong, there will be a lot of arrests. Better if Fry cannot be arrested because he is not even in the city.

Dick Ball has orchestrated the coup. In Snappy's Bar, behind the opera, he got to talking with a Frenchman who offered to take refugees to Gibraltar in a trawler for him. He can accommodate seventy-five men on the ship, for a fixed price of 225,000 francs. Captain and crew stand ready, and the guards at the port have been bribed.

Fry and Hirschmann distrust the offer. It sounds too good to be true. But ever since Hitler's meetings with Franco and Pétain, it has become increasingly difficult to get Spanish transit visas. Apparently, the dictators made a deal to make it even harder to reach Lisbon legally. At this point, hundreds of refugees are waiting on help from the Centre. Each day, heartbreaking scenes play out at the office on the Rue Grignan. And the Fittkos can take at most eight to ten people per week across the border. Fry thus reluctantly hazards the attempts with the trawler.

Sixty of the British soldiers stuck in Marseille and fifteen of the refugees facing the greatest danger, including Walter Mehring, are to await the ship in a remote boathouse after ten o'clock at night. Fry impresses upon all of those involved not to pay the captain until each and every passenger is on board. Then, together with Stéphane Hessel, he takes the train a hundred kilometers away to Tarascon to visit the beautifully preserved medieval fortress there.

After coming from the train station the following afternoon and about to change his shirt quickly in his room at the Splendide, he hears a timid knock at his door. Mehring is outside, as always on the verge of a nervous breakdown. They waited in the boathouse half the night for the trawler, and then Hirschmann showed up and sent all seventy-five men home, singly or in pairs so as not to attract too much attention.

At the office, Fry learns the whole story. The captain suddenly imposed new conditions. He needed the entire sum up front to buy the ship from its owner. Only then could he fetch the trawler and take the refugees aboard. Negotiations dragged on for hours. Time was running out. It was a war of nerves. In the end, Dick Ball handed over the money to the captain – and ever since he is nowhere to be found. They fell for the oldest scam in the world. They bought a ship that does not even exist.

New York, October 30, 1940

The ERC has searched for a long while and finally found someone who has agreed to take over Varian Fry's work in Marseille. The man's name is Jay Allen. He is a reporter with great journalistic ambition and a résumé that almost reads like Ernest Hemingway's. In the 1920s, he lived, like Hemingway, in Paris and later took over Hemingway's job as the European correspondent for the *Chicago Daily Tribune*. Like Hemingway, he went to Spain in the 1930s and reported on the civil war. At present, pacific New York bores him, and he wants to return to France. It will take another few weeks for Allen to gather all the necessary visas, but Mildred Adams, who maintains contact with Fry from the ERC office and is tired of his unilateral actions, writes him today already that Allen will soon take over his job and that he should start preparing to bid farewell to Marseille.

The Villa, Waiting, and Death

November 1940 to February 1941

Marseille, late October to early November 1940

The trio of them – Mary Jayne Gold, Miriam Davenport, and Jean Gemähling – are riding in a streetcar headed east, away from the sea, into one of the city's hilly, outlying districts. The weather has turned inclement, windy and rainy, and that has altered their daily rhythm. Up to this point, Fry's people have not only worked together, but have also frequently spent their evenings together in cafés all around the Old Port. They are a young team, almost all of them now in their mid-twenties or early thirties. Their work saddles them with a great deal of gravity and responsibility, so it is all the more important to create moments of relief. Since it has gotten colder, however, and food has become so scarce that restaurants are almost unable to offer anything anymore, they spend much too much time apart in their poorly heated hotels.

Mary Jayne does not feel like resigning herself to this situation. She would like to find accommodation for her old friends Daniel and Théodora Bénédite, for Miriam and herself, and perhaps also for shy Jean Gemähling, that are large enough for all of them. The odds of that are slim in the overcrowded city center, so they have begun looking farther afield.

Their streetcar has just passed a large cemetery when Mary Jayne catches sight of a stop called La Pomme and senses they may have arrived at the right spot for their search. The three alight and find themselves on a small arterial road running parallel to a somewhat more elevated railway embankment. There is a lot of green space here with trees and bushes, and the houses are not very close together. The three of them turn back in the direction of the city, walk a few hundred meters, and stop in a café to ask whether there is a house for rent in the area, but the owner has no tips to offer them.

A bit farther on, they spot an underpass leading to the other side of the railroad embankment and see a broad boulevard there flanked by plane trees and boxwood hedges. Without exchanging a word, they cross beneath the embankment and walk along the boulevard, past a sign announcing "Private property. No trespassing!" and through a brick portal into a small park. White lettering on the portal reads "Villa Air Bel."

"This is private property. Did you not see the sign?" A short older man, raking leaves between the plane trees, seems irritated.

"Beg your pardon," Jean Gemähling says, walking toward him a bit. "We're looking for a house. We'd like to rent something."

"There's nothing around here," the man replies.

"We'd like to rent a house here," Gemähling repeats as if he had heard nothing.

The response is more forceful: "Nothing to let!"

"We're Americans," Miriam says, "and we thought perhaps …"

"Americans, you say?" The man perks up.

"Yes," Mary Jayne confirms. "Do you know the property owner?"

The man introduces himself; his name is Dr. Thumin, and he himself is the owner. Evidently, he has more faith in the reliability and financial wherewithal of Americans than he does in those of his countrymen. All of a sudden, he recalls a house for rent. The three must continue along the boulevard, he says. He will fetch the keys.

The tree-lined avenue makes a gentle ascent up the hill, ending at a tall, latticed gate in a stone wall. The wall encloses a sprawling three-story manor house and an unkempt garden with a fountain, a greenhouse, and a terrace with two massive plane trees. Dr. Thumin unlocks the gate but requests they wait on the terrace until he has opened all of the shutters. They must not enter the rooms until they are bathed in light.

The Villa Air Bel hails from the nineteenth century and is still furnished in the style of that age. The ground floor features a gigantic salon with parquet flooring and a piano, a somewhat gloomy dining room, a much too large, old-fashioned kitchen with a coal stove, and the home's only bathroom. The zinc bathtub in it and the swan-necked faucets, Dr. Thumin recounts, were a wedding present for his grandmother. On the

The Villa Air Bel in Marseille

second floor are several bedrooms, all outfitted with mahogany furniture, along with a large library containing the classics of French literature and pictorial wallpaper that, like frescoes, depicts various mythological scenes. On the third floor, there are even more, somewhat smaller bedrooms. In all, there are eighteen rooms.

"Too big," says Mary Jayne. Then she asks the homeowner about the price of rent.

"1,300 francs a month." According to the black market rate, that comes out to around fifteen dollars.

The three attempt to conceal their surprise; it is scarcely more than a month's rent for a single hotel room along the Old Port. They promise Dr. Thumin to return for a second viewing with friends. They, too, are thrilled. Fry, who adores Greco-Roman mythology, is particularly taken by the wallpaper murals in the library. One motif on it shows Aeneas fleeing from a burning Troy – the archetype of the political refugee.

On November 1, Mary Jayne signs the lease. Miriam comes up with the idea of running the house as a sort of private hotel, hiring a cook and two housemaids, and inviting not just coworkers at the Centre to be co-tenants. She remembers Victor Serge, the homeless revolutionary who made an impression on her, and his friend, the writer André Breton, who urgently needs a roof over his head as well. Both have a wife and child, and the colder the autumn becomes, the more difficult it will be to get by without stable accommodation.

In the end, fifteen people move into the villa. Aside from the three-person Serge, Breton, and Bénédite families, there is Varian Fry, young Gussie Rosenberg, the Centre's doctor Marcel Verzeano, and the three discoverers of the house, Miriam, Mary Jayne, and Jean Gemähling. Only Albert Hirschmann disapproves of the move. To his mind, Fry of all people must be at the Centre's beck and call in cases of emergency; the route from the villa to the offices on the Rue Grignan is much too far.

Such qualms, however, cannot prevail against the charm of the Villa Air Bel. Fry loves the home's gloriously shopworn grandeur, but also the prospect of finally putting a bit more distance between himself and worries about his clients. From certain places on the terrace, there is a fabulous view onto the park and the city's rooftops, all the way to the sea. Living with friends amid Louis XIV and Empire-style furniture, with their own library, gilt-framed mirrors above the fireplaces, and landscape paintings on the walls so well suits his notion of a cultured and yet also eccentric life that he cannot resist, irrespective of what Hirschmann says.

Marseille, early November 1940

The situation at the borders remains confusing. Spain has again grown more generous in issuing transit visas, but surveillance on the French side is getting stricter and stricter. The Fittkos are still confident they can continue to get refugees over the mountains on the *route Líster* unmolested, but that could change.

Under these circumstances, Fry makes two decisions. First, he gives up searching for possibilities of escape by ship. After the failures of the age-worn yacht that almost sank with the four men from Le Vernet aboard and of Dick Ball's expensive phantom trawler, he is fed up with maritime adventures. He is now betting everything on an overland way and sends Hirschmann to the frontier to identify alternative routes as a precautionary measure in case the Fittko's route – which is now known at the Centre as the "F" route – should be blocked at some point.

Second, he wants to try to bring to Marseille as many exiles as possible still living in internment camps. It is infinitely complicated to obtain visas or to draft escape plans for people who can hardly be reached because they are stuck behind barbed-wire fences. He thus asks Daniel Bénédite to embark on a tour of several camps to document the conditions there. Bénédite is to write a report in which he can demonstrate to those in charge in Vichy what is being done to the prisoners in France's name and that the camps must be closed down at once.

Washington, D.C., November 5, 1940

Franklin D. Roosevelt wins the presidential election and is the first and only president of the United States to begin a third term in office. After his electoral victory, he changes little about the allocation of emergency rescue visas for refugees from Europe. The President's Advisory Committee for Political Refugees chooses whether to grant the visas mainly from the standpoint of national security. It continues to be swamped by the bureaucratically immensely time-consuming review of individual cases and only manages to process the applications at a sluggish pace.

Marseille, early November 1940

Dick Ball has vanished. He did not say goodbye and spoke to no one about leaving the city or planning a trip. One day he was here, the next he is gone.

After the business with the trawler turned out to be a scam, he was inconsolable with shame. No one faulted him for it – Marseille's mafia shows no regard for the hardships of refugees, which is no surprise. Still, Ball showed up at the Centre multiple times to tell Fry how embarrassed he was about the failure, saying he wanted to replace the lost sum from his own pocket, no harm must come to the aid program, he would repay every dollar. Then, suddenly, he was nowhere to be found: no trace of him, no message, no clue. Varian Fry is forced to pass along Ball's primary task – to accompany the refugees from Marseille to the Fittkos in Banyuls – to the Centre's doctor, Marcel Verzeano.

That is not the only parting of ways. Miriam Davenport's papers for her return journey to Ljubljana have arrived. She can pick up the necessary visas at the American consulate in Switzerland, then travel from there to Italy, onward to Yugoslavia, and back to her fiancé. Her departure is not as abrupt as Dick Ball's, but it is all the more painful. The thought of not being able to live with her friends in the Villa Air Bel after all, friends to whom she has felt intimately close over recent weeks, makes this goodbye especially difficult for her.

Marseille, early November 1940

André Breton is a well-known man in France, not solely because of his books, but also because of the scandals he provokes. He loves the insult, the spectacle, the éclat. Upon closer inspection, it is in fact a mistake to distinguish between Breton's art and Breton's scandals. Art that takes itself seriously must, to Breton's way of thinking, be scandalous, lest it be banal.

He is the son of a police officer, a protector of public order, but there is hardly anything he reviles more than well-kept order. The true, the beautiful, the good, once regarded as the very heart of art, the yearning for aesthetic harmony, for ideal measure, or for well-chosen proportion are, in his eyes, ridiculous fantasies. He wants to startle, shock, antagonize his audience. They should be ripped away from their customary ideas and views in order to learn to see the world with sharper eyes. If they find confronting the unfamiliar to be scandalous and react with resistance, that is no flaw, but an unavoidable side effect. Initially, Breton wanted to become a physician. He studied medicine, engaged with Freud's theory of the unconscious, and came to the conclusion that only a radically altered consciousness could make a different, better life possible.

Breton is not the only person to pursue such aims. For decades, essentially, modernist artists have been speaking of nothing but renewing the expressive means of art in order to develop different modes of thought and perception. In one way or another, all of them want to reveal hidden truths, violate taboos, and expose the self-delusions of bourgeois society. For that reason alone, Breton continues to find friends with whom he can appear and proudly proclaim their shared ideas as the central intellectual program of the age.

His allies like following him because Breton possesses a natural authority, a palpable charisma, and he takes joy in gathering groups around himself. He gave their movement the name surrealism and in several manifestos defined what their art set out to do – and not do. This passion of Breton's to specify precisely what the one true surrealism is, however, bears drastic consequences. As head of the group, he expects fealty and responds humorlessly to every form of deviation. Critics enjoy calling him, ironically, the pope of surrealism, and he in fact reserves the right to bless submissive devotees while excommunicating fractious ones and expelling them from his circle.

In Paris, three years ago, he organized the most important exhibition of surrealism worldwide, together with his friend Paul Éluard. Salvador Dalí, Max Ernst, André Masson, Marcel Duchamp, Man Ray, and others participated. They wanted not only to show their works, but also to turn the exhibition itself into an unsettling giant happening. Parked in the forecourt outside the gallery was a taxi swathed in ivy, containing a poseable doll with shark teeth. From hidden pipes in the vehicle's roof, water rained down onto the puppet. At the entrance, visitors were steered past fifteen brutally disfigured window mannequins into the interior space. There, 1,200 coal sacks hung from the ceiling, the whole floor was strewn with leaves and damp soil, and a brazier glowed in the middle. Coffee was roasted in one corner, and in another, four beds draped in satin stood amid reeds and puddles of water. Hysterical laugher recorded at a psychiatric clinic was played from loudspeakers, and during the vernissage, a naked actress bound up in iron chains leapt from a mountain of pillows and splashed around in an artificial pond before suffering a hysterical fit that seemed all too real.

With actions such as these, Breton and his disciples have by no means made only friends. They want to provoke – and many people are easily provoked. The surrealists are trashed, derided, insulted, making them even more famous. For several years now, however, this cultural battle has extended beyond the more insular milieu of art and culture. For Breton, the surrealist revolution goes hand in hand with the communist revolution. It is not just art he intends to change, but also the way people live together in society. He advocates for absolute revolt, total insubordination. "The simplest Surrealist act," he writes in one of his manifestos, "consists of dashing down the street, pistol in hand, and firing blindly, as fast as you can pull the trigger, into the crowd. Anyone who, at least once in his life, has not dreamed of thus putting an end to the petty system of debasement and cretinization in effect has a well-defined place in that crowd, with his belly at barrel level."

Of course, this is ultimately just a fantasy of Breton's, an instance of verbal radicalism in which he attempts to carry his provocations to the extreme. But what was once a lurid imagined scenario, the war has suddenly transformed into a politically life-threatening confession of faith. For the Nazis, now the new rulers in Paris, surrealism is not just "degenerate," but also communist art. And not only that – the Vichy regime also desperately needs scapegoats it can make responsible for France's military collapse. Marshal Pétain, a staunch anticommunist, demands the country turn back to traditional values, and his admirers at the newspapers stir up hatred against the decadence of an avant-garde that ostensibly weakened, if not crippled France.

At the moment, it is no cakewalk being a surrealist. Many of them have left Paris and moved south with the million-strong host of refugees. Breton first found a place to stay with friends in Provence and then moved into an abandoned fisherman's hut at the mouth of the Rhone with his wife and daughter. He was never one of the wealthy writers; his literary fame was always greater than his sales figures. Now, though, his financial situation is disastrous, and Mary Jayne Gold's invitation to move into the Villa Air Bel brings salvation for his small family.

Mary Jayne feels drawn not least to his charisma. He has something of both a chieftain and a shaman about him. On one of their first days at Air Bel, when she comes downstairs to the dining room, she sees Breton arranging some leaves and branches in the middle of the dining table. That dumbfounds her because, in her eyes, he is the opposite of a poet interested in table decorations. But Breton invites her to look more closely at the leaves, and she spots two large praying mantises. While the body of the male creature still mates with the female specimen, the female has already severed his head and begun consuming it.

"You see," Breton explains with peculiar satisfaction, "the two make love while she eats him." An arrangement that, to his mind, obviously has surreal qualities.

Fry, too, gets along well with him. He is familiar with Breton's ideas about modern art. On many points, they are in line with the ideas he espoused in his time at Harvard with the magazine *Hound & Horn*. He shares Breton's delight in provocation in any case, as he does his rage at cheap social conventions. He enjoys the conversations with Breton and the proximity to such an important artist and feels understood, as though among kindred spirits. Moving into the villa is a boon for him.

Marseille, early November 1940

Now, before his trial is to begin, Killer Raymond sends a friend to Mary Jayne. He is Corsican, conspicuously short, meticulously dressed, and has well-contoured, uniform features. This, Mary Jayne thinks, might be how a brother of Napoleon looked. The man's name is Mathieu, he met Raymond in prison, and he makes no bones about his criminal past.

Mathieu invites Mary Jayne on a stroll through town. He has only just been released from custody and is enjoying his newfound freedom. At a small bistro, all the waiters surround him and greet him like a long-lost friend; evidently, he is an important man in his milieu.

The trial, Mathieu says over an aperitif, will be a serious matter. Desertion was a grave mistake – it is quite possible for the sentence to turn out to be a tough one. Even if Raymond will certainly not be sentenced to death, it could happen that he will be sent away to a detention camp for years and Mary Jayne will have to wait a long time for him.

Luckily, however, Mathieu has sterling contacts in Marseille. Naturally, it is possible to bribe judges and buy a lenient sentence for Raymond. He knows a retired general with excellent connections to military justice. For an appropriate subsidy for this general and the magistrates in the impending trial, Mathieu is certain, Raymond will very soon be out of prison again. Then Mathieu names a high price.

Mary Jayne is not naïve. She can guess what opportunities Mathieu will have to double-cross her in this deal. She will never learn whether her money has ever reached the judges or whether it has any influence on the outcome of the trial. But it is Raymond who sent Mathieu to her, and it is Raymond she would like to trust. Besides, money plays a different role for her than it does for most people. If in cases of doubt there are ways to aid in getting her lover back to her sooner, then in her eyes even a high price is not too much to pay.

A few days later, Mathieu accompanies her to the court proceedings. The two find seats in the back rows of the public gallery, but Mary

Jayne has a good view of Killer. He is sitting up front at the edge of the prisoner's dock, leaning far forward, looking eager and remorseful. He comes across as the epitome of a young man gone wrong, gone astray. The expensive attorney Mary Jayne hired for him is worth every franc. He speaks of the defendant's difficult childhood, his desire to fight for France, the honorable medal he received on his deployment in Norway, the news that his former sergeant was with de Gaulle's troops and ordered him to return to his old unit. Raymond, the attorney stresses, has recognized the grave mistake of being enticed to desertion and requests just one thing of the court: to be allowed to continue serving France.

Then the lawyer raises his hand theatrically and addresses the judge directly. "And by this judgment let France show that her justice is still tempered by mercy and humanity. And let France show that she is free from political and foreign pressures."

The magistrate does not hesitate, imposing a suspended sentence of six months. By the end of the month, Raymond shall be released from prison. He nods as he hears the verdict and grins a little. Mary Jayne and Mathieu remain seated in their chairs for a moment as Raymond is led off by a police officer. Then they get up, and as they leave the courtroom, Mathieu whispers to Mary Jayne, "You see, I told you it would come out all right."

Vichy, mid-November 1940

The facts that Daniel Bénédite has compiled for his report on the internment camps cast France in a negative light. There are still a hundred twenty camps with a total of around sixty thousand civilian internees trying to survive under barbaric conditions. Many of them do not even own a straw mattress and must sleep on the bare ground. Their barracks have neither stoves nor windows; when it rains, water drips through the roof and collects on the floor. The unhygienic conditions are disastrous. There are too few latrines, no toilet paper, no sanitary pads for women. Dysentery and typhus rage rampant. Medical care is abysmal, and the death rate is high without camp authorities doing anything serious about it. To list one example, in the Gurs camp, around three hundred people die each month. These are numbers from summer and autumn; with increasing cold over the course of the winter, the number will grow bigger. At this point, prison conditions can no longer easily be distinguished from those in the Nazis' concentration camps.

Lena Fischmann, the ERC secretary, copies the report in great haste, and then Fry sets off for Vichy with Marcel Chaminade. As the former press assistant in the French Foreign Ministry, Chaminade is still in good touch with employees in the new regime. But even these connections do not help. The trip is a depressing failure.

The fate of the internees is of no interest to anyone in Vichy. The very atmosphere in the little spa town is dismal. Ministries are housed in hotels, their rooms tiny and unsuitable as offices. Officials work not at desks, but, as Fry did in the Splendide at the beginning, at dressing tables from which they have unscrewed the mirrors. Government documents pile up on beds or on the floor. Meetings have to take place standing or in the lobby.

Fry and Chaminade are not even let in to see the ministers or other decision-makers in the first place. They leave behind a carbon copy of Bénédite's report with everyone with whom they are allowed to speak. All of them are horrified at the conditions described, but no one cares to do anything. Fry would like to succeed in getting at least the sick, the children, and the aged released. He has also compiled a list with the names of the most prominent prisoners, including Peter Pringsheim, one of Europe's best-known physicists and a brother-in-law of Thomas Mann. Everywhere, though, he comes up against indifference.

At the American embassy in Vichy, it is similar. Although Fry inquires on multiple days, the ambassador is too busy to speak with him. The subordinate secretary who finally receives them treats him dismissively. Like Consul Fullerton in Marseille, he urges him to leave France at once. No one in the embassy is willing to supply visas for exiles in danger – the fate of the internees is simply irrelevant to the officials.

Montauban – Marseille, mid-November 1940

Hannah Arendt is on the run like hundreds of thousands of others, too. But for her, escape also provides outstanding illustrative material for her analysis of the modern state. The sprawling bureaucracy, above all, which she will later term "rule by Nobody," she gets to know firsthand in all its menace. Amid the small-scale war with the anonymous administrative machine in America, her ex-husband Günther Anders had to move heaven and earth to procure all the affidavits for her and Heinrich Blücher, without which one cannot obtain emergency rescue visas. Since Hannah Arendt worked for the Zionist Youth Aliyah in Paris, it was not just Varian Fry's Centre Secours, but also Jewish organizations that helped in successfully navigating this egregious obstacle course of regulations.

Now, the American consulate has informed Arendt and Blücher that visas are ready for them in Marseille. But just as soon as they have eked out this victory against American bureaucracy, French bureaucracy gets in their way. The police in Montauban are unwilling to issue them a *sauf-conduit* for their trip to Marseille, and without this document – that much is clear – they will run afoul of the strict checks at the Gare Saint-Charles. And so they borrow bicycles, exit the train before arriving at Saint-Charles, and trundle into the city illegally via side roads – without a *sauf-conduit* they have naturally also not received a residence permit for Marseille.

The next element of uncertainty is the hotel. At registration, they have to identify themselves and consequently reckon with the French or perhaps even the German authorities learning and checking their names. Luckily, there are no further difficulties at the consulate, and the visas are delivered to them without their having to wait a long time. The next morning, though, they receive the message at their hotel that Heinrich Blücher should report to reception. He does not hesitate, leaves his luggage behind, and immediately quits the building. Arendt acts clueless, pays for the room, and sits down to breakfast. When the hotelier approaches her and asks about Blücher, she leaps to her feet and loudly accuses him of being the sole reason her husband was marched off to the prefecture: "This is your fault."

Afterward, she meets Blücher in a café, and together they leave the city at once on their bicycles. While they are now the privileged owners of American entry visas, in essence nothing has changed for them in their precarious situation because the French will not issue any exit visas. They have no choice but to return to Montauban and continue keeping an eye out for a chance to get out of France.

Marseille, mid-November 1940

The relationship between Fry and the ERC in New York grows pricklier from week to week: too much tension on both sides, too much impatience, too many misunderstandings. Mildred Adams coolly informs Fry that his Centre is getting too expensive. It is necessary to save money. He must dismiss employees to lower costs.

Fry is outraged. In light of the situation in Marseille, such instructions seem unconscionable to him, especially coming from people sitting in America at richly laid tables in cozy homes taking no personal risks. He responds in the polemical and provocative tone he has mastered so well: "If you really want us to reduce the staff," he writes to the committee, "[...] you must tell us what category of people we are to deny our services to. Are we to refuse in future to bother with painters? If so we can drop one worker. Are we to ignore people in camps? If so we can let another go. Shall we in future ignore any person who is not in Marseille, or who cannot tell us what he wants to tell us in a letter subject to censorship? If so we can reduce the staff by perhaps two. Please don't tell us to reduce the staff to one or two, without also specifying what kind of work, if any, you want us to confine ourselves to in the future [...]."

It almost sounds as if the New Yorkers were at fault should the Centre not command unlimited financial resources. It sounds as if it were their secret intention to curtail aid for refugees. Fry's indirect reproaches are so absurd and scathing that his colleagues at the ERC gradually begin to doubt whether he is even still reachable by rational argument.

In Marseille, Fry has people living in a nightmare before his very eyes, desperate people for whom he is their last chance, and allies risking a great deal for their work and blindly putting their faith in him. To dismiss these people to save expenses is a morally untenable notion for him.

Again, Eileen assumes the thankless task of enjoining her husband by cable to see reason. After all, the committee is not idle. In October alone, it brought in $20,000 from donors. He must tone it down, she writes him, reminding him that he will return to New York at some point. Then, at the latest, he will again have to face the people he is now insulting.

André Breton in the library of the Villa Air Bel

Fry feels less and less like returning to America, however. On his excursions with Stéphane Hessel, he has positively fallen in love with the beauty of Provence. Living with the other residents of the Villa Air Bel, among whom he enjoys great respect, does its part to enhance even further his infatuation with the country. And he is happily willing to pay the price this love demands.

All the residents of the villa have entrusted the cook with their ration coupons, but she frequently returns from shopping with half-empty bags; the stores and markets have nearly been picked clean. The country is beginning to starve, and Fry, who was already slender, has now lost several kilograms. By this point, the stores available for dinner are so ridiculously meager that they prefer to forgo eating and sit together at the long table in the dining room and drink wine. For wine may still be had. Then, the mood very quickly relaxes; they sing French pop songs and listen to news from the BBC over the wireless.

On top of that comes the cold. Temperatures plummet, and autumn is rainier and stormier than usual in Marseille. There is a gigantic oven in the villa's kitchen and fireplaces in almost every room. But there is hardly any firewood to be found. During the day, they can heat only one room:

the library on the second floor where André Breton and Victor Serge take turns sitting at the desk and working on their new books. More and more often, the villa's residents cease removing their scarves or coats when they come inside the house. Warm water for washing in the one bathroom is quite out of the question.

And still, there is no holding Fry back in his enthusiasm for Marseille and Provence. He even tries to lure Eileen to France. "You could join me," he writes her, "and we could have a wonderful winter together. It is a beautiful, beautiful country." The man who runs the Quaker aid organization in the city has received a visit from his wife. Fry admits in his letter to Eileen to being "terribly jealous" of his good fortune.

Marseille, mid-November 1940

André Breton's own acolytes are starting to get on his nerves. Many of them have settled in Marseille after the great flight from the Germans. As soon as word got round among them that he now lived in the Villa Air Bel, a constant succession of friendly visits and courtesy calls began. Breton enjoys this homage, but they also interrupt him during his limited working time in the heated library. To put an end to them, he dispatches Gussie Rosenberg as emissary to Brûleur de Loups on the Old Port, the surrealists' favorite café. He has him announce that from now on the Villa Air Bel will be open to guests every Sunday between lunchtime and seven o'clock in the evening, and that Breton invites all of his friends, but otherwise will not receive visitors and does not wish to be disturbed.

Thus do the knights of a first-rate surrealist roundtable assemble in the villa's dining room around the long table on Sunday afternoons. They all became acquainted with one another in Paris in the 1920s: the Spanish painter Óscar Domínguez, with his bulldog face; the slight Victor Brauner, a painter as well, who lost an eye in a fight with Domínguez; the Romanian Jacques Hérold, who for years worked as an assistant to Brâncuși, but has now struck out on his own as an artist; the Lithuanian sculptor Jacques Lipchitz; along with Wilfredo Lam, who grew up in Cuba with a Chinese father and a Congolese mother and was long supported by Picasso; and, last but not least, the writer Benjamin Péret, one of the co-founders of surrealism and a long-standing companion of

Jacqueline Lamba, Jacques Lipchitz, André Breton, and Varian Fry

Breton's. The sculptor André Masson and the poet Réne Char, who at one time were part of the circle of surrealists but now maintain some distance, are likewise present as guests there on occasion.

Breton sits at the head of the table, his wife, Jacqueline Lamba, at his side. Even before meeting her husband, she worked as a painter and photographer, but earned her living as a mermaid-like nude underwater dancer at Le Coliséum, a cabaret in Montmartre. She is radiantly blonde and often wears splinters of colorful glass or tiny shards of mirror in her hair. There are few people capable of defying her charisma. She is smart, temperamental, and, as Breton says, almost scandalously beautiful.

Gatherings such as these are nothing out of the ordinary for the surrealists. For years, Breton has been convening such meetings to offer a forum for small-scale artistic experiments or debates, and probably also to consolidate group consciousness. Mary Jayne Gold, Jean Gemähling, and Varian Fry are admitted as passive observers. Gussie Rosenberg, who has been interrogating Breton for days about surrealism's ideas, is also permitted to attend the first session.

Benjamin Péret reads one of his poems to start. He often conjures lyrical dreamworlds far removed from any logic or temporal order – or he will sing the praises of feces and obscenities in extreme detail to shock his listeners. Amid the company of jaded surrealist colleagues, however, he is no longer able to spring an unpleasant surprise on anyone. Once he finishes, a big applause breaks out, with whistling and cheering. The circle abounds with goodwill and approval.

Then a game begins that bears the name *cadavre exquis* [exquisite corpse]. Breton has prepared a large sheet of paper, which he folds horizontally into as many segments as there are participants at the table. On the first segment, he sketches a random design without letting the others see it, then flips the page such that his drawing remains concealed, and passes it to the person next to him. On the next segment of paper, this person draws a second motif of his choice, which he in turn obscures by folding the paper once more and passing it to the third participant – and so forth until the last player has added his partial drawing. Afterward, the page is unfolded, revealing a jointly created image that unites the most varied ideas, styles, and themes into a grotesque amalgamation.

The game originated in the 1920s and was initially played in surrealist circles with words, not with drawings. In that version, all participants sit at a table with a sheet of paper in front of each, covertly write down a random word, then fold the paper so that no one else can read anything, and pass it to their seatmate, who notes down the next word. If everyone keeps to a prescribed grammatical structure, what thus arises are bizarre sentences that resist any rational semantic order. The first sentence to emerge in this way allegedly read "Le cadaver exquis boira le vin nouveau," or "The exquisite corpse will drink the new wine," which is rumored to have given the game its name.

The game with words, in a modified form, becomes a fixed ritual of these Sunday get-togethers. Breton places a hat on the table before him, and each person in this round table tosses in folded slips of paper with individual words or phrases. Then Breton mixes the slips, pulls them out one by one, writes down what is on them, and at the end reads the newly generated collaborative poem aloud. In most cases, individual lines invite complicated interpretations, which are subsequently hotly debated by the participants.

Fry and the three other observers utter not a word throughout. Nor does it occur to anyone to ask them for their opinion. Breton's Sunday guests often behave haughtily and pretentiously, viewing themselves as a circle of insiders whose knowledge those on the outside cannot access. During the week, however, when they come to the Centre's office one by one, they are modest and grateful whenever Fry or Mary Jayne or one of the others advises them on their visa problems.

Marseille, late November 1940

Charles Fawcett has decided to leave France. He wants to go to Great Britain to take part in the Battle of Britain. For months, British cities have been under constant bombardment by the German *Luftwaffe*. The comparatively small number of fighter pilots in the Royal Air Force tries to counter the attacks of this superior power, but casualties among the pilots are high. Churchill honored their courage in a speech before Parliament. "Never in the field of human conflict," he said, "was so much owed by so many to so few." Fawcett is greatly impressed by this; he wants to go to Great Britain and train to become a pilot.

As an American, he has no trouble obtaining an exit visa. For Fry, this presents a rare opportunity to have volatile messages smuggled into the British embassy in Madrid by a trusted courier. Fawcett can store some of the papers in one of his trumpet's valves. Others he conceals in hollow sculptures he fashioned while an art student in Paris. Because he is afraid of becoming nervous if he is searched at the border, he also draws a few pornographic pictures he hides rather perfunctorily in his luggage.

At first, everything at the border proceeds as he expected it would. Fawcett cannot suppress his anxiety, the customs agent becomes leery, discovers the drawings, confiscates them, and thus believes to have found everything there is to find. But then something happens with which Fawcett did not reckon. Several police officers pull him aside and interrogate him about his work for Fry in Marseille. Fawcett thinks he recognizes in one of them a man who offered to volunteer for the Centre – obviously not to help, but to investigate it. Luckily, Fry did not respond to this man's offer. Fawcett divulges nothing in the interrogation and is set free again. But from Spain, he has no opportunity to warn Fry about how hot on his heels the police now are.

Marseille, late November 1940

The Villa Air Bel gets another renter. It is Charles Wolff, the music critic Mary Jayne Gold met over the summer in Toulouse with Miriam Davenport. He is a brilliant, witty man whom Fry has hired for the Centre. Wolff comes from Alsace, speaks perfect German, and his primary task will now be to look after the many Jews who have been expelled from Alsace and Lorraine by the Nazis. Despite all appeals to frugality from the New Yorkers, Fry increases his expenditures even more with this move. As long as he can rely on donations from Mary Jayne, however, that does not bother him much.

Barcelona – Biarritz – Madrid, late November 1940

Right after arriving in Barcelona, Fawcett is about to report to the American consulate, but before he can enter the building, he is detained by the Spanish secret police. The officers are well informed about him, take him back to France, and turn him over to the Gestapo office in Biarritz. There, probably to unnerve him, they let him wait in a corridor for hours. Fawcett does in fact grow more and more anxious, for he is still carrying on him Fry's treasonous documents.

Eventually, he spots a high-ranking German officer approaching him in the hallway, accompanied by a very obsequious man, clearly a French informant. This companion gives Fawcett an idea. He leaps up, opens the hall door wide for them both, and follows them in a similarly very servile posture. He leaves just enough distance so that the officer does not notice him but remains close enough to them both to seem like he belongs with them. To his good fortune, they are headed across the courtyard of the police building to the exit. As soon as he has passed the boom gate in their wake, Fawcett hastens to the train station, jumps on the next train to Spain, and on the following day arrives at the British embassy in Madrid without being followed.

Marseille, December 2–5, 1940

When the first placards showed up in the streets of Marseille in late November announcing Marshal Pétain's visit, Albert Hirschmann warned everyone at the Centre. He knows the nervousness that strikes the police in a fascist country when the head of state comes to their town. He wants nothing to do with this and instead travels back to the Spanish frontier to continue his search for escape routes over the mountains. He has found a way leading to Spain via Andorra that seems quite promising to him.

Preparations for welcoming Pétain take on hysterical dimensions. One-story-tall wooden panels that read "Vive Pétain! Vive la France!" are installed along the boulevards. A gigantic portrait of the marshal bearing the commanding caption "Follow me!" hangs at the port. All shops, bistros, and restaurants are obligated to decorate their windows with photos of Pétain. In the display of one bookstore, Daniel Bénédite spots not just a picture of Pétain, but also one of the especially German-friendly prime minister, Pierre Laval – though the bookseller has laid out around the two photos several copies of Victor Hugo's novel *Les Misérables*.

To avoid being caught up in any raid in the city center, Fry asks his secretary Lena Fischmann to come to the Villa Air Bel one day earlier than Pétain's arrival so that they can work there. He has scarcely dictated the first few letters to her when two police cars drive up. Four officers from the detective division get out and take up positions in the villa's entrance as though intending to block a getaway route. A tall commissioner yells for all residents of the house to gather immediately in the hall.

"What are you planning to do?" Fry asks.

"Search the house, of course," the man snaps.

"May I ask who has given you the right to search this house?"

"We are entitled to do so," he barks. "No need to trouble yourself with this."

"Still, I'd like to see the search warrant," Fry persists.

"Oh, you want to cause trouble, do you?" the commissioner jeers.

"Not at all. But I would like to assert my rights and those of my friends."

The commissioner pulls a folded document from his pocket and hands it to Fry. Then the officials begin their work. According to French law, they may search private rooms only in the presence of the residents, so they are called upstairs from the hall, one after the other, to be present as witnesses while their rooms are turned upside down.

The enthusiasm of the accompanying officials is noticeably less intense than that of their commissioner. They find two typewriters, a small pistol with a mother-of-pearl handle in Victor Serge's room, and Breton's service revolver he kept after his time as a doctor with the military. Yet all concrete evidence of their work as escape agents Fry and his people are able to make disappear under the disinterested eyes of the searching men.

All the while, the commissioner snoops around in the dining room, rummaging through drawers and cabinets. Suddenly, in triumph, he holds up a piece of paper on which Breton has written in his idiosyncratic handwriting a single sentence – declaring the marshal a terrible moron: "Ce terrible crétin de Pétain."

"Look here," the commissioner beams. "Communist propaganda!"

"I object," Breton cries. "The sentence reads 'Ce terrible crétin de putain.'" ("Putain" means whore.) It is a harmless sentence, Breton explains, without any political background.

Everyone in the room is following the little dispute when suddenly Killer Raymond steps through one of the doors to the terrace. He has been released from prison this morning and is again wearing the uniform of a Foreign Legionnaire.

"Cherie," he calls out to Mary Jayne, setting down his suitcase. "Here I am! We must celebrate my release." Only then does he notice the odd situation he has happened upon. Because the officers are in plainclothes, they are not immediately recognizable as policemen. "What is going on here?"

"The police," Mary Jayne explains. "We're being questioned and searched." Since she knows how precarious Raymond's relationship to law enforcement is, she asks just in case: "Is everything okay?"

First, Raymond smiles, patting his breast pocket, which contains his official release papers. Then, all of a sudden, he begins muttering nervously and whispers to Mary Jayne that he has 40,000 francs worth of stolen money orders in his suitcase. His friend Mathieu asked him to hide them.

Mary Jayne is aghast. She has done a great deal to get her lover out of prison, but no sooner is he free than he again puts himself in danger of being arrested. Once more she has to try to rescue him. She whispers to Jacqueline Lamba to ask her to distract the policeman watching the hall a bit. Indeed, Lamba needs only two or three friendly remarks, plus a gentle swing of her hips, to win the official's undivided attention – and buy Killer the seconds he needs to reach into his suitcase and stuff the papers behind a picture leaning against the wall, unnoticed.

The search of the capacious house takes time. It is not until the afternoon that the commissioner gives up; his people have found nothing illicit. But instead of apologizing to the residents, he has them loaded into a police van and taken to the port. Killer rides along although, as a casual visitor to the villa, he is not even one of those arrested. He parts ways with Mary Jayne and the others only when it becomes clear that they are being taken to the S.S. *Sinaïa*, one of the large passenger ships moored at the docks. At this point, night has fallen, and as he is leaving, Killer promises to alert the American consul the very next morning so that he can free them.

The women are housed in the third-class cabins. For the men, there are sleeping berths in the cargo hold. Over six hundred people are on board, mostly foreigners, Jews, unhoused people, and petty criminals. They have all been more or less randomly arrested off the street. The only person who has prepared for being detained for a considerable time is jail-seasoned Victor Serge. He demonstrates for Mary Jayne how to sleep in a filthy bed without one's bare skin coming into contact with the pillow or the blankets. He has also packed books he now distributes because he knows how boring incarceration can become after only a few hours.

The next day, Fry waits impatiently for Consul Fullerton. Killer surely notified him. Yet neither Fullerton nor any of his employees show their face. The food is disgusting. For breakfast there is a hunk of black bread and a nondescript soup sweetened with saccharine, for lunch a piece of meat burned on the outside and still half frozen inside, and for dinner sweet soup again.

That afternoon, everyone is locked into the cargo hold for a few hours. It is cold, dark, and cramped. The feeling of being helplessly at the mercy of caprice sets in. When they are allowed on deck that evening, they learn that the marshal sailed past the *Sinaïa* on a pilot boat and one wished to spare him the sight of prisoners on deck.

Mostly, it is the uncertainty that is excruciating. None of the arrestees knows why they are being detained or for how long. No one may notify an attorney. Rumors circulate that they are all to be taken to an African internment camp.

After sundown, prisoners congregate on deck to sing popular tunes and battle songs – including the German song "The Peat Bog Soldiers," which was written by inmates in a concentration camp.

> We are the peat bog soldiers
> Marching with our spades
> To the moor
> Here amid this barren plain
> The camp has been erected
> Where razor wire bounds our domain
> And, joyless, we're neglected.

Mary Jayne stands there for a while and has moments of an acute sense of belonging. Since childhood, she has numbered among those spoiled by fate, having led a carefree life full of luxury. Now she is aboard a squalid prison ship and for the first time involved – not just through donations, but through personal commitment – in a fight like those sung about in freedom songs. However tiny her contribution might be, for the first time she is wholly part of a grand, serious cause.

Fry keeps trying to get in touch with the consulate. On a slip of paper, he writes a cry for help to Fullerton, tightly wraps the paper around a ten-franc coin, and throws both from the ship's deck to a boy wandering about the quay. At first, Fry is unsure whether the boy will actually deliver the message to the addressee or whether he will discard the note and view the coin as a gift. When a package is brought on board with sandwiches and one of Fullerton's calling cards hours later, however, it is clear that the consul knows where they are being held, but is unable or unwilling to free them.

The following day, Hiram Bingham joins them on board. He has searched the entire city for someone with the authority to order the release of Fry and the others, but he has been unable to reach literally anyone. All senior officials are out and about accompanying Pétain; all of them are jostling their way into his entourage. Whenever the marshal appears somewhere or rides past in his car, one sees more and more French people raising their right arms for the fascist salute in his honor.

Not until Pétain has departed are the prisoners gradually let off the ship. In total, Fry learns, more than seven thousand people were

Hiram Bingham, American vice consul, on the transporter bridge above Marseille harbor

arrested. All prisons and jails were overcrowded. In addition, the police had commandeered barracks, cinemas, and three large ships to take all *personæ non gratæ* off the streets for four days.

Marseille, mid-December 1940

Ever since Fry was freed from the *Sinaïa*, he has been tailed by men from the prefecture. Apparently, they are supposed to catch him doing something illicit so that he can finally be expelled. Luckily, an employee at the prefecture has warned him so that Fry can temporarily focus his full attention on the legal portion of his work.

What is much more unsettling is that two criminal detectives come into his office making inquiries about an associate "who calls himself Hermant." From the way they ask the question, there can be no doubt that they have uncovered Hirschmann's fake identity as Albert Hermant. With quick thinking, Fry answers that Hermant has not worked for the Centre in weeks and vanished without a trace. The officials content themselves with that and leave again, but now it is clear that Hirschmann, as a German refugee and a Jew, is in serious danger.

Marseille – Banyuls, December 13, 1940

Once again, it is Friday the thirteenth. When Hirschmann returns from the Spanish frontier in the morning and comes to the offices on the Rue Grignan, everything happens very quickly. Fry delivers the bad news to him that his cover is blown. For a moment, Hirschmann gazes out the window, then turns to Fry, smiles, and shakes his hand. There is not much to say. He heads directly to the train station, without again setting foot in his apartment, and catches the next train to Banyuls. He is carrying on his person the American visa Fry obtained for him. The Fittkos are to get him across the border, and like all the others, he plans to get a ship to New York from Lisbon. In a flash, the chapter of his life at the Centre Américain de Secours is over.

But there is trouble in Banyuls. Lisa Fittko has a high fever, is very weak and half unconscious. She urgently needs to be taken to the hospital in Perpignan. Her husband has already managed to get a rental car and the necessary gasoline but cannot himself drive because he would certainly be arrested on the way without a *sauf-conduit*. Hirschmann thus takes over the car. Together, they bed Lisa down in the back seat and try to shield her from the cold with blankets. Suddenly, Lisa's face is smeared in blood. The two men cannot find a wound; blood is seemingly trickling out of her mouth. Her breathing is shallow, and she is hardly responsive anymore. Only forty kilometers separate them from Perpignan, but during the drive, the distance feels longer and longer for Hirschmann.

Upon arriving at the hospital entrance, he initially has to leave Lisa lying in the car. At reception, he learns that there are no doctors in the building because of the weekend. They will return on Monday at the earliest, meaning in three days, but also perhaps not until Tuesday, as they have a second hospital to staff. Hirschmann has to bargain with the head nurse for a while. She does not want to admit Lisa until he pays for four weeks of care in advance. Luckily, he is carrying a lot of money: his emergency reserves for his escape to Lisbon. Lisa's condition is now so grim that the nurse assigns her a bed on the ward for the terminally ill.

Hirschmann hesitates to leave her alone, but she has lost consciousness, and he has to expect that the police are looking for him. He thus drives back to Banyuls. The next morning, Hans Fittko takes him across the border to Spain. Both are young and fit; the route takes them three hours. Then Hirschmann has left France behind him for good.

On the day Hirschmann arrives in Portbou, Fry writes to Eileen that he has never felt so lonely and abandoned as he does now. Hirschmann was a special friend, the only one at the Centre with whom he could speak without any inhibition because he was in the know about everything, even about the British soldiers they are smuggling out of the country. Fry has lost his closest confidant, the man with astonishing talents and the unerringly good mood. For the first time, he toys with the idea of quitting and returning to New York.

Marseille, mid-December 1940

Mary Jayne Gold and Killer Raymond are in love. The great distance between the worlds they each come from, however, is constantly palpable. Raymond does not get along with the residents of the Villa Air Bel. They are, for his taste, too out of touch with reality; the way they talk with one another, to his ears, is more smug than clever. Breton's regal bearing makes him mutinous. The others, in turn, see in him not much more than a young, rather unkempt bedfellow of Mary Jayne's. Only Victor Serge likes him because he reminds him of his own youth – when he robbed banks with anarchist friends.

And so, after a few days, Killer moves out of the villa. He takes a room at an hourly hotel, furnished with little more than a large bed and a wardrobe, the mirror of which reflects every movement on the bed. The room is not cheap but for Killer has a crucial advantage. Upon moving in, he is asked neither for his name nor for his papers. Owners of bordellos are not required to register their usually very short-term renters with the authorities.

Killer has to remain incognito because he has deserted once again. Sooner or later, the Foreign Legion would have sent him to Algeria or to one of the other colonies. He does not want to leave Marseille, though, on account of Mary Jayne and his friend Mathieu, who has since made him an associate in his criminal enterprises. As a result, Mary Jayne shuttles from now on between two disparate worlds. During the day, she works for the refugees at the Centre and lives at the villa. At night, however, she sleeps at Killer's in the bordello and feels like a gun moll from the movies whenever he places his revolver within reach on the bedside table before they go to bed.

Marseille, mid-December 1940

It is a normal workday at the Centre – initial interviews are held with potential clients, letters written to administrative authorities, or affidavits requested from American supporters – when Fry finds a note on his desk with an anonymous message after his lunch break. It consists only of a few words asking him to a meeting at the bar of the Hôtel Splendide. Fry hesitates, but his curiosity wins out in the end. When he enters the bar, he runs into the reporter Jay Allen and an older woman named Margaret Palmer. The two are his replacement. The ERC in New York has sent them to take over the Centre. The board views Fry's stay in France as finished; he is to return to America.

Allen is not quite forty, a stocky man with black, neatly parted hair and a somewhat chubby face. He drinks scotch with soda that he has obviously brought with him from New York; there has not been any for sale in Marseille now for weeks. His plan for handing over the Centre to him is simple. He asks Fry to show Margaret Palmer the ropes over the next few days; he is to explain all routine processes to her and introduce her to all important contacts as his successor. As soon as she knows everything through and through, Fry can leave.

As for him, Allen says, his journalistic work takes priority. To avoid at all being suspected by the police as an escape agent in the first place, he does not intend to set foot in the offices on the Rue Grignan – the workers there do not need to know him. Allen has contracts with several newspapers for which he is to report from all corners of France. He will travel a lot and does not want to be bound to Marseille. At the moment, he mostly wants to conduct an interview with Marshal Pétain. Every evening, he will phone Margaret Palmer, have her describe ongoing problems, and then make the necessary decisions.

Fry listens to Allen and, as so often, assumes an expressionless face; he wants to play his cards close to his chest. As soon as he is back in the office, however, his response is all the more decisive. He gathers his closest associates together for a war council. In his view, it is totally outrageous to run the Centre remotely, with its infinitely many intricate tasks, by placing a few evening telephone calls – especially since the French police could tap any line at any time. Jay Allen will destroy everything Fry has built over the previous months in short order. And so Fry asks his people to consider whether, under these circumstances, they want to share their carefully guarded information about escape plans, hideouts, and supporters with their new bosses. If not, they should convey that to the ERC.

His associates are horrified. Lena Fischmann drafts a telegram on behalf of everyone, warning against removing Fry. It would inevitably lead to the Centre's collapse and endanger the lives of hundreds of clients.

Fry himself does not stop at letters of protest. He is beside himself with rage, unable to see anything in his recall except targeted personal humiliation. No more thoughts about leaving Marseille, an idea he had entertained after Hirschmann's escape: instead, he now openly threatens the ERC with divorce. The Centre Américain de Secours was established by him, not by the New Yorkers. "This bureau," he writes, "is not your bureau: it is an independent aid organization founded by Americans living in France." From the money Fry receives from the Brits for the soldiers of theirs he is having smuggled out of the country, and from the amounts Mary Jayne Gold donates, the Centre can stand on its own two feet financially. A lucky break to add: a few days earlier, Fry was able to establish contact with a filthy-rich American woman currently living in Grenoble. She is an art collector named Peggy Guggenheim and without much hesitation she put 500,000 francs at the Centre's disposal.

As so many times in his life, Fry feels bossed around by incompetent people and is unwilling to take it. If the New Yorkers hold it against him that the State Department has been demanding he be recalled for months, that only makes the matter worse in Fry's eyes. He expects them to defend him against the department's charges, not give in. And if someone else from the committee is so inept to suggest that Jay Allen's famous name might indeed be useful in drawing the attention of the American public to the plight of the refugees, then Fry feels insulted in his pride as a journalist to boot. "If my name is mud," he writes, "then let me know so that I can sever all connections to you, however slight, once and for all."

The waves of anger crest higher and higher, and only a coincidence manages to mollify his feelings a bit, at least temporarily. Margaret

Palmer falls ill and is sidelined for two weeks. Apparently, she has a fragile constitution, and the meager food in Marseille does not become her. She talks for hours about the current condition of her digestion, Fry seethes in a letter to Eileen, even if no one wants to hear about it in such detail. As long as she is not in a condition to take up her duties at the Centre, there is no point to talking about Fry's replacement. And so he continues working as though nothing had changed and brushes off Allen.

Marseille, late December 1940

Someone must have denounced Bil Freier, the Centre's forger, because without having done anything treasonable, he is arrested one morning. Two police officers knock at the door of the garret room he occupies with his fiancée Mina. They do not even pretend to want to search the room to find evidence. "We know everything," they say, pointing to a small metal can in which Freier hides his work materials for illegal jobs. They open it and confidently remove paints, brushes, and stamps. Denial is futile; the presumptive evidence is too clear.

The policemen do not have a car and ride with Bil and Mina to the precinct on a public bus. Luckily, it is one of the old buses that still has an open platform in the rear, and Freier succeeds in tossing several incriminating documents overboard during the trip without being noticed.

With nothing to implicate her, Mina is released the following morning and heads directly to the office of the Centre. It is not the first time Fry learns of the arrest of one of his people, but this news hits him harder than usual. He gave Freier the idea to use his artistic talents to imitate signatures and draw little stamps on identification forms. He turned him into a forger. Fry hires a lawyer to do his utmost for Freier. The odds are not good, however; the body of evidence is too blatant.

Marseille, late December 1940

Among the points of contention between Fry and the New Yorkers is the question of the people for whom Fry requests American visas and the order in which he has them smuggled to Spain via the only path to escape available, the "F" route. He has been unable to get everyone to safety whose names are on the lists with which the committee sent him to Marseille – not by a long shot. Instead, he unilaterally sent other, less famous intellectuals and artists on their way.

To defuse the conflict, Fry decides to visit some of the most prominent candidates on his lists to actively offer them his assistance in fleeing to America. Yet most of those who have not initiated contact with the Centre of their own accord do not even want to be rescued in this way. Henri Matisse and André Malraux, for instance, are banking on the protection of the armistice agreement and intend to remain in France. Even Theodor Wolff, formerly editor-in-chief of the *Berliner Tageblatt*, turns them down, despite as a German Jew knowing very well what he can expect of the Nazis. He is seventy-two, lives in an elegant flat in Nice with a view of the sea, only just weathered an operation on his eyes, and feels too tired to flee from the Nazis to a different country yet again.

André Gide now lives in a hamlet called Cabris, in the countryside outside Cannes. He receives Fry very genially, serves tea and cookies, but also makes clear from the outset that he does not want to leave France. The Germans, he emphasizes, have gone to considerable expense to gain his sympathies and make him the literary poster child for the occupying government. Apparently, Gide mentions, they regard him as France's leading writer. But there is no way he will respond to their overtures; collaborating with the Nazis is out of the question for him.

Only Marc Chagall, now living in Gordes, a half-deserted village near Avignon, after his escape from Paris, can be won over to a rescue plan. As a Jew, he experiences the Pétain regime's antisemitic laws firsthand. He was born in Russia and received French citizenship three years ago, but now it is to be revoked again, as it is from all other immigrated Jews as well. As a further argument for his journey to America, Fry is able to present him with an invitation from the Museum of Modern Art in New York. And so he acquiesces. For the time being, however, he shall remain in Gordes. Not until Fry has gotten the necessary emigration papers together will he come to Marseille.

Marseille, late December 1940

After the fight with the New Yorkers has escalated, Fry can no longer count on their help obtaining immigration papers to the United States for all the refugees whose names he passes along to them. The committee now views Jay Allen as the responsible party in Marseille, even if so far he only cares about his journalistic work. Fry must thus again look for new ways to get people not on the committee's lists out of France.

In a situation such as this, he recalls the contact made by Albert Hirschmann with the Guérini brothers, the Corsican gangsters. Their restaurant, La Dorade, is just a couple of street corners away from the offices on the Rue Grignan, making it easy for Fry to cultivate the relationship during occasional lunches or dinners.

Charles, the man behind the register at this establishment who never shows any emotion and never drinks anything but mineral water, is well informed about everything happening in Marseille. Naturally, he also knows about the Centre's clandestine activities and can make Fry an offer. Now, half a year after the armistice, there are again more freighters plying the Mediterranean, and for his people at the docks, it is no trouble to get stowaways on board – for good pay. Nevertheless, when the refugees then come ashore in Syria, Egypt, Algeria, or Morocco, they have no visas for the respective countries and must expect to end up in jail. But a jail in the Middle East or North Africa is a better place than a concentration camp in Germany.

Provence, late December 1940

It is one of the harshest winters Marseille and its surrounds have ever experienced. The Côte d'Azur lies beneath a solid blanket of snow. In the countryside, farmers must break up the sheet of ice covering the troughs so that their animals can get to the water. The Rhone is frozen solid over long stretches. André Breton, who in autumn was still living in a fisherman's hut at the mouth of the river, can luckily say that he and his family are now quartered in the Villa Air Bel. But its inhabitants can scarcely heat the large house. Coal and wood are strictly rationed, and the allocations by way of the ration coupons are no longer sufficient. In their desperation, the residents fell a tree on the villa's grounds to make firewood.

On the day after Christmas, the temperatures in Marseille drop to minus eleven degrees Celsius (twelve degrees Fahrenheit), and in some places the thermometer even reads minus thirteen (under nine degrees

Fahrenheit). Tram service can only be maintained if the frozen railway switches are regularly thawed with blowtorches.

It is on these of all days that Fry must arrange the move of his Centre Secours. The rental agreement for the rooms on the Rue Grignan, which the leather trader had conveyed to them in September at no charge, expires at the end of the year. Fry has found a new office in a stately three-story bourgeois home at number 18, Boulevard Garibaldi. With four large, sunlit rooms, it offers more space and is located right in the city center, just a few buildings away from the main drag on La Canebière. The cost of rent, however, now imposes an additional burden on an already strained budget.

At the same time, bad news arrives from New York. Eileen has to inform her husband that the Foreign Policy Association's patience has finally run out. In August, the organization had been generous enough to allow him to go on leave from his duties as lead editor of Headline Books for the trip to Marseille, which, at the time, was not supposed to last longer than three weeks. Now, a good four months later, they have fired him and hired a successor.

Their dismissal hits Fry hard. He loved his work, which for him was a job close to his heart. But, he writes back to Eileen: "Compared to the human beings in my care here, even the headline books [*sic*] seem unimportant." It is simply impossible for him, he has written to his wife multiple times already, to abandon his work in Marseille: "This job is like death – irreversible. We have started something here we can't stop. We have allowed hundreds of people to become dependent on us. We can't now say we are bored and are going home."

Sanary-sur-Mer, January 6, 1941

The cold takes its toll. Franz Hessel is a diminutive, introverted man, among the greats in the world of literature. As a writer, he captured the mood of his favorite cities, Berlin and Paris, in wonderfully tender short stories. As an editor at Rowohlt Verlag, he discovered the hidden talents of numerous budding authors. As a translator, he introduced Germany to masterpieces by Balzac, Stendhal, and Proust. And what's more, in matters of love, he remains an inveterate romantic.

Before the First World War, he married the fashion journalist Helene Grund who seems like the perfect contrast to him: chic, impetuous, immoderate, and endowed with the measure of recklessness that he lacks. Helene Grund never thought much of marital fidelity and, in full candor, began an affair with one of Hessel's close friends, the art dealer Henri-Pierre Roché. Hessel obtained a divorce but could not let go of his wife, marrying her a second time even though she was unwilling to break up with Roché. Over the years, they were bound together by a love triangle that produced two sons, Ulrich Hessel and the Stéphane Hessel with whom Varian Fry has become friends on their joint excursions through Provence over previous weeks.

Franz Hessel is now sixty years old, but in spite of his age, he was incarcerated in Les Milles and Saint Nicolas like Lion Feuchtwanger. Life in the camps shattered him. After a bout of bacterial dysentery, he was so emaciated that the commandant of Saint Nicolas eventually released him. Since then, he has again been living with Helene and their son Ulrich in a narrow house in Sanary-sur-Mer, the only luxury of which is a cramped tower room where he has put his writing desk. For a few weeks, it looks as though he will recover. He works on a novel and tries to gain other authors for an anthology of stories about their experiences as refugees. It is to bear the title *Erzählungen am Lagerfeuer von Saint Nicolas* [*Stories from the Camp Fire at Saint Nicolas*].

But then the cold comes. Each morning, Hessel sets out with sacks and a wheelbarrow to gather wood from the forests of Sanary. Alfred Kantorowicz runs into him by happenstance. Hessel does not complain, but he is so exhausted that Kantorowicz has to prop him up and walk him home through the ice-cold wind. Hessel jokes that it is only the freezing cold that makes him stiff and inflexible. At home, he sits for a while in an unheated room, sighing deeply once or twice, and neither Helene nor Ulrich notice how he is doing. When Kantorowicz is about to visit him two days later, he has already died: quietly, without complaint or much fuss – just as he had lived.

To the surprise of his wife and son, once news of Hessel's death has made the rounds in town, an impressive procession of mourners shows up at his death bed. It is not just authors from the German exile community who know the role he played for literature who come, but also Sanary's many French inhabitants. The unprepossessing, always friendly man in the loden coat – who could be seen every day at the market or in a café, and who enjoyed watching them play pétanque along the harbor – made a bigger impression on them than was to be suspected.

On the day of the funeral, the weather turns. The cold yields to heavy, pouring rain. Hessel's writer friends wait in the paltry shelter of the cemetery wall. When the coffin and the family arrive, one of them, Hans Siemsen, recites a short poem by Joachim Ringelnatz at the graveside.

> When I pass, you must never cry,
> My love for you will also not die,
> Have a good cry, have a good laugh,
> Do well what you do on your own behalf.

After they have shaken the hands of Helene and his two sons, they depart, frozen and soaked, to warm themselves over grog at one of the cafés along the harbor that Hessel so loved to frequent. They sit together for a long while, staring into their mugs in silence.

Banyuls, January 14, 1941

Lisa Fittko is still doing poorly, but she has now regained enough strength to return to Banyuls. She had jaundice, she thinks. The doctor bet on scurvy. In the end, however, the diagnosis did not matter since there were no drugs or vitamin-rich foods that could have helped her anyway. On the ward where she lay, there were two rows of thirty beds with terminally ill and dying patients. Over the first two weeks, her fever was so high that she hardly noticed what was going on around her. Then, later, she would frequently hear the hours-long death rattles of many a patient, but it hardly scared her because she had grown used to it. Unable to visit her, her husband sent her letters regularly. Marcel Verzeano, who had taken over Dick Ball's task of escorting the Centre's clients to Banyuls, twice stopped by on the way back to Marseille and for a precious hour told her about her husband and about work.

When she is finally allowed to leave the hospital, the women on the dying ward collect safety pins for her to pin up her skirt tightly around her waist. She has grown so thin it would otherwise fall down around her feet. Her husband has found a new flat for them both in Banyuls. It is just a single room in one of the narrow, three-story buildings near the

Hans and Lisa Fittko in Marseille, 1941

port, and the apartment, ludicrously enough, is located directly above the city's customs office, but it has running water and a toilet.

Naturally, the pair are just as cautious as before, but by now, everyone in Banyuls ultimately suspects why they set out into the mountains on excursions with guests so often. No one is bothered by it. On the contrary, tacit agreement with what they do is widespread in town. No one snoops on them, and one of the customs agents even goes out to eat with them occasionally at the tavern and warns them if a refugee is acting awkwardly and is in danger of attracting attention.

For the time being, Lisa is too weak for the path through the mountains. Hans takes over the guiding work on his own. Neighbors can tell by looking at her how sick she was and try to help her without a lot of fuss. Since there is pork at the butcher shop for a change, she stands in line and hands the butcher her ration coupons. The man looks at her and asks:

"How much do you want?"

"Those are all the coupons I have," she says.

The butcher shakes his head. "I'm asking how much meat you want, not how many coupons you have."

Then he gives her an entire pound, an actual little roast, even though according to her ration card she is only due a hundred grams a week.

Marseille, mid-January 1941

By this point, Fry's biggest worries are Rudolf Breitscheid and Rudolf Hilferding. Over the past few days, the French police have, for the first time, arrested prominent exiles and handed them over to the Nazis. Fry knows that the two SPD politicians are right at the top of the Gestapo's wanted lists. If he intends to rescue them, he must act swiftly now – especially since he cannot predict how the power struggle with the ERC in New York will end and whether he will have the opportunity to help them later.

The two Rudolfs – as Breitscheid and Hilferding are wont to be called at the Centre – have had in hand all requisite paperwork to enter the United States for months now. It was only the French exit permits they could never get. Fry repeatedly offered to have the Fittkos get them over the border illegally. But they view themselves as statesmen with an international reputation and consider fleeing over the Pyrenees not only unworthy of them, but also ultimately pointless, since they think themselves so famous that they would also be recognized and arrested in Spain. Although the French have been detaining them in a guarded hotel in Arles since September, they have both so far trusted Marshal Pétain's regime to protect them from abuse by the Nazis.

Now, however, that the French police have handed over refugees to the Gestapo for the first time, Breitscheid and Hilferding have become more receptive to Fry's offers. To spare them the arduous route over the mountains, he intends to have them put on a cargo ship as stowaways by the Guérini brothers' gangsters and taken to Algeria. The plan is especially perilous, not least because of the long escape route from Arles to the port of Marseille. As soon as Breitscheid and Hilferding leave the hotel in Arles without authorization, the police will put all trains and buses to Marseille under strict surveillance.

But Charles – the Guérinis' man at La Dorade – also has a solution for that. Although there are hardly any more privately owned cars, one of his gangster friends has access to a big limousine and an official special permit to move freely throughout France in it whenever he likes. A tremendous privilege: obviously, the connections of the Corsican mafiosi in Marseille reach all the way to the highest ranks of the administration.

The evening on which the car's driver is to fetch the two SPD bigwigs and smuggle them to Marseille via roads still covered in snow, Fry spends at the Guérinis' restaurant. At the official curfew, Charles lowers the iron shutters over the entrance and windows, but his regular guests know a rear door through which they can still enter the establishment late. An English consular employee on whose behalf Fry has already taken some British soldiers out of the country joins him at his table. The man is drunk and, to Fry's irritation, begins speaking in allusions about their clandestine endeavors despite being within earshot of a shady Russian moneychanger who occasionally does black market deals for the Centre. Fry keeps trying to change the subject to something inconsequential. Under ordinary circumstances, he would leave the table and head home, but on this evening, he is too nervous to be alone. He wants to learn immediately and firsthand whether Breitscheid and Hilferding have arrived in Marseille undetected.

Eventually, the driver of the limousine comes in through the rear door and, without casting a glance at Fry, walks up to Charles, who as ever is sitting at the register behind the counter. The man is perceptibly furious.

"*Allez!* What's up?" Charles asks.

Without turning around, Fry can easily hear what is said at the counter.

"They changed their minds," the driver says.

"What?"

"They don't want to leave," he explains.

"What do you mean they don't want to leave?" Charles cannot really believe his ears.

The driver shrugs. "It's enough to make you crazy. I drive all the way to Arles to get two guys who are supposed to be in mortal danger. And when I get there, they tell me they've changed their minds; they don't want to leave! They can kiss my ass. Cowards!"

Pamiers – Marseille, mid-January 1941

Anna Seghers has spent a good three months at Madame Jeanne's in Pamiers. During this time, she has traveled multiple times to Marseille to obtain visas for her family's escape to Mexico. While doing so, she often froze miserably. As absurd as it may sound, she has come to know Marseille as a city of cold, storms, and snow. While the freeze may be subsiding a bit now, the low temperatures remain a problem because she was only able to take lodgings with the children in a cheap, poorly heated hotel in the Arab quarter.

Luckily, Seghers managed to finagle a visa from the Mexican consulate for her husband, too. Since Rodi must pick it up from the consul in person, the camp commandant of Le Vernet is prepared, just this once, to have him transferred to Les Milles. From there, Rodi will occasionally receive authorization to leave for two or three days so that he can finally see his family again and take care of his travel formalities in Marseille.

After those quiet weeks in Pamiers, Seghers is happy to be living in a large city again. One evening, she takes the children to the Old Port to show them a restaurant with a large oven that prepares a special dish in it called pizza. It is a round sheet of dough dressed with cheese, tomatoes, and other kinds of vegetables and then baked in the oven. When the flatbread is served at the table hot, at first glance it looks like a flat cake, but it has the savory taste of vegetables and spices. As they have at every waypoint along their escape, the children go to school in Marseille as well. The Lycée Thiers is conveniently located; it is not far from the hotel and the same distance with respect to the new office of the Centre Américain de Secours, where each week Seghers picks up a financial subsidy for the maintenance of her family.

The most important thing the family now needs, though, Fry is not permitted to pay for, according to the ERC's political rules: passage to Mexico. But on this point, Seghers is able to rely on her network of communist friends. Years ago, the Communist Party of the United States of America founded a League of American Writers, for which many leftist American authors have volunteered during the global economic crisis. Because Jewish and other aid committees are unwilling to pony up for the escape costs of the family of an obviously highly talented writer who is nevertheless loyal to Stalin, the League ultimately covers them. Altogether, the four ship tickets from Lisbon to America cost more than a small car.

Like countless other refugees in Marseille, Seghers now plans to go to battle for the still-missing French exit visas – when she hears a sensational rumor. Since the beginning of the year, the Ministry of the Interior in Vichy has been surprisingly generous when it comes to issuing visas for travel to French colonies. Formally speaking, these documents do not permit one to leave France, but still to journey from the motherland to certain overseas possessions: to Martinique, for instance, one of the isles of the Antilles in the southern Caribbean. And there is even a shipping line that regularly departs from Marseille for Martinique. That all sounds extremely enticing, even for exiles who have never heard about Martinique and do not have the slightest clue what to do there. For them, it is enough to know that this little island is far, far away from Europe – because that means it is far, far away from the Nazis.

Arles, mid-January to early February 1941

Breitscheid and Hilferding have also heard this unbelievable rumor. At the outset, they proceeded very cautiously, inquiring with the authorities in Arles whether it might be disadvantageous for them in some way to apply for such exit papers. The officials in the little provincial town did not know but were willing to ask the government in Vichy. Its answer came promptly and was striking; not the slightest danger for two men existed in France, the Ministry of the Interior informed them, and the desired visas for Martinique had been issued forthwith and were ready for them at the prefecture in Marseille.

It is evident even to Fry that, under these circumstances, the two Rudolfs no longer had any interest in being smuggled illegally to Marseille by a gangster. Still, he finds it difficult to trust the Vichy regime's sudden liberality. Since living in France, he has not heard of a single case in which an exile was permitted to leave the country with a genuine, officially approved exit permit.

A few days later, however, Breitscheid and Hilferding are sitting across from him in the Centre's new office, showing off to him with mild condescension the documents he had thought as out of reach as the moon. Fry congratulates them that he was wrong and privately reproaches himself for having advised the two men, again and again, to undertake illegal and hazardous actions to flee. The Ministry of the Interior even provided both of them with letters of recommendation. In them, the shipping business that runs the ocean line to

Martinique is requested to treat these high-ranking passengers with special courtesy.

These letters do not make a big impression, however. The booking office of the shipping company is located only a few hundred paces from the Centre. The clerk there cannot be bargained with. He informs Breitscheid and Hilferding that on the next available ship, the *Wyoming*, all first-, second-, and third-class cabins are already booked and that he can only offer them berths in a dormitory below deck. The two politicians imagined this passage would be considerably more pleasant, but Hilferding bites the bullet and has one of the last available berths reserved for him. Breitscheid, on the other hand, sees that as beneath his dignity. He suffers from insomnia anyhow and would rather wait for the next ship than settle for group accommodation.

When Fry hears about this, he is appalled. He still sees Breitscheid as facing great danger; every day the politician spends within striking distance of the Gestapo is, in Fry's view, an unnecessary risk. He implores him to put up with every imaginable discomfort in order to put Europe behind him once and for all. But after Fry's miscalculation in visa matters, Breitscheid doubts his competence more than ever. For a while he wavers with his decision – until it is snatched from his hands.

Five days before the ship's departure, an official in Arles informs the two SPD politicians that he must invalidate their visas at the behest of the Ministry of the Interior and that they may not leave their hotel again until further notice. Both are speechless, though they still cling to the hope of remaining under the continued protection of the French government. A week later, there is a knock at their hotel room doors. Policemen arrest them and take them to Vichy. In the car, Breitscheid complains, "Why do you torture us this way if you only want to extradite us in the end?" The official escorting them replies: "You have a very low opinion of France, sir."

In Vichy, the two men must spend the night in a police building. The next morning, they are taken to the border between the occupied and unoccupied zones and handed over to the Gestapo there.

Marseille, February 4, 1941

For almost five months now, Walter Mehring has been living at the Hôtel Splendide. As an allegedly seriously ill person, he must not be caught outside his room. He is condemned to idleness. Since he was magnificently networked with other exiled artists and writers during his years in Vienna and Paris, he was able to give Fry advice on occasion about selecting clients whom the Centre ought to support. Aside from that, all he could do was wait for any unforeseeable opportunity to flee.

That opportunity has now arrived. Mehring is among the first people to hear about the new Martinique route from the Centre. In fact, he, too, receives a travel permit with surprising ease, but since all accessible ships are already fully booked, the document is initially useless to him. Then, however, Fry learns that Breitscheid and Hilferding's visas were annulled, thereby freeing up Hilferding's berth on the *Wyoming*. The Centre immediately picks up the costs and secures the ticket for Mehring, to put him, finally, on his way to America.

On the day of departure, armed policemen bar the quay where the *Wyoming* is moored. The passengers are let through the cordons only one by one or as families, and officers of the Police Nationale thoroughly check their papers, routinely matching the names of those leaving with a card index behind their desk. The official checking Mehring's identification papers and visa takes no issue with anything until he turns to the index and finds a card in it bearing Mehring's name along with the comment "Exit from France prohibited."

The official shows Mehring the card. "I fear you will have to wait a few minutes. I have to inquire first." Then he vanishes into a side room to phone the prefecture. Mehring is terrified. He collapses onto a bench, distraught, and begins making peace with his life – to the extent he is capable of formulating a coherent thought.

Mehring has that modicum of luck with which many unimaginable things are possible in Vichy France. Ten agonizing minutes later, the officer returns to him, and it is obvious he is no sympathizer with the Nazis or the Pétain regime. He hands Mehring all his documents and smiles: "I suspect this has to do with a different Walter Mehring. You may board."

Paris, February 11, 1941

Rudolf Hilferding has been severely maltreated on the way to Paris already. In La Santé prison, where the Gestapo houses its detainees, he is tortured and dies in his cell during the night from February 10 to 11. A short while later, Rudolf Breitscheid is taken to Berlin and transferred to Berlin's Gestapo prison on Prinz-Albrecht-Strasse.

Marseille, February 14, 1941

When Fry learns of the two men's extradition, he is stunned. There is now nothing more he can do for them, except inform the public about their fate and the deplorable role Marshal Pétain's regime played in this case. He is so upset that even at risk of being wiretapped, he reaches for the phone and calls the *New York Times* bureau in Vichy to pass along all the facts and details.

In the afternoon, he is paid a visit by one of the many clients whom the Centre supports with weekly payments but who is still waiting in vain for an exit. The man is an impressive personage: tall, stout, rhetorically brilliant, and highly intelligent. His name is Alfred Apfel, and in the years before Hitler's ascent to power, he was among Germany's most well-known attorneys. In sensational political trials, he defended leftist artists and authors like George Grosz and Carl von Ossietzky, thus incurring the wrath of the National Socialists.

Fry has not yet recovered from the shock of Breitscheid's and Hilferding's betrayal and is happy to be able to discuss their political backgrounds with a man as experienced as Apfel. The two of them fear that the government will soon extradite additional famous exiles. Since Apfel was on the first list of exiles who were expatriated by the Nazis in 1933, along with Breitscheid, Feuchtwanger, and Heinrich Mann, Fry considers him to be in particular danger as well. He strongly advises him to be especially careful in the coming days.

Apfel hesitates. He goes pale, his face registers pain, and he clutches at his chest and neck.

"I … I … I don't know. I think I'm having a heart attack," he gasps.

Fry leaps up and manages to catch him before he slides from the chair onto the floor. Together with Marcel Verzeano, the Centre's physician, he carries the heavy man into a side room. They try everything at their disposal in the way of first aid. They tear open his collar to give him air and listen to his chest for heart sounds.

But they have no chance. Apfel is beyond help. After half an hour, Verzeano must declare him dead.

Spring in France

February to June 1941

Marseille, mid-February 1941

The battle between Fry and the ERC in New York rages on. The situation is still unresolved. Under no circumstances does Fry want to turn over the Centre to his designated successor, Jay Allen, and the New Yorkers want to force Fry's return to America, once and for all. He was hired, they reproach them, for only four weeks and to rescue a few famous artists and has not had a valid contract with the committee in a long while. Mildred Adams in particular, who feels beholden to Allen, accuses Fry of having become a radical during his stay in France. In internal memoranda to other members of the ERC board, she enumerates some of his sins: he lives in Villa Air Bel "with Victor Serge, an old Bolshevik," and rescues predominantly "German Jews" or former "Spanish combatants." In other words, she considers him politically unreliable and a liability for the committee's collaboration with the State Department.

The State Department is apparently of the same view and makes Fry feel its might. Now, after six months in France, Fry's passport is expiring, and he must request a renewal. In essence, a routine matter, but Fry learns from Consul General Hugh Fullerton that there are strict instructions to renew his passport only if he agrees to return to the United States at once.

Fry is bewildered and agitated. He can see in these instructions nothing but a brutal attempt at blackmail on the part of the State Department, for without his American passport, he is of course robbed of an important safeguard. The department demonstrates to him how much he is at their mercy, but by doing so, if nothing else, they provoke the defiance of Varian the Contrarian. In that case, he writes to Eileen, he will simply remain in Marseille without a passport; he will not allow himself to be strong-armed. But what distinguishes him as an American without identification papers in wartime from the refugees he is trying to help?

Montauban, mid-February 1941

Hannah Arendt and Heinrich Blücher find themselves facing one of the most difficult decisions of their lives, and they must make it quickly. The government in Vichy, they have learned from reliable sources, has become noticeably more generous in issuing exit papers since the turn of the year. Why, nobody knows, and nobody knows the criteria by which Pétain's ministries select the exiles who may leave the country.

Right away, Arendt and Blücher try their luck by applying to leave – and receive positive answers! Suddenly, their waiting is at an end. At one stroke, there are no more bureaucratic obstacles between them and the salvation of being abroad. They have valid transit visas for Spain and Portugal and entry visas for the United States. The path to freedom is open to them.

Since October, however, Hannah Arendt's mother has been living with them in Montauban. She is now sixty-six years old and still does not have any visas, neither for Spain and Portugal, nor for America. Deciding whether to leave without her is enormously difficult for them. Fortunately, however, Arendt ran into a Russian friend from Paris in Montauban who is willing to care for her mother until her visas have arrived. Besides, she hopes to be able to do more for her from America than if she were to stay in France.

To the very end, doubts remain about the regime's sudden generosity, but the customs agents do indeed allow Hannah Arendt and Heinrich Blücher to pass. The country that, with no explanation, has long treated them as prisoners now sets them free, with no explanation. In Spain, too, they encounter no trouble. Not until they are in Lisbon does their streak of luck end. All ships to the United States have been booked for months to come. After Vichy opened its border just a crack, a torrent of refugees made for Portugal. Again, Arendt and her husband must gear up for an unforeseeable period of waiting – now, though, in a country where they are largely safe from the Nazis.

Marseille, February 1941

Max Ernst is wearing the sheepskin jacket of a shepherd when he arrives at Villa Air Bel. He has spent months in internment camps, first in Les Milles, then in Saint Nicolas. From Saint Nicolas, the tent city, he fled twice and covered the seventy kilometers to his atelier on the river Ardèche. The first time, he was denounced by a deaf-mute neighbor and taken back to the camp by the police in handcuffs. The second time, he was forced to realize that there was no place for him to flee. His girlfriend, the painter Leonora Carrington, had suffered a schizophrenic episode in his absence, had sold their house together, and had disappeared to Spain.

Now he is sitting in the villa's only barely heated dining room, cutting a picturesque figure with his tanned face, his prominent, beak-like nose, and his bright blue eyes. With his abrupt movements and the thick fleece jacket, he comes across like a giant bird blown in from the outside and now puffing up its feathers against the cold.

He is no stranger at this dining table. Varian Fry may be meeting him for the first time, but ten years earlier, as a student at Harvard, he had printed pictures by him in his magazine *Hound & Horn*. And Max Ernst is connected to André Breton in particular by a complicated common history. For almost twenty years, he numbered among the most important painters of surrealism for Breton. In Breton's eyes, he has the incomparable ability to wrest everything he depicts in his paintings out of the quotidian, familiar world and shift it all into new, surprising – which is to say: surrealist – associations. The major exhibitions Breton organized were for him not complete unless he was able to show works by Max Ernst in them.

Ernst is friends not just with Breton, though, but also with the second great pioneer of surrealism, Paul Éluard – and two years ago an irremediable conflict broke out between Éluard and Breton over key political questions, but it was also a bit about the wounded vanity of two huge artist-egos. Breton has long opposed the Stalinist course of France's communist party and on this point demands absolute loyalty from his entourage. Éluard, however, would not submit to him and in 1938 published a propagandist poem in the Stalinist party newspaper *Commune* as a sign of his resistance. Consequently, Breton formally shut him out of the surrealist movement and demanded his devotees break off all personal contact with Éluard. Max Ernst was not willing to issue a total condemnation of that sort, for which reason Breton likewise excluded him from his surrealist circles.

At the Villa Air Bel, though, Breton does not possess the power to pronounce such verdicts of banishment. He is a guest in this motley community, not the man of the house. And so he must put up with it if Ernst's charm and the charisma of his art win over the others' sympathies.

Max Ernst painted incessantly in Les Milles and Saint Nicolas. He took the finished works with him on his various flights and has now also recovered his works and those of Leonora Carrington that were stored in his home on the Ardèche – all in all, an impressive number of paintings. To make their transport nimbler, he has removed many of the canvases from their stretchers, stacked them up, and rolled them together into heavy sausages. Now he unrolls them, one by one, and enjoys showing them like an actor enjoys stepping on stage. The residents of the villa are enthralled. The paintings seem like windows into a fantastic world full of monsters and vines beneath resplendently clear skies. Quite a few of Leonora Carrington's paintings seem to respond to those by Max Ernst; it is like eavesdropping on the painted dialogue of two lovers. Within a few days, the housemates organize an exhibition. Since not all pictures find an appropriate spot on the walls of the house, Max Ernst suggests hanging some of them from the branches of the winter-bare plane trees on the terrace, where they dance gently in the wind and glow.

For a short time, Air Bel becomes the gathering place of French avant-garde art. It is not just Breton's inner circle of surrealists who come, but also many of those who had distanced themselves from Breton. René Char, André Masson, Jacques Lipchitz, and not least Marcel Duchamp – all of them want to see the exhibition in the trees. Because it has grown warmer again, a long table is set up on the terrace beneath the plane trees and covered in a white cloth. At that point, however, the hosts stand there embarrassed because there is almost nothing to eat; they can only offer wine.

For Max Ernst, the exhibition is an attempt to reconcile with Breton. As ever, he considers the rift on Éluard's account unnecessary. Breton, though, remains unyielding. He enjoys being photographed, and photographed often, in front of the villa with his devotees, but takes care that

Jacques Hérold (standing), Max Ernst, and Daniel Bénédite hang pictures by Max Ernst and Leonora Carrington in a tree in front of the Villa Air Bel

Max Ernst, one of the most important surrealist painters, is not visible in the pictures.

Marseille, late February 1941

The Centre's four rooms on the Boulevard Garibaldi are overcrowded. On some days, up to twenty people work here now. Ever since the exiles have been able to obtain exit visas from the French authorities, Fry has enlarged his team without regard for the costs and has reorganized the office's work.

On the terrace of the Villa Air Bel, February 1941

Until now, they have focused on paying out small amounts each week to refugees stuck in Marseille to render their survival possible – and have secretly smuggled some of them out of the country illegally. They have succeeded in doing so around three hundred fifty times. Now, the Centre essentially functions as a travel agency. The main obstacle to escape is no longer the missing exit visas; it is the endless bureaucracy. Fry and his people help the exiles wind their way through the jungle of administrative bodies, book tickets for crossings, or search for aid organizations in America or the rest of the world willing to pay for these crossings. Each case is different. For some, it is more convenient to travel to Martinique. For others who have the entry permit for the United States or other countries, it is better to get to Lisbon by land and wait there for a ship.

Among the clients are celebrities like the physicist Peter Pringsheim, writers like Siegfried Kracauer and Hans Sahl, important sculptor Jacques Lipchitz, and theater producer Ernst Josef Aufricht, on whose stage Brecht's *The Threepenny Opera* became a global sensation. In the end, however, the difference between well-known and unknown refugees plays no role for Fry anymore. He now wants to rescue as many people as the capacities of his office allow, provided he can find money to do so – and the French do not expel him.

Alongside the licit ways, however, there is still demand for illicit exits. Why even now some exiles are denied the requisite visas is initially inscrutable – until they succeed in bribing an employee at the prefecture in Pau who obtains for Fry a copy of a list of prohibited individuals. According to the will of the Gestapo, no one on it may leave the country, and the French authorities follow these instructions.

Fry studies the list very thoroughly and finds a few of his clients on it, too. Some of them, he realizes with pleasure, the Centre got out of the country weeks hence. Apparently, Hitler's Gestapo is not as well informed as it likes to claim it is, if it is still hunting in Marseille for people who have been in Manhattan or Hollywood for ages. In addition, Fry is happy that his Underground Railroad still runs smoothly after five months, and from this point on sends to the Fittkos in Banyuls first and foremost those people on the Gestapo list.

Marseille, February and March 1941

It is not just against external opposition that Mary Jayne Gold and Killer Raymond must defend their *amour fou*, but also against inner opposition. Only over time do they grasp how much courage and will they need for this. Mary Jayne has decided not to condemn the circles in which Raymond lives, but to study them as an ethnologist would a foreign people. She overlooks more minor instances of theft or fraud with a shrug and tries to persuade herself that the principal criminal energy comes from Mathieu, the gang leader.

It comes to a head in a first serious crisis when Raymond boasts about having shot a police informant with Mathieu and buried his corpse on the grounds of the Villa Air Bel. It never becomes entirely clear whether this murder actually took place or whether Raymond fabricated it to maintain his grim reputation. Fry is nevertheless worried. The Centre cannot afford to be implicated in a crime. With others from the house, he searches the park grounds, but fortunately they find no freshly disturbed soil anywhere.

Mary Jayne is self-confident, educated, wealthy. That holds an enormous attraction for Raymond, but it also makes him wary. In his world, women usually do not have much of a say. Mathieu's girlfriend does what Mathieu wants; she cooks, she cleans, she stays quiet, and – if Mathieu demands it of her – she sleeps with other men. Mary Jayne, on the other hand, makes Raymond feel her independence. One cold winter's evening, he brings her a fur coat he stole on one of his hauls, but Mary Jayne, spoiled by fashion, has different standards. She finds the coat so ugly that she will not wear it under any circumstances. She makes excuses – it does not fit; it is not the right size – but Raymond notices that his present is not good enough for her.

Mary Jayne also feels unnerved by the liaison. She has never experienced such an adventuresome passion. For a shockingly long time, she succeeds in turning a blind eye to a fact that is immediately apparent to the others. Raymond is very young, just twenty-one, almost ten years her junior. Although there was talk about his age in the court proceedings because of his desertion, she always wanted to believe his assertions that he was already twenty-eight. The age difference makes the relationship between them even more imbalanced. Next to her, Raymond comes off not as her lover, but as a boy toy she exploits. Then again, when he affects the tough guy, the killer, some of her friends get the impression that she is addicted to him, ultimately in thrall to him, sexually. Both offend her; both embarrass her.

One evening, Mathieu and Raymond pay an unannounced visit to the Villa Air Bel. They burst into the dining room where the Centre's employees are sitting together, and shout and point at the people at the table with their hands in their coats, like gangsters in the movies hiding revolvers in their pockets. It is unclear what they want, but they behave so menacingly that Dagobert the poodle – essentially Raymond's best friend – crawls underneath the table and cannot be lured out again. Apparently, they believe they can intimidate the Centre's scaredy-cat intellectuals with cheap tricks, unsuspecting that Daniel Bénédite and Jean Gemähling possess far more military combat training than they let on. Eventually, the two leave the house just as abruptly as they came.

The next day, Fry talks to Mary Jayne and asks her to move out of the villa so as not to endanger the work of the Centre. It is not easy for her, but she realizes that Fry is right. Her connection to Raymond harbors risks she cannot ask of the others.

Marseille, March 14, 1941

When Fry comes to his office in the morning, he receives a brief message that ends a long conflict. Jay Allen has been arrested. A few days earlier, he had set out for Paris for research without a *sauf-conduit* and then was about to return to the unoccupied zone. While attempting to cross the demarcation line illegally, he was apprehended by a patrol. Now he will be detained in a prison for several weeks and then deported.

The argument between Fry and the New Yorkers is thus decided. Since his potential successor must leave the country but he can remain in Marseille, the committee must come to terms with Fry and his mode of operation, whether they like it or not.

Marseille, March 1941

To provide more variation during the Sunday gatherings at the Villa Air Bel, André Breton needs a deck of tarot cards. Because his understanding of surrealism has always bordered fairly closely on the world of esotericism, it should surprise no one if he is interested in the art of cartomancy. He asks young Gussie Rosenberg to keep his eyes peeled on his courier routes through Marseille for stores selling the playing cards. Although one of the most common decks bears the name Tarot de Marseille, Rosenberg is unable to scare one up anywhere in town. The following Sunday, consequently, Breton invites seven painters to join him in designing a surrealist tarot deck. He of course adds his wife Jacqueline Lamba to the group, plus Victor Brauner, Óscar Domínguez, Wilfredo Lam, and Jacques Hérold. André Masson and Max Ernst, whom he had actually banished from his inner circle, are permitted to be in on it as well. Is a reconciliation with him possible after all?

The eight of them not only develop new designs for the face cards, but also replace the traditional card suits. They transform clubs into "keyholes of knowledge." In place of spades come the "black stars of the dream." Diamonds become the "blood of the revolution," and hearts "flames." They name their new deck *Jeu de Marseille* after its place of origin. Unfortunately, they lack the time to design the necessary number cards this Sunday as well, and so the group project remains incomplete.

Marseille, mid-March 1941

For a good two months now, Bil Freier has been in police custody awaiting trial. Together with five other men, he has been crammed into a two-man cell. The food is wretched, and the constant confinement makes many of them aggressive. But Freier cannot be gotten down; he distracts himself. With paper and tusche that Fry's attorney brought him in jail, and despite the lack of space, he draws two long comic strips that he calls graphic novels because he can think of no better name for them.

At first, it looks as though Freier is very fortunate. The judge before whom he is brought after his arrest is evidently no proponent of the Vichy regime. He asked him a few routine questions, and once he heard Freier had studied art, he steered the conversation to painters like Murillo, Velázquez, and Rembrandt. He turned the interrogation into a chat among art aficionados. Presumably, he wanted to prevent Freier from implicating himself with some sort of thoughtless statement or confession.

After, the judge delayed the trial using all the rules of juridical art to let the dust settle a bit on the case. Today, then, he has had Freier retrieved from his cell, discussed the matter again with Fry's attorney, and then summarily halted the proceedings. There is no more talk of the unambiguous evidence against Freier; he may leave court a free man.

Fry is enormously relieved and has found Freier and his fiancé Mina a hiding place in an empty hotel. The rooms there are oddly furnished, with mirrors hanging everywhere, even on the ceiling. Eventually, the couple figure out that Fry has found them accommodation in an erstwhile bordello.

His luck does not last, however. Freier no longer has any identification papers; his forged *carte d'identité* was taken from him in jail. A friend brags about having excellent connections with an official at the prefecture, but when Freier applies for real papers, he is immediately arrested and carted off to Le Vernet camp.

Grenoble, mid-March 1941

Peggy Guggenheim has lost her car. More precisely, she has misplaced it: a pretty blue Talbot convertible with a long nose and a hatchback. She parked it in a garage, that much she can still recall. But since no gasoline has been dispensed to civilians in France for over half a year now, she was not able to use the vehicle and by this point has simply forgotten in which garage it is parked.

In principle, the car does not matter to her – she does not need it herself – but now it turns out that it would be useful to rescue her art collection. She thus goes from garage to garage in Grenoble with René, her art shipper, to locate the automobile. The two make good progress at first, until Peggy Guggenheim realizes that she has feelings for René, and she starts an affair with him. That delays the search considerably. Peggy loves being distracted by interesting men. She is an unattached woman and does not understand why she should do without this pleasure.

At the moment, though, delays are inconvenient because, rationally speaking, it is high time to get out of France. Peggy Guggenheim is a Jew, she has both of her children with her, and the government in Vichy keeps passing new antisemitic laws. The American consul in Grenoble warns her not to remain in the country a day longer than necessary. There are rumors circulating that sooner or later the French will hand over not only famous exiles to the Nazis, but all Jews as well.

But Peggy Guggenheim does not want to be spooked. At this point, she is forty-one years old and has been living in Europe for years. Her father was an industrialist and left her a considerable fortune with which she was long at loose ends, until her friend Samuel Beckett gave her the idea three years ago to collect avant-garde art. In another friend, Marcel Duchamp, she found the most competent advisor imaginable and opened a gallery in London. She learned quickly and purchased early paintings by Wassily Kandinsky, Yves Tanguy, Picasso, Giacometti, and Paul Klee.

It was last summer in Paris, however, when she made the haul of her life. As Hitler's troops were marching up to the French border and war could have broken out any day, countless artists wanted to leave the country as fast as possible and urgently needed cash for their travel funds. She thus drove from studio to studio, carrying a well-filled

Peggy Guggenheim in London, 1939 (In the background, the painting *Le Soleil dans son écrin* by Yves Tanguy)

briefcase, and bought up magnificent works for a song, including several Picabias, a Braque from his Cubist phase, a Gris, a Léger, and early works by Delaunay, Man Ray, and Mondrian, plus surrealist paintings by de Chirico, Miró, Magritte, and Victor Brauner, and sculptures by Brâncuşi, Lipchitz, André Masson, and Hans Arp. After only a few weeks, she had assembled a world-class collection.

Three days before the Germans marched into Paris, she was sitting outside Café de Flore, wondering with André Breton and other friends how she might get to Megève, near Grenoble, where her children were waiting for her. There was no other way but to risk driving the overcrowded streets south in her Talbot. She was reluctant to part ways with her newly acquired artistic treasures, but René promised her to pack them up well and send them on after her.

Everything has since arrived in Grenoble unscathed and for now is being stored in the basement of the municipal art museum. But how can she get this unparalleled collection to America safely, now, in these uncertain times of war? What René suggests to her is fairly unusual and a bit illegal, but otherwise easy to carry off. After they have actually tracked down the Talbot in one of Grenoble's garages, they will pack all the sculptures and paintings into the car, put a few lamps, blankets, plates, and pots on top, declare it altogether not as valuable cultural assets, but as household effects, and thus ship it, disguised, to New York.

When Guggenheim steps off the train at Marseille Saint-Charles to supervise the loading of the car at the port, an old friend of hers is already waiting on the platform. Victor Brauner belongs to the innermost circle of surrealists around Breton, but as a Jew and native Romanian, he is at risk of being arrested and taken to an internment camp at every roadside check. He hides away, disguised as a shepherd, in the mountains north of Marseille and hopes that Peggy Guggenheim can intervene with the American consulate and obtain a visa for him.

Victor Brauner is also among the interesting men with whom Peggy Guggenheim has a fling. Naturally, she will undertake everything she can to get him out of France. First, though, they shall spend the evening at Brûleur de Loups along the port, the surrealists' favorite café. And there they run into Max Ernst.

Marseille, late March to early April 1941

Toward the end of winter, food in France becomes scarcer and scarcer. The last stores have been used up, and there is nothing to harvest in the fields or gardens. Some employees of the Centre show concrete signs of malnourishment. Fry has lost ten kilograms and must literally tighten his belt so as not to lose his suit trousers. For two weeks, there is no bread anywhere in the city. Then cargo ships carrying grain from America arrive, gifts of solidarity from the United States to France. French bakers put little American flags on the bread baked with it. It is hard to imagine, Fry writes to Eileen, a more effective way to win sympathies for America.

Marseille, March 24, 1941

The *Capitaine Paul Lemerle* is anchored off depot no. 7 at Marseille's international port. It is a plain, mid-sized freighter, twenty years old, and already a bit ramshackle. It has cargo holds in its prow and its stern, low-slung superstructures, and four cabins for the crew. It is neither a pretty ship nor an elegant ocean liner, but access to it is more closely guarded than to a government palace. Police riot squads in helmets armed with automatic pistols seal off the quay in several rows. Up to the gangway, passengers have to walk through a dense cordon of guards warily eyeing their every step. The effect is that of a band of convicts being led single-file onto their galley.

The cargo ship is to put to sea in the afternoon and to take more than two hundred passengers across the Atlantic to Martinique. The forward hold is loaded with freight; in the aft one, ship's carpenters have erected two separate dormitories with bunked cots made from rough wooden planks, one for the women and the other for the men. In the ship's stern, there are several long tables with benches, also made from boards of spruce, where meals for largish groups can be eaten. And on both sides along the bulwark, cramped wooden cabins are lined up to serve as latrines: port side for men, starboard side for women.

Fry and his people have succeeded in securing forty spots aboard the ship for the Centre's clients. They are proud of their success, each ticket having cost them around 10,000 francs. Included among those who can finally leave are André Breton and Victor Serge with their families, the painter Wilfredo Lam, and – Fry is particularly happy about this – two of the four men from the old resistance group Neu Beginnen whom Mary Jayne Gold was temporarily able to pry loose from Le Vernet in October, but whose escape then failed. Other aid organizations have snagged tickets for their candidates, too. Anna Seghers is on board with her husband and two children, along with Alfred Kantorowicz and his wife. In addition, there is a young, highly talented ethnologist of Jewish derivation for whose passage the Rockefeller Foundation in New York paid: Claude Lévi-Strauss.

Yesterday, all the passengers had to present their papers at the port office to get the last approval stamps for their exit. No one expected any difficulties; everything had been verified a dozen times. Yet when Kantorowicz showed his passport to the official, he fared similarly to Walter Mehring before the departure of the *Wyoming*. The official disinterestedly rummaged through a card index, stopped short, found a card with Kantorowicz' name on it, signaled to two policemen, and had him arrested. At one stroke, it was all over for him. He was wanted, Kantorowicz learned; there was a warrant out for his arrest. The two policemen searched him for weapons and led him through labyrinthine corridors to the office of the harbor commander. The latter was, absurdly enough, a colonel in the French air force. Yet Kantorowicz knew him, of all people, through French friends and was aware he thought Pétain's policy of collaboration a disgrace for France. He thus mentioned these friends' names to him, at which point the colonel tore up the arrest warrant, stamped Kantorowicz' passport, and advised him to leave the port office as quickly as possible.

Up to the last moment, it remains unclear who is actually allowed on board the *Capitaine Paul Lemerle* and who is not. At the last minute, by request of the Spanish military mission, all Spanish men fit for military service between the ages of eighteen and forty-eight are separated from their families on the quay and sent back. They are to be handed over to Franco. These men's farewells from their families, whom they may never see again, are heart-wrenching.

When Victor Serge, experienced in matters of prison, descends into the ship's stern to the men's dormitory, he realizes what he has stumbled into. The *Capitaine Paul Lemerle* is a floating internment camp. The cavernous cargo hold has no windows and is ventilated only by the entry hatch. Straw mattresses lie atop the low wooden cots, but there are no blankets. Still, everyone aboard knows how lucky they may consider themselves to have won a spot to freedom on this cargo ship. When they

Refugees on the *Capitaine Paul Lemerle*, including Victor Serge (far left), Jacqueline Lamba (second from left), and Wilfredo Lam (third from left)

finally put to sea, everyone gathers on the stern to watch first the port, then the city, and finally Notre-Dame de la Garde with the giant golden Madonna on its spire vanish in the distance.

By the time the ship reaches the North African coast, the heat in the cargo hold has become unbearable, and passengers move their straw mattresses onto the deck to sleep. The cooking is done there, too, in large field kitchens: a porridge prepared each day alternately from rice with dried peas, rice with beans, or rice with lentils. In addition to that, the latrines spread the stench of resin-exuding, urine-soaked lumber.

Breton cannot stomach the incessant lack of space on board. He paces restlessly on deck until Claude Lévi-Strauss introduces himself and joins his peregrinations, and they engage in discussions of aesthetics and ethnology. Even more peculiar is the encounter between Anna Seghers and Victor Serge. Five years earlier at the Writers Congress in Paris, Seghers tried every which way to prevent a declaration of solidarity in support of Serge, who was serving time in a Siberian penal camp as a prisoner of Stalin. Now, the two of them must flee Europe on the same ship. Naturally, Serge knows what role Anna Seghers played at the time, but he also knows that she will not be able to be dissuaded from her political convictions and prefers to avoid her.

After a month-long sea voyage, the *Capitaine Paul Lemerle* enters the broad bay of Fort-de-France, the capital of Martinique. The passengers are overcome by the tropical splendor of the forests and mountains stretching out before them. Finally, they are safe – though nowhere near free, as they are soon made to realize. They are taken from the ship by boat straight to an internment camp called Le Lazaret, the island's former leprosy ward.

When Anna Seghers comes ashore at the camp with her family, a gray-haired man in bathing trunks approaches and greets her jauntily in a familiar tone: "Anna, Anna, what a pleasant surprise it is to see you wash up here on the blue waves of the Caribbean."

It is the writer Kurt Kersten, a friend from her years in Berlin. Kersten was lucky enough to get to Bordeaux so early during those chaotic weeks of war in France that he was able to get himself to safety from the advancing German troops on a French ship. He has now been living on Martinique for nine months and cannot get off the island again. None of the letters sent to refugee committees to free him from Le Lazaret have yet born fruit. Because he reached Martinique, he no longer counts as seriously threatened, and the aid organizations are understandably focusing their actions on the many persecuted persons still within reach of the Nazis and thus in mortal danger. Kurt Kersten is safe, but for now is also at an impasse.

Vichy, March 29, 1941

By request of the German military authorities, the government in Vichy establishes a *Commissariat general aux questions juives* (CGQJ). From this point forward, French measures to identify and remove from public life all people of Jewish descent – foreigners as well as French citizens – are to be coordinated by this "Commissariat-General for Jewish Affairs."

Banyuls, April 1, 1941

The gendarme charged with fetching Lisa and Hans Fittko and bringing them to the police station does not get far. Just a few paces past the front door, he is stopped and forced to justify himself. He does not find that easy; he stammers about, struggling for words, trying to mollify the situation. The Fittkos feel well and truly sorry for him.

According to a new directive from Vichy, each and every foreigner and non-resident must vacate the areas close to the border within a week. It is yet another attempt by the regime to halt illegal aid to escapees once and for all. The provision also affects the Fittkos. They must leave Banyuls, and they realize that their work for the Centre is thus about to end after half a year.

The landlady Mademoiselle Rosa, however, does not agree with this ordinance in the least. When Hans and Lisa step out the front door with the gendarme, she is just returning from the market with her shopping bag on her arm. She immediately accosts the police officer, asking where he plans on going with her renters. The new law, she says, does not affect the Fittkos because they are not outsiders; they have been living in town for a long time. Two other women stop to cajole the police officer, an older man joins them, and a crowd forms. The policeman defends himself. It was not his idea that foreigners are not allowed to live in Banyuls, but a decree by the government.

Mademoiselle Rosa shouts: "Foreigners? But these are our neighbors." Why would the gendarme now suddenly call them foreigners?

The others chime in to agree with her. A woman at the window in the building across the street shouts that the two of them are indeed from town.

Only when the gendarme promises that monsieur and madame will return in just a few minutes does the commotion subside.

It is not a big scene, just a small, friendly incident on the street. But for the Fittkos, it goes to show yet again how far the support of many French people for Hitler's foes reaches. Without the help of these French men and women, without their courage to take in and hide strangers, not one refugee would have been able to survive in France for more than a few weeks.

Before Lisa and Hans Fittko went to Banyuls for Fry, they had assembled all the documents they needed to escape abroad. In the interim, the precious visas from that time have long since expired, and they must both fight through the jungle of requests for help, affidavits, and authorizations to replace them once more. For this reason, they relocate to Cassis, thirty kilometers south of Marseille, where Lisa's brother is lying low with his family. From there, they can easily reach both the Centre and the American consulate, both of which are to support them in this fight. Fry and Hiram Bingham promise to do their utmost, but the bureaucratic hurdles have since grown higher. It will take months until the path is cleared of them, months during which Lisa and Hans must again go to ground and any unforeseen inspection could cost them their lives.

Marseille, April 2, 1941

Max Ernst has shown Peggy Guggenheim his exhibition at the Villa Air Bel like a deft master of ceremonies. Peggy Guggenheim is not especially fond of his new works, however, which offends him a little. She would rather have some of his early paintings already shown in large exhibitions, thus ensuring their high market value. Because Max Ernst needs money for a new start in America, he eventually sells her the pictures for two thousand dollars, though he will not get the majority of the money until he is in New York.

To seal the deal with a drink – but also because he is celebrating his fiftieth birthday today – Max Ernst invites Peggy Guggenheim and Victor Brauner to dinner at a black market restaurant where, for hard currency, they are served an astonishingly copious multicourse meal. By now, Peggy Guggenheim is quite taken by Max Ernst's charm. She begins falling in love with him, but does not want to snub Victor Brauner, her current lover, so she only flirts with him discreetly.

But when Ernst says goodbye to her after the meal, she makes herself clearer. He asks her: "When, where, and why will I see you again?" She answers with clear demands: "Tomorrow at four at Café de la Paix, and you know exactly why!"

Marseille, April 9, 1941

Fry has only just arrived at the Centre this morning when his telephone rings and Bella Chagall reports with alarm that her husband has just been arrested. Fry is shocked and appalled. It was only a few days ago that he had asked Marc Chagall and his family to relocate from remote Gordes to Marseille. He has gathered all the documents for them and wants to send them over the border to Spain. Now, because they complied with his request, they have practically walked right into a trap set by the police.

Apparently, a large-scale raid is underway, and Jews are being arrested in all of the city's hotels and taken to the police precincts to be registered. Fry's horror turns to fury. He dials the number of the police official in charge at the prefecture.

"You have just arrested Monsieur Marc Chagall," he says in a voice of hard-won self-control.

The official is not particularly impressed by this finding since he does not know who Marc Chagall is. Only when Fry explains to him that Chagall is one of the world's greatest living artists does he take notice.

"Should news of his arrest leak, for any reason," Fry adds, "the entire world would be horrified, the Vichy government would suffer considerable embarrassment, and you, presumably, could expect a severe reprimand."

"Thank you for phoning me. I will see to the case at once."

As soon as Fry has hung up, Daniel Bénédite embraces him excitedly. "That's how you have to talk to them, boss."

"If he isn't out in half an hour," Fry says, "we'll call the *New York Times*."

Half an hour later, Bella Chagall calls back to share that her husband was just brought back to the hotel by the police.

Big cheers at the Centre. Fry's associates congratulate him. He is delighted and smiles, then removes his glasses, wipes them clean, and has them give him the next client's file. Taking a stand for a world-famous man to protect him is comparatively easy; to rescue an anonymous refugee is all the more difficult.

Marseille, late April 1941

Hiram Bingham receives a letter of protest from Eleanor Roosevelt on his desk. God knows it is not the first indignant letter she has addressed to the consulate in Marseille. As ever, she eschews no conflict if it concerns assisting refugees from France. This missive, however, is different than the rest. In this case, she is not objecting because the consulate is approving too few emergency visas for entry to the United States, but because in her opinion it has issued one visa too many.

It has to do with Max Ernst and his wife Luise Straus-Ernst. Bingham has in front of him a joint visa for the pair of them. He has informed them of this, and as soon as the French authorities approve their exit, they can get on their way. But now Eleanor Roosevelt has learned the couple has been divorced for fifteen years. In her eyes – and not just in hers – this is more than an excusable error. In puritanical America, one is a stickler for such things. Quite a few unmarried couples Fry sent on their way across the Atlantic from Europe have already had to be married at sea by the captain of their ship so that they could disembark in New York as legally approved spouses.

Luise Straus-Ernst is a feisty character, not easily intimidated. She was one of the first women to write a doctoral thesis at the University of Bonn. With Max Ernst, Hans Arp, and others, she founded the Cologne branch of Dadaism after the First World War. Their collective exhibitions caused marvelous scandals; all of Cologne's art world was in uproar, and the artists were variously accused of blasphemy, pornography, or anarchism. At the point her husband fell in love with Gala Éluard and went to Paris, Luise split up with him and from then on wrote for some of Germany's best newspapers as an art critic and journalist.

In 1933, she had to flee the Nazis as a Jew. Bingham is aware of the risk she runs if he revokes the visa he has already issued her. He thus invites her and Max Ernst to meet with him at the consulate to discuss this business with both of them at once.

Eleanor Roosevelt's information is accurate, the two confirm; they have been divorced since 1926. Max Ernst tries to treat the matter lightly and suggests he and Luise could get married again to clear up this bothersome bureaucratic problem. The suggestion is either rash or not meant seriously, however, because shortly after their divorce, Max Ernst married Marie-Berthe Aurenche, fifteen years his junior, in Paris. While this marriage only exists now on paper, it is still legally valid.

In addition, his former wife has a low opinion of his idea. "Max, you know it's nonsense," she says. "We have been living apart for a long time now, and neither of us has ever resorted to fraudulent means." She hopes to be able to come by a visa some other way, and not just as the wife of a famous painter. After all, she is a renowned journalist. "Who knows? Maybe all this isn't even necessary. I'm an optimist."

Marseille, May 1941

Mary Jayne Gold is sitting under the drying hood at the hairdresser's. Killer Raymond has arranged to pick her up there when she is finished. He storms into the salon an hour too early and behaves like an intractable teenager. It is yet again about money and jealousy. Raymond is furious because Mary Jayne still donates substantial sums to the Centre despite Fry's request that she move out of Villa Air Bel – the house she found and rented. Yet she treats him like a cheap street urchin.

"Killer, you're impossible."

"I'm impossible? You're impossible! You don't love me. You never say 'I love you.' Say it at least once. Say it! Say it, goddammit!"

"What is wrong with you? What do you want?"

"I can be a devil. You'll see."

"Killer, don't do anything stupid – please …"

"See? You can't say it. Fine, you'll see I can be a devil. You said it yourself."

Raymond rushes out of the salon, leaving Mary Jayne behind, baffled. Does he really want her to make declarations of love – beneath a drying hood with curlers in her hair? She is sick of the endless quarrels with him. She feels tired, very tired.

A few hours later, Marcel Verzeano visits her in her hotel. He knocks at her door, and as soon as she sees his face, she knows he comes bearing bad news. Killer has broken into her old room at the Villa Air Bel, ransacked everything, and stolen her jewelry. Only the cook and the housekeeper were home, and no one could stop him.

When Mary Jayne arrives at the villa, the others are very considerate of her. She numbly begins cleaning up her room. It looks as if a fight had taken place. The small drawers of the secretary where she stored her jewelry are wrenched open, two of them lying on the floor.

Then, Mathieu, Raymond's gangster boss, pulls up in front of the villa in a car. He has found out, he says, where Raymond has gone to ground – in Cannes – and offers to drive there at once with Mary Jayne to retrieve her jewelry. Although her friends at the Centre advise her against it and attempt to protect her from herself, she plops into the passenger seat and has Mathieu take her to Cannes.

During the ride, Mathieu confesses his love for her. He has worshipped her ever since they first met, and he offers to kill Raymond for Mary Jayne as revenge for the robbery. It is clear he wants to replace him as the man at her side, as the lover of a filthy rich American woman. Mary Jayne does not pursue the matter further and takes a room at the Carlton in Cannes because she expects a luxury hotel will provide her a bit of protection from the men with whom she must deal at the moment.

The following day, Mathieu does in fact manage to persuade Raymond over the phone to meet at the Carlton's café terrace. Raymond parks a black sports car outside the hotel and climbs out of the vehicle with a girl in expensive clothes. The conversation relaxes once he realizes that Mary Jayne has not yet alerted the police about the theft, and once she recognizes that his escort is only a prop of sorts for his impressive entrance. At first, there is extensive talk about when the jewelry can be bought back from the fence who now has it in his possession. Mary Jayne has ultimately resigned herself to never seeing it again, though. Toward evening, she relocates negotiations to her hotel room, throws out both Mathieu and the girl soon thereafter, and as soon as she is alone with Raymond, it does not take long for him to kneel before her armchair, lay his head in her lap, and passionately beg her for forgiveness and for them to reconcile.

The power of their attraction to one another is still great enough to disregard many other considerations. In the end, though, they both know that Raymond's breach of trust cannot be patched up again for the long haul. Moreover, it is high time for him to put Marseille and the gangster underworld behind him if he wants to have a chance at a relatively tidy life. He thus decides to enlist with de Gaulle's French troops in London and asks Mary Jayne to help him search for a way to flee there.

At first glance, that seems easy, considering she works for a highly effective office of escape agents, but when she speaks with Fry in Marseille, he firmly rebuffs the idea. Daniel Bénédite and Marcel Verzeano have admittedly scouted out a way to escape to Spain via Andorra that now replaces the Fittkos' "F" route, but Fry must not, for any reason, endanger the many supporters working for him along this route. In his view, Raymond is a much too shady candidate for him to want to entrust with information about the new route. For Fry, the safety of his helpers outweighs Raymond's life – as it does the considerable contributions with which Mary Jayne has supported the Centre as well.

For Mary Jayne, this is a bitter disappointment, even if she ultimately accepts the reasons for Fry's refusal. Even so, she thinks she can sense the open disdain with which Fry treats Raymond gradually rubbing off on her. Fry cannot comprehend what about Raymond, in spite of everything, still binds her to him.

It is Charles Wolff, Mary Jayne's old friend from Paris, who eventually puts her in contact with a criminal Spanish trafficker. For a substantial sum, the man is willing to get Raymond over the mountains the very next day. Mary Jayne is both happy and disconsolate; Raymond is finally at the point of giving up his criminal life in Marseille, yet at the same time, she must live without him in return.

When he sets out at dawn, he has very precise, somewhat theatrical ideas of their farewell. Shortly before the meeting spot he has arranged with the smuggler, he asks Mary Jayne to stand back beneath a tree with Dagobert: his blonde lover together with her black poodle.

"You don't move until I'm out of sight. Okay?"

"Okay."

He kisses Mary Jayne once more.

"I will be a good soldier. Promise. You'll see."

Then he takes a few steps to the trafficker, turns around to face her, gazes upon Mary Jayne for a few seconds as though committing her image to memory for life, and raises his hand.

She waves back.

Then the two men walk along the street to the next intersection. Dispirited, Mary Jayne leans back against the tree, watching them. At the intersection, Raymond turns around to her once more, raises his hand again briefly, then follows the smuggler into the cross street, and is gone.

New York – Marseille, May and June 1941

Once again, Fry tries to lure his wife to France. It is spring, and southern France showcases its beauty in the most glorious of colors. Fry's letter to Eileen, though, is not just about scenic allure, but also about jealousy and sexual deprivation. "I would like to have you back in my bed very much, for despite all your suspicions, I always sleep alone." He writes that he visited a bordello a few times with Otto-Albert Hirschmann, but it did not agree with him. Ever since Hirschmann had to flee, he has been there a couple of times by himself, but then felt even lonelier.

Eileen's sympathy with her husband's loneliness is limited, seeing as how he has every opportunity to put an end to it if he really wanted to. She will soon turn forty and does not want to give up hope of having a child. For that reason alone, his absence for a wholly indefinite period of time strikes her as too long. "I think," she writes, "a year's separation is enough if we are to take up life together again … if you stay beyond August I think we'd better call it a day for both our sakes. […] I should like to feel that some real warmth of feeling was still possible for me with you, and if not with you then with someone else."

Letters still take around three weeks to cross the Atlantic. Over such intervals of time, it is difficult to have a sensitive dialogue about questions like these. Eileen has heard a great deal about her husband from refugees who have arrived in New York, including insinuations that he might have a homosexual relationship with Daniel Bénédite. She would like all the more to hear him declare his commitment to her and to their marriage, but the tone of his reply comes off as flatly sober. "I don't think we shall find the separation has been too long. On the contrary, I think we shall find it has been a good thing for both of us. Neither of us has found any substitute for the other; perhaps for that reason we shall respect one another more in the future … Yet I agree that a year is long enough: in another we should probably be compelled by biological necessities to find substitutes, however unsatisfactory."

That is not what Eileen wants to hear from her husband after ten months apart, so she tries to draw him out of his shell once and for all with her next letter. "How is your Danny?" she writes, making clear to him how dissatisfied she is with the distanced tone of his replies. "Your letters are not calculated to soothe and reassure hurt feelings and suspicions."

Still, little is to be accomplished by confronting her husband with accusations of this sort. Instead, they provoke more his defiance and his predilection for polemics than his empathy. Eileen might have suspected as much. The answer Fry gives her to her question about Danny is ice-cold and very condescending. "What extremely *nasty* digs, my dear, so unworthy of your intelligence."

Canfranc, June 1941

Max Ernst lacks the patience to wait any longer. He is afraid of ending up in an internment camp again and wants to put France in his wake for good. His exit papers are incomplete, but he figures he has a chance of getting through to Spain anyway if he does not use the train station at Cerbère, but the one in Canfranc, deep in the country's interior. He rolls up the canvases of the pictures he hung at the Villa Air Bel and stuffs them in his suitcase. Other paintings he has left on their stretchers he ties up into a big bundle. Unfortunately, he is now destitute again and in need of fifty dollars in travel money, but neither Peggy Guggenheim nor Marc Chagall can loan it to him. By chance, he happens upon Varian Fry on the street and tells him his sorrows. With some hesitation, Fry reaches into his briefcase and slips him sixty dollars.

The train station at Canfranc resembles a palace. Though it is narrow, it is two hundred forty meters long, has three ornate cupolas, and seventy-five doors on each of its long sides. The narrower-gauge French trains stop on one side and the wider-gauge Spanish trains on the other; in the station concourse between them, border and customs formalities are completed.

Aside from Max Ernst, only thirteen other passengers are on the train. They are traveling up into the Pyrenees via Toulouse and Pau. Canfranc station is located between the mountains at an altitude of almost 1,200 meters. Max Ernst's hope that the French border agents might be more generous here amid the montane solitude than in Cerbère is dashed, however. The official who checks his papers notices immediately that his exit visa is invalid and confiscates his passport.

Without identification papers, Max Ernst can expect to be arrested at the next police checkpoint and taken to a camp once again. Nevertheless, he walks to the Spanish checkpoint on the other side of the train station with his luggage. Before the customs agents there can ask for his passport, he unties the package with the framed pictures and unrolls the canvases from his suitcase. The officials are surprised and impressed. They help Max Ernst spread out his works across the elongated concourse hall as in a gallery. The other passengers, too, stop and stroll along the pictures, marveling.

The disturbance in the train station attracts the French border agent to the impromptu exhibition. He looks around for a long while, then invites Max Ernst into his office.

"Monsieur," he says there, "I love talent. You have a great deal of talent. I admire it." Then he returns his passport to him and walks with him to the trains.

"This one," he explains, "is the one traveling to Spain. The other is headed back to Pau, the nearest prefecture," and adds: "Take care not to board the wrong train."

Then he says goodbye, vanishes into his office, and does not show his face again until Max Ernst has bundled his paintings back together and departed on the correct train to Madrid and Lisbon.

The Long Goodbye

June to November 1941

Vichy, June 2, 1941

The regime of Marshal Pétain issues a second "Law on the Status of the Jews." The occupational bans for Jews decreed in the first law of October 1940 are broadened. And at universities, from this point forward, a *numerus clausus* is in effect for Jews in certain subject areas (medicine, law) to exclude them from university study. In addition, all Jews must register themselves with the police. With the addresses collected, future arrest and deportation lists can be compiled.

Marseille, June to August 1941

The Centre finds itself in a curious conflict. On the one hand, since the beginning of the year, Fry and his people have been getting more refugees out of the country than ever before, often dozens a week, mostly Jews. At the end of May, Fry once more conducted an interim assessment and arrived at over one thousand people they were able to help escape from France so far. On the route through Andorra, they illegally smuggle refugees to Lisbon who are at acute risk. For Jews especially, the danger is growing more and more concrete; since May, thousands of foreign Jews have been arrested in Paris and its surrounds and incarcerated.

On the other hand, the bullying and threats against the Centre are becoming more and more severe. Every couple of days, police officers show up at their door, flash search warrants, and systematically turn the office or the villa upside down. A group of French fascists announces that it will attack the Centre if it "continues aiding Jews and dirty Gaullists." Then, suddenly, a young Frenchman appears at the office and wants to speak with a "Captain Smith" from the Royal Air Force to pass him secret maps of German airports. Fry hauls the fellow straight out the door and from the window observes him crossing the Boulevard Garibaldi and meeting two men on the other side of the street whom Fry takes for criminal detectives: apparently an agent provocateur. Eventually, Bénédite is lured into a trap by an informer during a black market transaction and forced to spend a few weeks in jail.

Mary Jayne Gold sank into depression after saying goodbye to Killer Raymond and, as soon as she had her visas together, left for the United States. The State Department has recalled Hiram Bingham from Marseille and replaced him with a vice consul who sees it as his most important mission to obstruct any path to salvation in the United States for refugees. In this way, bit by bit, Fry loses many confidants whom he could trust blindly.

What proves even more serious is a scheme on the part of the American embassy in Vichy. It has sent word to the French government that Fry's passport has long since expired and that it would not protest were he to be detained and expelled. Indeed, Fry receives a summons from the police chief of Marseille shortly thereafter. Maurice de Rodellec du Porzic hails from a noble Breton family steeped in tradition, was a naval officer in the First World War, and is regarded as a staunch acolyte of Marshal Pétain.

Fry shows up for the arranged meeting punctually, but must wait almost an hour before he is admitted to the police chief. De Rodellec du Porzic is a man in his mid-forties with a sharply drawn part and the hair at his temples shaved short. In his gigantic office, he has placed his desk in front of the window such that his interlocutors are blinded by the incident sunlight and can only make out the silhouette of his face. For a long while, he leafs through Fry's police dossier in silence. Then he looks up and threatens to prosecute him for various offenses he has allegedly committed. Fry remains calm, knowing that de Rodellec has no evidence against him, and he tells him as much, too.

"In the new France, we do not require any evidence," de Rodellec replies. The regime in Vichy had put an end to the idealist notion that it is better to allow a hundred criminals to escape than to arrest one innocent person. "We think it better to arrest a hundred innocent people than to let one criminal go."

"I see," Fry retorts, "that we have very different ideas of human rights."

"Indeed," de Rodellec agrees. "I am aware that they still believe in the antiquated notion of human rights in the United States." But, he claims, it is only a matter of time before the United States also tosses these silly ideas overboard. "We've realized that society is more important than the individual. You will also come to understand that."

De Rodellec allows a short pause, and then he asks Fry to leave France. If he refuses, he will arrest him and have him locked away in some provincial city far from Marseille so that he can cause no further harm.

Fry does not take this threat all that seriously either, but he is aware that the regime could declare him *persona non grata* at any time and expel him. He intends to buy as much time as possible. With each day the Centre continues to work, it can rescue more refugees – especially now. He quickly tries to calculate the maximum grace period the police chief will grant him.

He will, he says, send a cable to New York at once for them to search for his successor. Even under favorable conditions, that will take a good four weeks. "Could you give me until August 15?"

Clearly, de Rodellec does not wish to haggle over dates and agrees.

With this nod from the police chief, Fry realizes, his farewell from Marseille has irrevocably begun.

Berlin, June 22, 1941

On Hitler's orders, the *Wehrmacht* attacks the Soviet Union.

Washington, D.C., July 1, 1941

President Roosevelt signs a new law that tightens the requirements for immigration to the United States. The emergency visa problem is ended. From now on, refugees must not only file a biographical sketch and a moral affidavit as well as demonstrate considerable financial assurances, but also submit a close relatives statement. This document compels them to provide information about the residences of all close relations. Those with family members in Germany or in countries occupied by the Germans will not receive a visa. Officially, this is to prevent the Gestapo from blackmailing refugees into espionage or sabotage after they immigrate by threatening relatives of theirs who remain at home. Because it is nearly impossible for refugees to prove with official documents where their relatives currently reside in war-torn Europe, however, American visas have become de facto unobtainable.

Vichy, July 22, 1941

The regime in Vichy passes a resolution on the "Aryanization" of Jewish businesses and Jewish property. From now on, Jews shall be dispossessed without compensation. The *Commissariat general aux questions juives* (CGQJ) assumes the task of selling the assets in question and funneling the profits made into state coffers.

Marseille, August 29 to September 7, 1941

Fry has already overrun the departure date agreed to with de Rodellec by two weeks. He still moves about the city freely without changing his habits or hiding. He has no desire for the impression to arise in retrospect that he willingly followed the instructions of the Vichy regime with respect to his exit. His notorious spirit of resistance will not allow it. They will have to come and arrest him; he will not leave the country until he is forced to do so.

Since the emergency visa program was halted, the Centre must focus on placing refugees in other countries, in Mexico or Cuba, Morocco or Brazil. Fry and his people were already doing that before, too, and since the bureaucratic hassle of forcing through rescue visas against pushback from the State Department has now ceased to exist, in a certain sense their work has even gotten easier.

Fry is sitting as his desk when two criminal detectives enter his office around midday to arrest him. The two men are sheepish. Their mission is embarrassing to them, that much is palpable. They inform him politely that Fry will have to stay in jail until he can be transported to the border and expelled. As they take him to their vehicle, a secretary remains with Fry and rides along to verify where he will be held.

Over the course of subsequent hours, the employees of the Centre make him their most important client. Bénédite travels to Vichy to prevent or at least delay Fry's deportation by political means. The others phone all employees of the police and intelligence agency they know who are well-disposed to them to find a way to get Fry out of jail. But there is no remedy in Marseille for an arrest warrant ordered personally by police chief de Rodellec.

Fry is put up for the night not in a cell, but in a kind of conference room, yet with only a large table and no bed. He tells the inspector on duty the next morning that it is "uncomfortable to sleep on a table, but entirely possible." The man assigns him a personal bodyguard who is not to let him out of sight until he is on the train in Cerbère trundling across the border. Fry points out to the inspector that he cannot be deported in the short term at all because he has no valid transit visas for Spain and Portugal. The inspector, however, scoffs; this simple bureaucratic problem will be solved by the customs agents at the border.

The bodyguard, Inspector Garandel, is a jovial man with a half-bald head and concerns about France's good reputation. Fry, he says, should please not believe the French are barbarians. His assignment is also noticeably disagreeable to him. Fry reassures him: "That's only *some* French people. One might also say just *one* Frenchman ..."

Garandel first takes Fry to the Centre so that he can clear out his desk, then to the Villa Air Bel, where he can pack his suitcases. At Saint-Charles station, the two ascend the splendid open-air staircase that Fry descended for the first time upon his arrival in Marseille exactly one year and fifteen days ago. At the top, Fry turns around and takes one last look at the city bound up for him with the loveliest, the saddest, and the most intense experiences of his life. His gaze falls upon the large neon sign of the Hôtel Splendide, where it all began, upon the Boulevard d'Athènes, which runs straight toward the Centre's office, and, beyond, upon the hill with the basilica Notre-Dame de la Garde, the Madonna on its tower gleaming in the evening sun.

On the platform, his closest associates have assembled before the train, which is ready for departure. Together, they squeeze into the compartment the police have reserved for Fry. Because Inspector Garandel is sitting among them, they cannot freely discuss the future of the Centre on the journey. Instead, they pass around a bottle of cognac and listen to Garandel tell anecdote after anecdote from Marseille's underworld in his Southern French accent.

When the train arrives in Cerbère, Fry experiences a small moment of satisfaction. As he had predicted at the police prison in Marseille, the customs officials refuse his passport because the necessary exit and transit visas are missing. The document must be sent back to Marseille again so that the authorities there can add to it the countless stamps and signatures for which Fry so often fought on behalf of his clients. Experience has shown that can take weeks.

In accordance with orders, Fry is supposed to spend this time in prison in Perpignan, Inspector Garandel informs him. But Garandel does not even think about carrying out his superiors' order and instead puts him up in a hotel near the beach. This last deferral before his deportation provides Fry with the opportunity to make the fundamental decisions about the Centre's future with his people. Because the committee in New York has not found a successor for Fry, Jean Gemähling is to take over leadership officially. He is a Frenchman and not a Jew, which might simplify negotiations with the regime. Behind the scenes, Daniel Bénédite will hold the reins, Marcel Verzeano will also continue taking refugees over the Pyrenees illegally, and Charles Wolff will be in charge of the Villa Air Bel as the head of the household.

After only five days, much faster than anticipated, Fry's passport returns from Marseille with all the requisite visas. Fittingly, it is a dreary,

Varian Fry (right) with Daniel Bénédite at the office of the Centre Américain de Secours

rainy day when Fry boards the train for Cerbère with Inspector Garandel and the others. Upon arrival, Garandel allows them time for a farewell dinner at the train station restaurant. It is a taciturn meal. Even Fry has lost any inclination for gallows humor. They sit together calmly; profound connections have formed through the perilous work of the foregoing months. Everyone is aware of the gravity of this forced parting. It may well be that they will never see each other again. Then Fry rises, asks everyone at the table to move closer together, and snaps one last photograph.

Afterward, each of them embraces him as though wishing to hold onto him and not let him leave. Danny Bénédite is particularly crushed. He just cannot believe what is happening. "You can't leave us, though," he whispers to Fry. "You're more Frenchman than American now."

When Fry at last steps onto the platform, it turns out that, of all people, the American ambassador in Vichy, William D. Leahy, is waiting for the same train and, with him, several American journalists, too. Fry consciously keeps his distance from Leahy – who is partially responsible for his expulsion – and remains standing on the door's footboard when the train eventually begins moving to wave for the last time to his friends lined up beside one another beneath the station's projecting roof.

Even at the train station in Portbou and on the train to Barcelona, Fry maintains his distance from Leahy and does not exchange a word with him. Nevertheless, the journalists traveling along are firmly convinced it cannot be a coincidence if these two men are leaving France on the same day by the same train. On September 7, the *New York Times* reports that "Leahy Takes Fry with Him into Spain." In the short article, it reads that Leahy met Fry beforehand in Perpignan and permitted him to travel with him even though Fry's Centre had helped mostly leftist and communist refugees. Leahy and the State Department are furious about the false report and strongly suspect that Fry put it out to compromise Leahy.

Cassis, September and October 1941

The harbor town of Cassis is encircled by the cliffs of the calanque as though by a protective wall. The Vichy regime's decrees seem to lose much of their power on their way over these mountains. Hans and Lisa

Fittko have been living here for six months almost completely out in the open. The town's officials caution them again and again because their papers are not in order, but no one even thinks about arresting them or locking them away in a camp as the laws actually prescribe.

Fry's promise to obtain rescue visas to the United States for the Fittkos has died a political death on the long path through official channels. Fry has since been expelled and the rescue visas abolished. But Fry's associates have not forgotten what the couple did for the Centre's clients and were able to procure visas to Cuba for them as an alternative. The exit visas are confirmed, the tickets for the ship, the SS *Colonial*, booked and paid for. As far as it is humanly possible to judge, nothing more could go wrong.

But then Lisa Fittko's parents are arrested in Mâcon, a town north of Lyon. The police officer responsible is a zealous friend of the Nazis and wants to have them carted off to a German concentration camp. Lisa Fittko asks the Centre to persuade him to release her parents. When none of the letters and telegrams have an impact, she roams from one aid committee in Marseille to the next, from the Red Cross to the Quakers, to the Unitarians, to the Jewish and evangelical groups, tells their story everywhere, and still finds no one with a clue about how to change the officer's mind. Time is short. The SS *Colonial* will put to sea in the next few days. In her desperation, Lisa Fittko is at a complete loss about what to do, but what she cannot do is depart for freedom and leave her parents behind on their way to a concentration camp.

Then a friend asks whether she has tried the Swedish consulate yet. At first, it sounds like a far-fetched suggestion, but Sweden has officially taken over the diplomatic mission of the German Reich in France's unoccupied zone. If the officer in Mâcon is in fact such a great admirer of the Nazis, then a Swedish protest might make an impression on him.

The afternoon of that very same day, Lisa Fittko is sitting across from the Swedish consul. He is a tall, slender man in his early forties. His name is Folke Sixten Berglund, and he listens to her intently, but remains aloof. He says he sees no possibility of helping her without overstepping his political jurisdiction.

"Maybe you could summon my parents to your consulate?" Lisa asks. Once they are in Marseille, a way to hide them will present itself.

But Berglund brushes this aside. He does not know Lisa's parents, and there is no legal reason why he should summon them. Any attempt to intervene in the matter on her behalf would be unlawful and could cost him his job.

This effectively ends the conversation. There is nothing more to say. Lisa does not get up, however – and neither does the consul. The two sit facing one another for a long time without saying a word and without moving. The silence weighs on both of them.

Eventually, the consul asks whether Lisa's parents are Jews and where they come from.

Lisa nods and says her family comes from Vienna.

"What did your father do there?"

"He was the editor of a magazine."

"What sort of magazine?"

"A literary magazine. Pacifist."

Again, they sit a long while in silence facing one another. Then, Berglund gets up, walks into an adjoining room, types up a summons for Lisa's parents, and presents her with it in exchange for the promise that her father and mother will never, under any circumstances, set foot in the consulate. Minutes later, at Marseille's main post office, Lisa addresses the letter with the summons to the police officer in Mâcon and mails it.

The letter indeed performs the miracle she had hoped for. After a week, her parents step off the train in Marseille. Lisa picks them up at the train station and brings them to Cassis, but all they have left are five days together. After that, she has to set out for the SS *Colonial* and to Cuba with her husband. Her parents have neither identification papers nor tickets. They cannot come along. Whether she will ever see her parents again and how they are supposed to survive in France is unclear. They wave farewell to one another, but Lisa Fittko does not feel anything anymore: no pain, no fear, no longing, nor any anticipatory excitement about Cuba. She is empty, gutted.

Barcelona – Lisbon, September and October 1941

Fry is in no hurry. After arriving in Spain, he does not continue on the fastest path to Lisbon, but first stays for a few days in Barcelona. The city impresses him. Having been there before briefly three times, he now wants to get to know it better. He stays at the España, a glamorous Art Nouveau hotel just a few steps from La Rambla. He wanders the streets, overwhelmed by life in peace time, without nightly blackouts, with open dance halls, with well-stocked shelves in the stores, and with cafés in which there is real coffee with real milk and real sugar.

What he feels, however, is not the relief of having escaped war, but his old predilection for depression. The faces of all the refugees the Centre was unable to rescue, he writes to Daniel Bénédite, catch up with him. He estimates that far more than 15,000 people have contacted them over the course of the past year. In light of their limited means, they had to discuss each individual case in their conferences and decide whom they could help and whom they could not.

Fry feels guilty. He blames himself for having been too undiplomatic, too quick to anger, and too dogmatic. Maybe – no, probably – he could have achieved more if he had acted more sociably, if he had made an effort to incline Consul General Fullerton and Ambassador Leahy more toward his mission instead of plunging into ever new and enervating confrontations.

Part of his uneasiness is that he does not know what is next for his marriage. He has changed greatly over the past year, he warns Eileen in a letter. His life has become more intense than ever before. "But I do not think I shall ever be quite the person I was when I kissed you good-bye at the airport […]. For the experience of ten, fifteen and even twenty years have been pressed into one. Sometimes I feel as if I had lived my whole life […] since I first walked down the monumental stairway of the Gare St.-Charles […]."

In Lisbon, too, Fry takes his time. He endeavors to perfect the Centre's Underground Railroad further. Refugees who flee illegally are not just smuggled across the borders by their guides, but also across Spain, from one hidden safe house to the next, to shacks, barns, remote old churches. For the very last leg from the Portuguese border to Lisbon, however, there is no trustworthy guide, and Fry tries to find a suitable man.

Not until October 1 does he go to the Pan Am office to book his return flight to New York. He presents his old ticket from the previous August and learns that it has expired long ago. As a result, he has to send a cable to the committee in New York and ask for the money for a new ticket. It costs $525, more or less the equivalent of a good used car.

To use the additional waiting time well, Fry assists the Unitarian aid organization that handles refugees who have gotten stuck in the city involuntarily. He still wavers. Eileen informs him that, on November 4, a fundraising dinner will take place in New York in honor of Jay Allen, his old adversary. Allen was released from the French prison because Roosevelt's administration exchanged him for a German journalist arrested in America. If Fry is still not back in New York by this date and able to speak for himself, Allen intends to dedicate the event to him: "This dinner should not be for me, but for V[arian]M[ackey]F[ry]."

Fry is not in a celebrating mood, though. Returning to New York does not excite him. "I *prefer* the blackout," he writes to Bénédite, "and would gladly trade even an occasional bombardment for what lies in wait for me in America. But I have to go home … to the hard geometry of New York." On November 1, his Clipper takes off from the broad delta of the Tagus off Lisbon. On November 2, he lands in the East River at LaGuardia.

What Happened Afterward

Daniel Bénédite (1912–1990) continued leading the Centre after Fry's expulsion. With his wife Théodora, Jean Gemähling, and other coworkers, he succeeded in smuggling around three hundred more refugees out of France until the Centre was shut down for good by the police in July 1942. The deportations of Jews from the occupied zone began in March 1942 and in August from the unoccupied zone to the concentration camps and death mills of the Germans. What Fry and his people had long feared now came to pass. In a joint operation by the SS, the French police, and the government in Vichy, from 1942 a total of 75,000 French and foreign Jews were handed over to the Nazis and murdered.

Varian Fry (1907–1967) was faced with a number of people with whom he was on the outs after his return to the United States. The president of the Emergency Rescue Committee, Frank Kingdon, had not forgotten Fry's unilateral actions in Europe. He forbade him from calling himself a representative of the committee and declared subsequent collaboration with him "undesirable." The State Department, moreover, let it be known that it would not issue any visas for clients of the ERC as long as Fry remained associated with the committee.

In 1942, Eileen Hughes Fry divorced her husband, and in the same year, the FBI began surveilling him. Only after a lengthy search did Fry find another job: as an editorial assistant at the left-liberal news magazine *The New Republic*. After holding leadership roles at *The Living Age* and the Foreign Policy Association, this occupational backsliding bothered him, especially since his problems with authority had not diminished.

Between 1942 and 1944, Fry wrote his memoirs of his year in Marseille. He had difficulty working because he again suffered from depression. When his book *Surrender on Demand* was published in 1945, it did not receive a great deal of attention. In the euphoria of victory, the American book market was not particularly interested in stories about past wartime suffering, and even less in a critical view of the measures taken by the State Department that had made it difficult for Jews and other persecuted persons to escape from Europe to safety.

When Fry left *The New Republic* in March of 1945, the unhappiest period of his professional career began. He had been unable to reconcile himself to the magazine's – in his view too friendly – reporting on the Soviet Union. With his raging anticommunism, however, he made no friends among liberal Americans who, in those years, faced the communists witch hunts of Senator Joe McCarthy and the House Un-American Activities Committee. Fry was employed by several newspaper editorial teams, though regularly let go after a short while because of political differences. His attempt to establish himself as an entrepreneur with sound and educational film studios soon failed as well.

In his private life, he had more luck for a time. In 1950, he married the twenty-seven-year-old journalist Annette Riley who looked up to her husband – sixteen years her senior – and admired him for his work as an escape agent. The couple had three children together, but bit by bit, the lack of recognition Fry labored under cast its first shadows over their marriage. By that point, he was working for various companies as a freelance public relations and commercial copywriter, most notably for Coca-Cola – and, to supplement his income, as a teacher of Latin, ancient Greek, and history.

In 1963, he turned to the International Rescue Committee (IRC), a large aid organization for refugees that had been founded at the urging of Albert Einstein. With the assistance of the famous artists he, in turn, had rescued from France, Fry suggested compiling a portfolio of original lithographs to be sold to art collectors and donors in sizeable quantities. The IRC subsequently financed a lengthy stay for him in France, where many of the artists had returned, but most put him off or turned him down outright. After two years of soliciting, Jacques Lipchitz was the only one who had delivered a lithograph to him.

This failure hit Fry hard. He alternated between bitterness, aggression, and depression. Living with him grew difficult, but he was surprised and dismayed when his wife spoke about getting a divorce.

In April of 1967, Varian Fry experienced the only tribute during his lifetime for his actions as an escape agent. In the presence of his family, he was awarded the Chevalier class of the Order of the Legion of Honor at the French consulate in New York. Mary Jayne Gold and Albert O. Hirschman attended the ceremony. This belated recognition effected only a marginal improvement in Fry's mental health. In August, he and his second wife divorced. In early September, he began working as a Latin teacher at Joel Barlow High School in Redding, Connecticut. On September 13, 1967, he was found dead in his home. According to the autopsy, Varian Mackey Fry died of a stroke – at the age of fifty-nine.

In 1994, he was recognized by Yad Vashem as "Righteous Among the Nations." His son James planted a tree at Yad Vashem in his father's honor in 1996. The acting American secretary of state, Warren Christopher, took part in the ceremony. "We have come," Christopher said in his speech, "to pay tribute to Varian Fry – a remarkable man and a remarkable American. Regretfully, during his lifetime, his heroic actions never received the support they deserved from my government, particularly the State Department."

Mary Jayne Gold (1909–1997) completed her degree in psychology after her return to the United States and specialized in criminal psychology. In 1980, she published her memoirs of her time in France under the title *Crossroads Marseille 1940*. As a still very wealthy woman, she spent a large portion of the year living in her villa in Gassin near St. Tropez. She gave it the name Air Bel.

Miriam Davenport (1915–1999) was bound to Mary Jayne Gold and Varian Fry by a close friendship over her lifetime. Together with her Yugoslavian husband Rudolph Treo, she took a circuitous route home to the United States, via Switzerland and Portugal, in 1941. There she continued working for the ERC, which was later merged with the International Rescue Committee (IRC). In 1946, she divorced Treo and married a second time. From 1951, she worked as a painter and sculptor and earned her doctorate in French literature of the eighteenth century as well.

Raymond "Killer" Couraud alias *Jack William Raymond Lee* (1920–1977) was sentenced in absentia to ten years in prison after fleeing from a French court. He arrived in London in October of 1941, where at first he joined de Gaulle's troops. Not long after, under the name Jack William

Raymond Lee, he transferred to the Special Operations Executive (SOE), a strike force of the British secret service. He was gravely injured on several deployments behind enemy lines. In July of 1944, he was part of a six-person commando operation tasked with killing Field Marshal Erwin Rommel. The assassination failed because Rommel was injured in a strafe attack and taken to a field hospital shortly before the SOE group reached his quarters. After the liberation of France, Couraud alias Lee left the British army and became a member of the French general staff. Mary Jayne Gold referred to her efforts to resocialize Killer Raymond during her year in Marseille as her most important contribution to the war against Hitler.

Albert O. Hirschman (1915–2012) joined the U.S. Army after the United States entered the war in 1941 and was deployed to North Africa and Italy. After the end of the war, he became director of the Western European division of the office that devised the Marshall Plan for the American government. In 1952, he moved to the World Bank, for which he spent four years working on development programs in Bogotá, Colombia. After his return to the United States, he taught at Yale, Columbia, Harvard, and Princeton University as a professor of economics. In 1970, he published the study *Exit, Voice, and Loyalty*, which is still regarded today as a standard work in economic theory.

Hiram Bingham IV (1903–1988), like Varian Fry, reaped professional disadvantages for his efforts to rescue refugees. In 1941, he was abruptly transferred by the State Department to Portugal and, later, to Argentina, where he left the diplomatic service in 1946. Because he hardly ever spoke about his actions in Marseille, his family learned nothing about his connection to Fry and the ERC. Not until after his death did his relatives discover documents that Bingham had kept from his time in Marseille and give them to the United States Holocaust Memorial Museum in Washington, D.C. In 2002, the Constructive Dissent Award was posthumously bestowed on Bingham by Secretary of State Colin Powell for his meritorious service.

Stéphane Hessel (1917–2013) joined the French Resistance, was arrested in Paris in the summer of 1944, sentenced to death as a spy, and transferred to Buchenwald. He survived because he assumed the name of a murdered fellow prisoner at the concentration camp. After 1945, he entered France's diplomatic service and worked for the French mission to the United Nations, among other posts. In 2010, he published the essay "Time for Outrage!" ["Indignez-vous!"] in which he sharply criticized political intransigence in the face of looming catastrophes – from climate change to migration policy to the financial crisis – and called for resistance. The slender volume sold millions of copies around the world.

Charles Fawcett (1915–2008) joined the Royal Air Force in London after fleeing from France. He had to abandon his training as a pilot, however, when a tuberculosis infection was diagnosed. No sooner had he convalesced, than he joined the Foreign Legion and took part in the liberation of France in 1945. Later, he fought in the Greek Civil War for the British against troops of the Communist Party of Greece. In the late 1940s, he was discovered as an actor and acted in around a hundred, mostly Italian films. He interrupted his film career to rescue refugees from the Hungarian Uprising of 1956, to participate in the civil war during the Congo Crisis, and, after 1979, to support the mujahedeen in Afghanistan in their battle against Soviet military forces.

Jean Gemähling (1912–2003) was arrested and interrogated multiple times as the nominal head of the Centre. In 1942, he went to ground, joined the French Resistance, and became the head of its intelligence service. After the war, he spent twenty years working for the French Atomic Energy Commission.

Charles Wolff (1905–1944) settled in Toulouse after the police had shut down the Centre in Marseille and became the leader of the French Resistance there. In May 1944, the fascist *Milice française* arrested him. He died while being tortured, without betraying the names of other members of the *Résistance*.

Leon "Dick" Ball, who had taken Alma Mahler-Werfel, Franz Werfel, Nelly and Heinrich Mann, and Golo Mann over the Pyrenees, vanished without a trace in November of 1940. To this day, in spite of all inquiries, no evidence regarding his subsequent fate has been found.

Justus "Gussie" Rosenberg (1921–2021) failed in his attempt to escape to Spain in 1941. Jean Gemähling took him on in the intelligence service of the French Resistance as a kind of apprentice. After the Allied landing in Normandy on June 6, 1944, Rosenberg attacked German troops in the French hinterlands with other resistance fighters, and was struck by a bullet. Later, he joined American troops as a translator and was wounded a second time. After the end of the war, he attended university first in France, then in the United States, and later taught literary history and political science at various American colleges. Shortly before his death, he published his memoirs of his years in France under the title *The Art of Resistance* (2020). He was the only employee of the Centre who publicly voiced criticism of Fry: "Even if the ERC helped many intellectuals and artists escape from France, in my opinion, Fry does not merit much recognition for it personally. He merely fulfilled his duties." One reason for this skeptical judgment may stem from the fact that Fry never undertook an attempt to rescue a still very young Rosenberg from France, even though he faced great danger as a Jew. As an active underground combatant who was involved in skirmishes with German troops multiple times, to boot, Rosenberg had probably also developed different notions of courage than Varian Fry.

Bil Spira alias *Bil Freier* (1913–1999) was a particularly upsetting case for Varian Fry. None of the attorneys he tasked with freeing Spira from Le Vernet were able to prevent the illustrator from being handed over to the Germans in 1942. According to Fry's information, the trail went cold at Auschwitz; he thought him dead. But Spira survived the extermination camp and was liberated from the concentration camp at Theresienstadt at the end of the war. He returned to Paris, took up his job as a caricaturist again, and worked primarily for French and Swiss newspapers.

Lisa Fittko, born *Elizabeth Ekstein* (1909–2005), and *Hans Fittko* (1903–1960) initially lived in Cuba and worked at an educational institution for Jewish refugees. After they had gotten married, they were able to relocate to the United States in 1948 and settle in Chicago. Lisa Fittko's parents survived the war in Cassis. Hans Fittko died in 1960 at the age of only fifty-seven. In 2000, he was posthumously honored in Yad Vashem as "Righteous Among the Nations." Since this title is given only to non-Jewish rescuers in the Holocaust, Lisa Fittko could not be included in this tribute. Her book about the couple's actions as escape agents was published in 1985 under the title *Mein Weg über die Pyrenäen* [English, 1991: *Escape through the Pyrenees*].

Rudolf Breitscheid (1874–1944) was deported by the Gestapo after his arrest, first to Sachsenhausen and later to Buchenwald. He died on August 24, 1944, in a bombing raid on Buchenwald by the United States Air Force.

Hannah Arendt (1906–1975) arrived in New York with her husband *Heinrich Blücher* (1899–1970) in May of 1941. Both initially kept their heads above water as journalists and teachers before receiving professorships in the 1950s at various colleges and universities. Hannah Arendt's magnum opus *The Origins of Totalitarianism* was published in 1951 [in German as *Elemente und Ursprünge totaler Herrschaft* in 1955], followed by numerous other influential books and essays. She ranks among the most important political thinkers of the twentieth century.

Lion Feuchtwanger (1884–1958) published his story about fleeing from France already in 1942: *Unholdes Frankreich* [English, 1941: *The Devil in France: My Encounter with Him in the Summer of 1940*]. The following year, he again moved into a villa with an ocean view, this time of the Pacific, in Los Angeles. With several new novels and film adaptations of earlier books, Feuchtwanger was one of the most successful exile authors in the United States. The memoirs of *Marta Feuchtwanger* (1891–1987) were published in 1983 as *Nur eine Frau* [*Just One Woman*].

Heinrich Mann (1871–1950) was unable to gain a foothold as a writer in America. His works went largely unnoticed there, and his memoirs *Ein Zeitalter wird besichtigt* [*Surveying an Age*] were published in Stockholm in 1946 without great success. Financially supported by his brother Thomas, he lived in Los Angeles. *Nelly Mann* (1898–1944) found occasional work in Los Angeles as a nurse. She was never able to overcome her dependence on alcohol and pills. Suffering from her social isolation, she committed suicide in 1944 after several failed attempts.

Franz Werfel (1890–1945) completed his novel about the life of Saint Bernadette in only five months after arriving in the United States, a novel he had sworn in the grotto at Lourdes to write if he were to be rescued: *The Song of Bernadette*. The book was a smashing success, exceeding even the sales figures of Werfel's perhaps most important novel, *The Forty Days of Musa Dagh*. His heart disease advanced, and in 1945 he died of a heart attack in Los Angeles at the age of only fifty-four. *Alma Mahler-Werfel* (1879–1964) continued to be the epicenter of large cultural circles. In 1952, she relocated to New York.

Anna Seghers, born *Annette Reiling*, by marriage *Netty Radványi* (1900–1983), was able to leave Martinique after a month and travel onward to New York. Because the family only possessed transit visas, they had to continue their journey from there to Mexico. In 1942, Anna Seghers' novel *The Seventh Cross* [*Das siebte Kreuz*] was published in English translation and became a worldwide bestseller. In Mexico, she wrote her big exile novel, *Transit*, in which she incorporated memories of her stay in Marseille. In 1947, she returned to Germany, became a member of the SED [Socialist Unity Party of Germany], and from 1952 to 1978 was president of the Writers' Union of the GDR.

Walter Mehring (1896–1981) escaped via Martinique to Florida. He received a one-year contract as a scriptwriter for a film studio in Hollywood, which was intended for him as a springboard, but he only produced a very few works, many of which remained fragmentary. In 1953, he returned to Europe and lived in Berlin, Hamburg, and Munich, almost without an income, before spending his final years in Switzerland.

Hertha Pauli (1906–1973) arrived in New York in 1940. She learned English lightning fast and initially wrote young adult books and, later, several biographical novels that were published in the United States. Starting in the 1950s, she regularly traveled to Austria, where she published her books again in German, but continued to live in America.

André Breton (1896–1966) arrived in New York in 1941 after a short stopover in Martinique. In New York, he published the surrealist journal *VVV* in collaboration with Max Ernst, Marcel Duchamp, and the

American painter and sculptor David Hare. In 1942, *Jacqueline Lamba* (1910–1993) left Breton and married David Hare three years later. By 1946, Breton had returned to France; Lamba did not do so until 1955. Breton organized further important exhibitions with works by surrealist artists, the last of these in the year before his death.

Marc Chagall (1887–1985) lived in the United States and Mexico from 1941 to 1948, and then he returned to France. He received commissions from many countries, took part in the Venice Biennale and in Documenta in Kassel. Some of the most important museums around the world staged extensive retrospectives of his works.

Victor Serge (1890–1947) arrived in Mexico, like Anna Seghers, in 1941. He continued to be assailed harshly by Stalin's devotees and survived attempts on his life. He died of a heart attack during a taxi ride in Mexico City. Suspicion that the infarction could be traced back to poisoning was unable to be disproved.

Max Ernst (1891–1976) and *Peggy Guggenheim* (1898–1979) married after arriving in New York and split up again two years later. With his fourth wife, painter and writer Dorothea Tanning, Max Ernst first lived in Arizona and then, from 1953, back in France. Peggy Guggenheim returned to Europe in 1948, settled in Venice, purchased a palazzo on the Grand Canal, and showcased her collection there in her own museum.

Luise Straus-Ernst (1893–1944), Max Ernst's first wife, never managed to leave France. She went into hiding in Manosque, a small town sixty kilometers north of Aix-en-Provence. She worked there from time to time for the French writer Jean Giono. In 1944, she was arrested, deported to Auschwitz, and murdered there.

Epilogue

> No paradox of contemporary politics is filled with a more poignant irony than the discrepancy between the efforts of well-meaning idealists who stubbornly insist on regarding as "inalienable" those human rights, which are enjoyed only by citizens of the most prosperous and civilized countries, and the situation of the rightless themselves. Their situation has deteriorated just as stubbornly, until the internment camp [...] has become the routine solution for the problem of domicile of the "displaced persons."
>
> Hannah Arendt (1951) *The Origins of Totalitarianism*, p. 279

The tale of a mass exodus of eight to ten million people is larger than any book that tells it. The story of the German and Austrian exiles alone who joined the trek of refugees by the thousands is so complex that it exceeds the scope of any reasonable portrayal. Anyone wishing to tell these stories must limit himself to the example of individuals. That, however, distorts the historical picture. Alongside every person mentioned in this book stood hundreds or thousands of others who had the same right to be memorialized. What's more, some of the fates related here were tightly intertwined with those who could not be recounted so that the book would not become unwieldy.

This book hews closely to what its protagonists reported about their escapes. Even so, those weeks and months in France were not a good time for keeping meticulous notes. Secrecy was important. All too candid chronicles, were they to fall into the wrong hands, could have put people in mortal danger. For that reason, much was written down only after the war – sometimes long after. As a result, errors have slipped in: the dating of quite a few events, for instance, or their sequence do not always match with the historical facts. To the extent possible, I have amended such obvious mistakes and replaced codenames used for persons or places with the historically correct ones.

Memories are generally precarious stuff. One example: Justus "Gussie" Rosenberg writes in his book *The Art of Resistance*, published in 2020, that eighty years earlier, on September 13, 1940, he led the famous group of refugees including Franz Werfel and Heinrich Mann over the mountains to Spain along with Leon Ball. Neither in Alma Mahler-Werfel's diary entries nor in Varian Fry's *Surrender on Demand*, which provide concordant information about this escape, however, is Rosenberg's participation mentioned. Who was actually there and who was not will perhaps never be able to be determined. In such instances of contradictory memories, I have as a rule been guided by the records that came about shortly after the events and not decades later.

What is surprising is how little recognition Varian Fry and his people have received in Germany – although German cultural history owes them quite a lot. Until now, anyone wishing to learn something in German about Fry and his Centre Américain de Secours was reliant upon the translation of his book *Surrender on Demand*. But for historically understandable reasons, it remained incomplete. For example, it largely disregards Fry's conflicts with the Emergency Rescue Committee or with his wife in New York and relates little about clients' experiences while fleeing or about his associates' living conditions in Marseille.

Even in comprehensive biographies of the writers to whose rescue Fry fundamentally contributed, he and his Centre are seldom accorded more than one page – and the information found in these few lines is, often enough, incorrect. Fry is passed off either as a Quaker, a Unitarian, a diplomat, or a university professor. In some autobiographies, like that of Heinrich Mann, he is not even mentioned, almost as though aid in escape for prominent authors were a sort of service industry, the staff of which need not be mentioned by name. As a kind of recompense, Fry is celebrated in an especially thick biography of Thomas Mann for the courageous abduction of Lion Feuchtwanger from the Saint Nicolas camp, which he had nothing to do with.

To this day, there is no German-language biography of Varian Fry. In light of his adventuresome efforts on behalf of German exile literature, you could be forgiven for thinking he had already merited one. This book cannot be a substitute for that, focusing as it does on the history of escapes from France between May of 1940 and August of 1941. In the United States, two biographies of Fry have appeared: *A Quiet American*

(1999) by Andy Marino and *A Hero of Our Own* (2001) by Sheila Isenberg. In German, political scientist Anne Klein provides information about the political background of Fry's work in her excellent dissertation entitled *Flüchtlingspolitik und Flüchtlingshilfe 1940–1942* [*Refugee Policy and Refugee Aid from 1940–1942*]. I owe much to these books and to the autobiographies of Varian Fry and Mary Jayne Gold.

What seems to me especially likeable about Fry's book is not least that he never gives the impression he is telling the story of a singular hero. Time and again, he makes clear how little one individual could achieve at the time and the great extent to which the survival of persecutees was dependent upon a tacit collaboration among many people who – often while risking their lives – refused, as though it were self-evident, to accept the vile laws the National Socialists and other fascists had concocted. Or, to borrow the words of Lisa Fittko: "none of us could have survived without the help of French people in every corner of the country – French men and women whose humanity gave them the courage to take in, to hide, and to feed these displaced strangers."

Acknowledgments

Many people have supported me in my work on this book in different ways. I would like to thank: Karin Graf and Franziska Günther from Agentur Graf & Graf, who helped me with valuable advice and corrections; Stefanie Hölscher, for her patience and care in editing, and Martin Hielscher, for always being a friend and important conversational partner for me; Christoph Buchwald, whom I pestered with questions about Walter Mehring; Jürgen Hillesheim, who kept me from looking for traces of Bertolt Brecht where none were to be found; Peter Stephan Jungk, who provided me with information about Franz Werfel; Jean Mattern, for his interest and for a long discussion on the Île de Ré about Varian Fry; and my son Nicolas Wittstock, who drew my attention to the book *Der totale Rausch* [English: *Blitzed: Drugs in the Third Reich*] by Norman Ohler on his podcast "Political Economy Forum." I owe special thanks to the translator Cornelia Geiser, who helped me with tremendous stamina and resourcefulness in my search for a street map of Marseille from 1940 when I was about to give up. I owe special thanks as well to: Pierre Sauvage, who was so generous as to make several indispensable photographs available to me for this book; Joachim Schnerf, who helped me gain clarity about the persecution of the Jews on the part of the Vichy regime; as well as historian Laurent Joly, who answered my questions about Vichy with great receptiveness and precision.

I could not have written this book without the nearly infinite treasures of books in the Deutsche Nationalbibliothek and in the collection of the Deutsches Exilarchiv in Frankfurt am Main. There, Sylvia Asmus, Regina Elsner, and Katrin Kokot in particular came to my aid. To them I offer my deep thanks. I also used Frankfurt's Universitätsbibliothek J.C. Senckenberg, as well as the archives of the Akademie der Künste, Berlin, and the Monacensia im Hildebrandhaus, Munich. On questions about transatlantic (radio) telephone conversations in 1940, curator Lioba Nägele from the Museum of Communication Frankfurt provided me with information. I likewise owe thanks to Laurence Ritter from the Fondation du Camp des Milles – Mémoire et Éducation for important information about the history of the camp Les Milles.

And last but not least, I would like to think Annette Wittstock for the joyous curiosity and unstinting endurance with which she accompanied me to this book's countless locales in Paris, Marseille, Aix-en-Provence, Sanary-sur-Mer, Cassis, Banyuls-sur-Mer, Cerbère, and Portbou, as well as on the Fittko route through the Pyrenees.

Illustration Credits

Page 3	United States Holocaust Memorial Museum, courtesy of Annette Fry
Page 23	Bettmann/Kontributor/Getty Images
Page 33	Courtesy of the Hannah Arendt Bluecher Literary Trust/Art Resource, NY
Page 39	ullstein bild/adoc-photos
Page 47	United States Holocaust Memorial Museum Collection, gift of Miriam Davenport Ebel
Page 59	Akademie der Künste, Berlin/Anna-Seghers-Archiv, Nr. 3759
Page 74	ullstein bild/ullstein bild
Page 75	ÖNB/Wien, Pf 36 714:C (1). Photo by Edith Glogau
Page 87	Courtesy of the University of Southern California, on behalf of the USC Libraries Special Collections (https://usclibstore.usc.edu/Feucht/Feucht-Gallary-1/i-wqR7vHT/buy)
Page 91	© Varian Fry Institute
Page 108	Library of Congress, public domain (LC-USZ62–91 232; http://hdl.loc.gov/loc.pnp/cph.3b37576)
Page 114	Wikipedia Commons (Robert Valette – Own work, CC BY-SA 3.0, https://commons.wikimedia.org/w/index.php?curid=4250933)
Page 123	Collection Christophel/Alamy Stock Photo
Page 130	Collection Walter Cruciani
Page 143	Photo: Antoni Campañà
Page 157	Associated Press/Alamy Stock Photo
Page 174	Hans Puttnies/Gary Smith: *Benjaminiana: Eine biografische Recherche*. Gießen 1991 (© Portbou City Council)
Page 178	Justus Rosenberg: *The Art of Resistance: My Four Years*

	in the French Underground: A Memoir. London 2020 (courtesy of the author)
Page 203	© Varian Fry Institute
Page 214	© Varian Fry Institute
Page 216	ullstein bild/United Archives
Page 224	United States Holocaust Memorial Museum, courtesy of Hiram Bingham
Page 235	© Varian Fry Institute
Page 247	© Varian Fry Institute. For the artworks visible in the tree: © VG Bild-Kunst, Bonn 2024
Page 248	© Varian Fry Institute
Page 254	© RMN-Grand Palais/Gisële Freund/RMN-GP/Dist. Photo SCALA, Firenze. For the artwork visible in the background: © VG Bild-Kunst, Bonn 2024
Page 257	United States Holocaust Memorial Museum, courtesy of Dyno Lowenstein
Page 274	United States Holocaust Memorial Museum

Bibliography

Aaron, Nikolaj. *Marc Chagall.* Reinbek bei Hamburg: Rowohlt-Taschenbuch-Verlag, 2003.

Arendt, Hannah. *Hannah Arendt: The Last Interview and Other Conversations.* Brooklyn, NY: Melville House, 2013.

Arendt, Hannah, and Günther Anders. *Schreib doch mal "hard facts" über Dich: Briefe 1939 bis 1975.* Edited by Kerstin Pütz. Munich: C.H. Beck Verlag, 2016.

Arendt, Hannah, and Walter Benjamin. *Arendt und Benjamin: Texte, Briefe, Dokumente.* Edited by Detlev Schöttker and Erdmut Wizisla. Frankfurt am Main: Suhrkamp, 2006.

Arendt, Hannah, and Günter Gaus. *Gespräch mit Hannah Arendt.* Munich: Piper, 1964.

Baruch, Marc Olivier. *Le régime de Vichy.* Paris: Éditions La Découverte, 1996.

Bénédite, Daniel. *La filière marseillaise: un chemin vers la Liberté sous l'occupation.* Paris: Éditions Clancier Guénaud, 1984.

Birman, Carina. *The Narrow Foothold.* London: Hearing Eye, 2006.

Blücher, Heinrich. *Versuche über den Nationalsozialismus.* Edited by Ringo Rösener. Göttingen: Wallstein Verlag, 2020.

Böttger, Steffi. *Für immer fremd: Das Leben des jüdischen Schriftstellers Hans Natonek.* Leipzig: Lehmstedt Verlag, 2013.

Breton, André. *Les manifestes du surréalisme.* Paris: Éd. du Sagittaire, 1946.

Breton, André. *Manifestoes of Surrealism.* Translated by Richard Seaver and Helen R. Lane. Ann Arbor: University of Michigan Press, 1969.

Bruttmann, Tal, Laurent Joly, and Barbara Lambauer. "Der Auftakt zur Verfolgung der Juden in Frankreich 1940: Ein deutsch-französisches Zusammenspiel." *Vierteljahreshefte für Zeitgeschichte* 60, no. 3 (July 2012): 381–407.

Carroll, Donald. "Escape from Vichy." *American Heritage*, July 1983. https://www.americanheritage.com/escape-vichy.

Churchill, Winston. *The Second World War.* London: Cassell & Co. Ltd, 1948.

Conradi, Peter. *Hitlers Klavierspieler Ernst Hanfstaengl: Vertrauter Hitlers, Verbündeter Roosevelts.* Frankfurt am Main: Scherz, 2007.

Convents, Ralf. *Surrealistische Spiele: vom "Cadavre exquis" zum "Jeu de Marseille."* Frankfurt am Main: Peter Lang, 1996.

Cziffra, Géza von. *Im Wartesaal des Ruhms*. Bergisch Gladbach: Lübbe, 1985.

Davenport Ebel, Miriam. "Miriam Davenport Ebel Memoir, 'An Unsentimental Education.'" https://www.varianfry.org/webpages/ebel_memoir_en.htm.

Dearborn, Mary V. *Mistress of Modernism: The Life of Peggy Guggenheim*. Boston, MA: Houghton Mifflin, 2004.

Doerry, Martin. *"Nirgendwo und überall zu Haus": Gespräche mit Überlebenden des Holocaust*. Munich: Deutsche Verlags-Anstalt, 2006.

Eiland, Howard, and Michael William Jennings. *Walter Benjamin: A Critical Life*. Cambridge, MA: The Belknap Press of Harvard University Press, 2016.

Ernst, Jimmy. *A Not-so-Still Life: A Memoir*. New York: St. Martin's/Marek, 1984.

Ernst, Max. *Max Ernst: die Schriften*. Edited by Gabriele Wix. Cologne: Verlag der Buchhandlung Walther und Franz König, 2022.

Feingold, Henry L. *The Politics of Rescue: The Roosevelt Administration and the Holocaust, 1938–1945*. New Brunswick, NJ: Rutgers University Press, 1970.

Feuchtwanger, Lion. *Der Teufel in Frankreich: Erlebnisse 1940*. Berlin: Aufbau Taschenbuch Verlag, 2018.

Feuchtwanger, Lion. *Ein möglichst intensives Leben: Die Tagebücher*. Edited by Nele Holdack, Marje Schuetze-Coburn, and Michaela Ullmann. Berlin: Aufbau, 2018.

Feuchtwanger, Lion. *The Devil in France: My Encounter with Him in the Summer of 1940*. Translated by Elisabeth Abbott. Los Angeles, CA: USC Libraries/University of Southern California, 2009.

Feuchtwanger, Marta. *Nur eine Frau*. Munich: Langen Mueller, 1983.

Fischer, Lothar. *Max Ernst: In Selbstzeugnissen und Bilddokumenten*. Reinbek bei Hamburg: Rowohlt, 1969.

Fittko, Lisa. *Mein Weg über die Pyrenäen: Erinnerungen 1940/41*. Munich: Carl Hanser, 1985.

Flohr, Marie-Christin, and Carsten Jakobi. "Das siebte Manuskript: Die abenteuerliche Entstehungs- und Editionsgeschichte von Anna Seghers' Roman *Das siebte Kreuz*." *Argonautenschiff: Jahrbuch der Anna-Seghers-Gesellschaft* 26 (2018): 151–63.

Flügge, Manfred. *Die vier Leben der Marta Feuchtwanger: Biographie*. Berlin: Aufbau-Taschenbuch-Verlag, 2012.

Flügge, Manfred. *Heinrich Mann: Eine Biographie*. Reinbek bei Hamburg: Rowohlt, 2006.

Flügge, Manfred. *Stéphane Hessel: Ein glücklicher Rebell*. Berlin: Aufbau, 2012.

Flügge, Manfred. *Traumland und Zuflucht: Heinrich Mann und Frankreich: mit zahlreichen Abbildungen*. Berlin: Insel Verlag, 2013.

Frucht, Karl. *Verlustanzeige: Ein Überlebensbericht*. Vienna: Kremayr & Scheriau, 1992.

Fry, Varian. *Assignment: Rescue*. New York: Four Winds Press, 1968.

Fry, Varian. *Auslieferung auf Verlangen: Die Rettung deutscher Emigranten in Marseille 1940/41*. Edited by Wolfgang D. Elfe and Jan Hans. Translated by Jan Hans and Anna Lazarowicz. Frankfurt am Main: Fischer Taschenbuch Verlag, 1995.

Fry, Varian. *Surrender on Demand*. New York: Random House, 1945.

Gold, Mary Jayne. *Crossroads Marseilles, 1940*. New York: Doubleday & Company, 1980.

Guggenheim, Peggy. *Out of This Century: Confessions of an Art Addict*. New York: Universe Books, 1979.

Hanfstaengl, Ernst. *Zwischen weißem und braunem Haus: Memoiren eines politischen Außenseiters*. Stuttgart: Deutscher Bücherbund, 1972.

Hannah Arendt im Gespräch mit Günter Gaus ("Zur Person," 1964), 2013. https://www.youtube.com/watch?v=J9SyTEUi6Kw.

Hasenclever, Walter. *Briefe*. Edited by Bert Kasties. Vol. II: 1933–1940. Mainz: Hase & Koehler, 1994.

Hasenclever, Walter. *Gedichte, Dramen, Prosa*. Edited by Kurt Pinthus. Reinbek bei Hamburg: Rowohlt, 1963.

Herzog, Günter. *Anton Räderscheidt*. Cologne: DuMont, 1991.

Hessel, Stéphane. *Danse avec le siècle*. Paris: Éditions du Seuil, 1997.

Hilmes, Carola, and Ilse Nagelschmidt, eds. *Anna Seghers-Handbuch: Leben, Werk, Wirkung*. Berlin: J.B. Metzler Verlag, 2020.

Hilmes, Oliver. *Malevolent Muse: The Life of Alma Mahler*. Translated by Donald Arthur. Boston, MA: Northeastern University Press, 2015.

Hilmes, Oliver. *Witwe im Wahn: Das Leben der Alma Mahler-Werfel*. Munich: btb, 2005.

Hirschman, Albert O. *A Propensity to Self-Subversion*. Cambridge, MA: Harvard University Press, 1995.

Isenberg, Sheila. *A Hero of Our Own: The Story of Varian Fry*. New York: Random House, 2001.

Jasper, Willi. *Der Bruder, Heinrich Mann: Eine Biographie*. Frankfurt am Main: Fischer Taschenbuch Verlag, 1994.

Jeske, Wolfgang, and Peter Zahn. *Lion Feuchtwanger: Der arge Weg der Erkenntnis*. Munich: W. Heyne, 1986.

Jungk, Peter Stephan. *Franz Werfel: A Life in Prague, Vienna, and Hollywood*. Translated by Anselm Hollo. New York: Grove Weidenfeld, 1990.

Jungk, Peter Stephan. *Franz Werfel: Eine Lebensgeschichte*. Frankfurt am Main: S. Fischer, 1987.

Jüngling, Kirsten. *"Ich bin doch nicht nur schlecht": Nelly Mann: die Biographie.* Berlin: List, 2009.

Jünke, Christoph. *Streifzüge durch das rote 20. Jahrhundert.* Hamburg: LAIKA-Verlag, 2014.

Kantorowicz, Alfred. *Exil in Frankreich: Merkwürdigkeiten und Denkwürdigkeiten.* Frankfurt am Main: Fischer Taschenbuch Verlag, 1986.

Kesten, Hermann. *Deutsche Literatur im Exil: Briefe europäischer Autoren 1933–1949.* Munich: Desch, 1964.

Kitson, Simon. *Police and Politics in Marseille, 1936–1945.* Leiden: Brill, 2014.

Klarsfeld, Serge. *Vichy-Auschwitz: le rôle de Vichy dans la solution finale de la question juive en France.* Paris: Fayard, 1942.

Klein, Anne. *Flüchtlingspolitik und Flüchtlingshilfe 1940–1942: Varian Fry und die Komitees zur Rettung politisch Verfolgter in New York und Marseille.* Berlin: Metropol, 2007.

Klein, Wolfgang. *Paris 1935: Erster Internationaler Schriftstellerkongress zur Verteidigung der Kultur: Reden und Dokumente mit Materialien der Londoner Schriftstellerkonferenz 1936.* Berlin: Akademie-Verlag, 1982.

Koestler, Arthur. *Scum of the Earth.* New York: The Macmillan Company, 1941.

Lahme, Tilmann. *Golo Mann: Biographie.* Frankfurt am Main: S. Fischer, 2009.

Leo, Maxim. *Wo wir zu Hause sind: Die Geschichte meiner verschwundenen Familie.* Cologne: Kiepenheuer & Witsch, 2019.

Lévi-Strauss, Claude. *Tristes tropiques.* Terre humaine. Paris: Plon, 1955.

Lévi-Strauss, Claude. *Tristes tropiques.* Translated by John Weightman and Doreen Weightman. New York: Penguin Books, 2012.

Lorey, Annette. *Nelly Mann: Heinrich Manns Gefährtin im Exil.* Würzburg: Königshausen & Neumann, 2021.

Loring, Marianne. *Flucht aus Frankreich 1940: Die Vertreibung deutscher Sozialdemokraten aus dem Exil.* Edited by Wolfgang Benz. Frankfurt am Main: Fischer Taschenbuch Verlag, 1996.

Lottman, Herbert R. *The Fall of Paris: June 1940.* New York, NY: HarperCollins Publishers, 1992.

Loyer, Emmanuelle. *Lévi-Strauss.* Paris: Flammarion, 2015.

Loyer, Emmanuelle. *Lévi-Strauss: A Biography.* Translated by Ninon Vinsonneau and Jonathan Magidoff. Cambridge, UK: Polity Press, 2018.

Mahler-Werfel, Alma. *And the Bridge Is Love.* New York: Harcourt, Brace, 1958.

Mahler-Werfel, Alma. *Mein Leben.* Frankfurt am Main: Fischer Taschenbuch Verlag, 1963.

Mann, Golo. *Erinnerungen und Gedanken: Lehrjahre in Frankreich.* Edited by Hans-Martin Gauger and Wolfgang Mertz. Frankfurt: S. Fischer, 1999.

Mann, Heinrich. *Ein Zeitalter wird besichtigt*. Reinbek bei Hamburg: Rowohlt, 1976.

Mann, Klaus. *Tagebücher: 1934–1935*. Edited by Joachim Heimannsberg, Peter Laemmle, and Wilfried F. Schoeller. Munich: Spangenberg, 1989.

Mann, Thomas. *Diaries 1918–1939: 1981–1921, 1933–1939*. Edited by Hermann Kesten. Translated by Richard Winston and Clara Winston. New York: Harry N. Abrams, 1982.

Mann, Thomas. *Tagebücher 1935–1936*. Edited by Peter de Mendelssohn and Inge Jens. Frankfurt am Main: S. Fischer, 1978.

Mann, Thomas. *Tagebücher 1940–1943*. Edited by Peter de Mendelssohn and Inge Jens. Frankfurt am Main: S. Fischer, 1982.

Mann, Thomas, and Erich von Kahler. *Briefwechsel 1931–1955*. Edited by Michael Assmann. Hamburg: Luchterhand Literaturverlag, 1993.

Mann, Thomas, and Heinrich Mann. *Briefwechsel 1900–1949*. Edited by Hans Wysling. Frankfurt am Main: Fischer Taschenbuch Verlag, 1995.

Marino, Andy. *A Quiet American: The Secret War of Varian Fry*. New York: St. Martin's Press, 1999.

Mayer, Michael. "'Die französische Regierung packt die Judenfrage ohne Umschweife an': Vichy-Frankreich, deutsche Besatzungsmacht und der Beginn der Judenpolitik im Sommer/Herbst 1940." *Vierteljahreshefte für Zeitgeschichte* 58, no. 3 (2010): 329–62.

Mehring, Walter. *Chronik der Lustbarkeiten: Die Gedichte, Lieder und Chansons, 1918–1933*. Edited by Christoph Buchwald. Walter Mehring Werke. Düsseldorf: Claassen, 1981.

Mehring, Walter. *Staatenlos im Nirgendwo: Die Gedichte, Lieder und Chansons 1933–1974*. Edited by Christoph Buchwald. Walter Mehring Werke. Düsseldorf: Claassen, 1981.

Mehring, Walter. *Wir müssen weiter: Fragmente aus dem Exil*. Edited by Christoph Buchwald. Walter Mehring Werke. Düsseldorf: Claassen, 1979.

Melchert, Monika. *Wilde und zarte Träume: Anna Seghers' Jahre im Pariser Exil 1933–1940*. Berlin: Bübül Verlag, 2018.

Meyer, Thomas. *Hannah Arendt: Die Biografie*. Munich: Piper, 2023.

Natonek, Hans. *Letzter Tag in Europa: Gesammelte Publizistik 1933–1963*. Edited by Steffi Böttger. Leipzig: Lehmstedt, 2013.

Nieradka, Magali Laure. *Der Meister der leisen Töne: Biographie des Dichters Franz Hessel*. Hamburg: Igel-Verlag, 2014.

Ohler, Norman. *Blitzed: Drugs in the Third Reich*. Translated by Shaun Whiteside. Boston, MA: Houghton Mifflin Harcourt, 2017.

Ohler, Norman. *Der totale Rausch: Drogen im Dritten Reich*. Cologne: Kiepenheuer & Witsch, 2015.

Pauli, Hertha. *Der Riss der Zeit geht durch mein Herz: Erlebtes, Erzähltes.* Frankfurt am Main: Ullstein Taschenbuch, 1990.

Pauli, Hertha. "Flucht." *Aufbau: American Jewish Weekly in German*, October 11, 1940.

Pauli, Hertha. "Tagebuch einer Flucht: II. Kampf um ein Schiff." *Aufbau: American Jewish Weekly in German*, October 25, 1940.

Pauli, Hertha. "Tagebuch einer Flucht: III. Rettung." *Aufbau: American Jewish Weekly in German*, November 1, 1940.

Philipp, Michael, ed. *Gurs: Ein Internierungslager in Südfrankreich: 1939–1943: literarische Zeugnisse, Briefe, Berichte.* Hamburg: Hamburger Institut für Sozialforschung, 1991.

Pistorius, Peter. "Rudolf Breitscheid, 1874–1944: Ein biographischer Beitrag zur deutschen Parteiengeschichte." Universität Köln, 1970.

Polizzotti, Mark. *Revolution of the Mind: The Life of André Breton.* New York: Farrar, Straus and Giroux, 1995.

Prater, Donald A. *Thomas Mann: A Life.* Oxford: Oxford University Press, 1995.

Quinn, Gregory. "The Marine Air Terminal at LaGuardia: The Age of the Flying Boat," October 15, 2015. https://portfolio.panynj.gov/2015/10/15/the-marine-air-terminal-at-laguardia-the-age-of-the-flying-boat/.

Radványi, Pierre. *Au-delà du fleuve, avec Anna Seghers.* Paris: Le temps des cerises, 2014.

Radványi, Pierre. "Einige Erinnerungen." *Argonautenschiff: Jahrbuch der Anna-Seghers-Gesellschaft* 3 (1994): 185–92.

Radványi, Pierre. *Jenseits des Stroms: Erinnerungen an meine Mutter Anna Seghers.* Translated by Manfred Flügge. Berlin: Aufbau-Verlag, 2005.

"Raymond Couraud." In *Wikipedia*, April 17, 2023. https://en.wikipedia.org/w/index.php?title=Raymond_Couraud&oldid=1150385135.

Richter, Horst. *Anton Räderscheidt.* Recklinghausen: Bongers, 1972.

Rosenberg, Justus. *The Art of Resistance: My Four Years in the French Underground: A Memoir.* New York: William Morrow, 2020.

Rousso, Henry. *Le régime de Vichy.* Paris: Presses universitaires de France, 2007.

Rudolph, Katharina. *Rebell im Maßanzug: Leonhard Frank: die Biographie.* Berlin: Aufbau, 2020.

Rysselberghe, Maria van. *Les cahiers de la Petite Dame: notes pour l'histoire authentique d'André Gide*, 4 vols. Paris: Gallimard, 1973.

Sahl, Hans. *Das Exil im Exil.* Frankfurt am Main: Luchterhand Literaturverlag, 1990.

Scheck, Raffael. *Hitler's African Victims: The German Army Massacres of Black French Soldiers in 1940.* Cambridge, UK: Cambridge University Press, 2006.

Scheurmann, Ingrid. *Neue Dokumente zum Tode Walter Benjamins*. Bonn: Arbeitskreis selbständiger Kultur-Institute, 1992.

Scheurmann, Ingrid, and Konrad Scheurmann, eds. *For Walter Benjamin: Documentation, Essays and a Sketch*. Translated by Timothy Nevill. Bonn: Arbeitskreis selbständiger Kultur-Institute, 1993.

Scheurmann, Ingrid, and Konrad Scheurmann, eds. *Für Walter Benjamin: Dokumente, Essays und ein Entwurf*. Frankfurt am Main: Suhrkamp, 1992.

Scheurmann, Ingrid, and Konrad Scheurmann, eds. "New Documents on Walter Benjamin's Death." In *For Walter Benjamin: Documentation, Essays and a Sketch*, 265–99. Bonn: Arbeitskreis selbständiger Kultur-Institute, 1993.

Schneider, Rolf. "Die Blindheit Adolf Hitlers: Rolf Schneider über Ernst Weiß: *Der Augenzeuge* (1940)." In *Romane von gestern – heute gelesen. Band III: 1933–1945*, edited by Marcel Reich-Ranicki, 264–70. Frankfurt am Main: Fischer Taschenbuch Verlag, 1996.

Schöck-Quinteros, Eva. "Dora Benjamin: Stationen einer vertriebenen Wissenschaftlerin (1901–1946)." *boujour.Geschichte* 4 (2014): 1–26.

Schoenberner, Franz. *Innenansichten eines Aussenseiters*. Munich: Kreisselmeier, 1965.

Schoenberner, Franz. *The Inside Story of an Outsider*. New York: Macmillan, 1949.

Schramm, Hanna. *Menschen in Gurs: Erinnerungen an ein französisches Internierungslager (1940–1941)*. Worms: Heintz, 1977.

Schulz, Georg-Michael. *Walter Mehring*. Hannover: Wehrhahn Verlag, 2013.

Seemann, Annette. *Ich bin eine befreite Frau: Peggy Guggenheim*. Berlin: Ebersbach & Simon, 2018.

Seghers, Anna. *Briefe, 1924–1952*. Edited by Christiane Zehl Romero and Almut Giesecke. Werkausgabe 5/1. Berlin: Aufbau-Verlag, 2008.

Serge, Victor. *Mémoires d'un révolutionnaire, 1901–1941*. Paris: Éditions du Seuil, 1951.

Serge, Victor. *Memoirs of a Revolutionary 1901–1941*. Edited and translated by Peter Sedgwick. New York: Oxford University Press, 1963.

Sösemann, Bernd. *Theodor Wolff: Ein Leben mit der Zeitung*. Munich: Econ, 2000.

Später, Jörg. *Kracauer: A Biography*. Translated by Daniel Steuer. Cambridge, UK: Polity, 2020.

Später, Jörg. *Siegfried Kracauer: Eine Biographie*. Berlin: Suhrkamp, 2016.

Spira, Bil. *Die Legende vom Zeichner*. Edited by Konstantin Kaiser and Vladimir Vertlib. Vienna: Döcker, 1997.

Stern, Jeanne. "Das Floß der Anna Seghers." In *Über Anna Seghers: Ein Almanach zum 75. Geburtstag*, edited by Kurt Blatt, 77–91. Berlin: Aufbau-Verlag, 1975.

Sternheim, Thea. *Tagebücher 1903–1971*. Edited by Thomas Ehrsam and Regula Wyss. Göttingen: Wallstein, 2011.

Straus-Ernst, Louise. *Nomadengut: Autobiografie 1914–1942*. Edited by Ulrich Krempel. Hannover: Sprengel Museum Hannover, 1999.

Sullivan, Rosemary. *Villa Air-Bel: World War II, Escape, and a House in Marseille*. New York: HarperCollins, 2006.

Tomkins, Calvin. *Duchamp: A Biography*. New York: H. Holt, 1996.

Velder, Christian. *300 Jahre Französisches Gymnasium Berlin*. Berlin: Nicolai, 1989.

Voswinckel, Ulrike, and Frank Berninger, eds. *Exil am Mittelmeer: Deutsche Schriftsteller in Südfrankreich 1933–1941*. Munich: Allitera, 2005.

Wagner, Frank, Ursula Emmerich, and Ruth Radvanyi, eds. *Anna Seghers: Eine Biographie in Bildern*. Berlin: Aufbau, 1994.

Walter, Hans-Albert. *Deutsche Exilliteratur 1933–1950*. Vol. 3: *Internierung, Flucht und Lebensbedingungen im Zweiten Weltkrieg*, 4 vols. Stuttgart: J.B. Metzler, 1988.

Warburg Spinelli, Ingrid. *Erinnerungen: Die Dringlichkeit des Mitleids und die Einsamkeit, nein zu sagen*. Hamburg: Luchterhand Literaturverlag, 1990.

Weinzierl, Ulrich. *Alfred Polgar: Eine Biographie*. Frankfurt am Main: Fischer Taschenbuch Verlag, 1995.

Weissweiler, Eva. *Lisa Fittko: Biographie einer Fluchthelferin*. Hamburg: Hoffmann und Campe, 2024.

Weissweiler, Eva. *Notre Dame de Dada Luise Straus-Ernst: Das dramatische Leben der ersten Frau von Max Ernst*. Cologne: Kiepenheuer & Witsch, 2016.

wolfparisblog. "„Dadurch, dass ich zum Glück die Kinder habe, ist alles doppelt schwer." Anna Seghers im Pariser Exil 1933–1940." Paris und Frankreich blog, November 19, 2018. https://paris-blog.org/2018/11/19/dadurch-dass-ich-zum-glueck-die-kinder-habe-ist-alles-doppelt-schwer-anna-seghers-im-pariser-exil-1933-1940/.

Wollheim, Mona. *Begegnung mit Ernst Weiß: Paris 1936–1940*. Munich: Kreisselmeier, 1970.

Young-Bruehl, Elisabeth. *Hannah Arendt: For Love of the World*. New Haven, CT: Yale University Press, 1982.

Zehl Romero, Christiane. *Anna Seghers: Eine Biographie 1900–1947*. Berlin: Aufbau Taschenbuch, 2020.

For information about the weather, I am grateful, among others, to the website created by Vincent Huck: *Année 1940, conditions météo remarquables. Année 1941, conditions météo remarquables.* https://www.prevision-meteo.ch/almanach/1940, accessed on August 24, 2023. Searching through the online archives of the *New York Times* was a pleasure. I was able to cross-reference countless details on the databases of *Deutsche Biographie*, *Künste im Exil*, the *Institut für Frauen-Biografieforschung* (Hannover/Boston), and *Wikipedia*. I owe thanks to the makers of these portals.

Index

Illustrations indicated by page numbers in italics